"Erik Goodwyn is prominent among that small but growing band of psychologists who use an evolutionary perspective to build a unifying science of humanity. In this encyclopaedic compilation of insights, derived from an impressive variety of sources, Goodwyn demonstrates how the therapeutic power of ancient ritual practices can be mobilized by modern clinicians, whether they be psychotherapists, physicians or psychiatrists. Through ritual, Goodwyn shows us, we can activate phylogenetic structures as old as our species and summon their limitless resources to our aid."

– Anthony Stevens, author of *Archetype Revisited: An Updated Natural History of The Self*

"Erik Goodwyn has delivered a definitive piece on ritual. The book provides a fascinating and erudite tour-de-force that bridges depth psychology and anthropology, drawing also upon biology and cognitive science, so as to explore the many layers of its topic. The author deftly pulls together these diverse sources of information towards building an integrative conceptual framework. The narrative is well-informed and informative. Goodwyn's engaging style makes it highly accessible, a pleasure to read."

– Raya Jones, School of Social Sciences, Cardiff University, UK

"In place of rituals that once pulsed with our blood and breathed with our breath, today we accumulate facts, information, procedures. We are not even sure what they all add up to. At the end of the work day, we addictively shop, consume, imbibe drugs, scan the internet—in search of something greater and more enduring. Meaning is the pattern that connects, and Dr. Erik Goodwyn would have us live more meaningful lives by understanding and accessing the timeless and archetypal patterns carried by rituals. Ritual, he argues, links the conscious mind with unconscious processes, critical because our self-conscious purposiveness lacks the evolutionary wisdom to which unconscious processes still have access. This book considers questions such as: How might we more effectively initiate teenagers into adulthood, women into menopause, patients struggling with the journey of dying? How is it that the'placebo effect' works—often more powerfully than the active ingredient in prescribed drugs—and how could ritual harness that power? How might healing words replace technical jargon in doctor/patient encounters? Goodwyn explores dozens of such scenarios, applying research from the fertile intersection of anthropology and psychology. The results are fascinating and highly valuable for anyone in the healing or helping professions."

– Jerry M. Ruhl Ph.D., depth psychologist, co-author of *Living Your Unlived Life*

"Drawing on a 'web of interaction' between biology, psychology, and culture, Erik Goodwyn creates an inspiring interdisciplinary theoretical model for ritual in clinical practice. Arguing that rituals are an overlooked resource, Goodwyn brings together the skills of a perceptive clinician with ritual scholarship to reveal deep insights about a therapeutic process that has its roots in the very origins of humankind. This is an original work of the utmost importance, it gets to the heart of human soul, and it will change lives."

– Dr Susan Greenwood, past lecturer and Senior Research Fellow, University of Sussex, UK

Healing Symbols in Psychotherapy

Ritual scholars note that rituals have powerful psychological, social, and even biological effects, but these findings have not yet been integrated into the practice of psychotherapy and psychiatry. In *Healing Symbols in Psychotherapy* Erik D. Goodwyn attempts to rectify this by reviewing the most pertinent work done in the area of ritual study and applying it to the practice of psychotherapy and psychiatry, providing a new framework with which to approach therapy. The book combines ritual study with depth psychology, placebo study, biogenetic structuralism, and cognitive anthropology to create a model of interdisciplinary psychology.

Goodwyn uses examples of rituals from history, folklore, and cross-cultural study and uncovers the universal themes embedded within them as well as their psychological functions. As ritual scholars show time and again how Western culture and medicine is "ritually impoverished" the application of ritual themes to therapy yields many new avenues for healing. The interdisciplinary model used here suggests new ways to approach problems with basic identity, complicated grief, anxiety, depression, meaninglessness, and a host of other problems encountered in clinical work.

The interdisciplinary approach of this accessibly written book will appeal to psychotherapists, psychiatrists, and Jungian analysts as well as those in training and readers with an interest in the science behind ritual.

Erik D. Goodwyn, M.D., is Assistant Professor in the Department of Psychiatry and director of psychotherapy training at the University of Louisville, USA. He was an officer in the Air Force for seven years, during which time he cared for patients from both military and civilian backgrounds. He has published articles in the fields of psychology of religion, psychodynamic theory, and spirituality in mental health, and his previous books include *The Neurobiology of the Gods* (Routledge, 2012) and, with Susan Greenwood, *Magical Consciousness: An Anthropological and Neurobiological Approach* (Routledge, 2016).

Healing Symbols in Psychotherapy

A Ritual Approach

Erik D. Goodwyn

Routledge
Taylor & Francis Group
LONDON AND NEW YORK

First published 2016
by Routledge
2 Park Square, Milton Park, Abingdon, Oxon OX14 4RN

and by Routledge
711 Third Avenue, New York, NY 10017

Routledge is an imprint of the Taylor & Francis Group, an informa business

British Library Cataloguing in Publication Data
A catalogue record for this book is available from the British Library

Library of Congress Cataloguing in Publication Data
Names: Goodwyn, Erik D., 1970– author.
Title: Healing symbols in psychotherapy : a ritual approach / Erik D. Goodwyn.
Description: New York : Routledge, 2016. | Includes bibliographical references.
Identifiers: LCCN 2015035052| ISBN 9781138120266 (hardback) |
ISBN 9781138120280 (paperback) | ISBN 9781315651811 (ebook)
Subjects: LCSH: Ritual–Psychology. | Signs and symbols. | Ethnopsychology. |
Psychotherapy–Religious aspects. Classification: LCC BL600.G66 2016 |
DDC 203/.8–dc23LC record available at http://lccn.loc.gov/2015035052

ISBN: 978-1-138-12026-6 (hbk)
ISBN: 978-1-138-12028-0 (pbk)
ISBN: 978-1-315-65181-1 (ebk)

Typeset in Times
by Out of House Publishing

Contents

Part I

Foundations

At the intersection of psychology and anthropology is the ritual. Of primary interest in this volume are the questions: what do rituals do? How do they work? Why do we do them? And most importantly: how can we apply the study of ritual to clinical practice in psychiatry and psychotherapy? In order to answer these questions, it is important to explore the relationships first between psychology and anthropology, and then between psychology, anthropology, and cognitive science so that we really know what we're getting into. This is because radically interdisciplinary work must put some thought into the way psychology, anthropology, and the other disciplines have related to one another in the past. In this first part, I will first review the relationship between depth psychology and anthropology with respect to ritual, followed by a chapter on the biology and cognitive science of ritual, at all points asking our main question: what can we learn from the best minds in ritual study, and how can we potentially use it to mold clinical practice? In order to provide a truly interdisciplinary answer to this question, I will develop what I am calling a "dynamic interdisciplinary" model of psychology.

In the second part, having provided a model for understanding ritual from a multidisciplinary perspective, I review the specific theories of ritual that have emerged in the past from each discipline. In Chapter 3, we will look at the cognitive science of religion and ritual and develop my concept of "psychological resonance"—a concept with wide applications in the study of folklore in general, but with specific applications to psychotherapy. In Chapter 4, I review the various anthropological theories of ritual, ranging from the early theorists to more recent developments. In Chapter 5, we begin the full application of ritual study to clinical practice by treating modern medical encounters in a ritual context, beginning with the biological effects of rituals as "placebo" effects; I also review the effects of ritual from the perspective of the biogenetic structural model. Finally, in Chapter 6 we will use what we have learned and compare it with common psychodynamic concepts that likely apply to ritual, including projection, narrative construction, and meaningful coincidence among other effects, and we will explore how the study of ritual can inform these psychological concepts and lend itself to suggestions for therapy.

In the third part, I cover various examples of rituals from history, anthropology, folklore, and cross-cultural study to deepen our understanding of ritual. Various types of rituals are discussed, ranging from magical inscriptions uncovered by archeology and history in Chapter 7, to curing rituals discussed in Chapter 8, to the manipulative magic rituals of Chapter 9, to life-stage and cultural transition rituals discussed in Chapter 10, to perhaps the most elaborated and intense rituals of all: those dealing with death and the dead, discussed in Chapter 11. In these chapters we will look at ways to apply the principles of these various examples of ritual to modern clinical encounters.

In the final part of the volume I will explore the main points we can take away from the present study, including a discussion of the common elements found in rituals and their functions, and we will end with a look at how we might construct new rituals as part of the "technology" of ritual structure and function, with an eye to applying it to clinical theory and practice.

Chapter 1

The Study of Ritual

Depth Psychology and Interpretive Anthropology

Every civilized human being, however high his conscious development, is still an archaic man at the deeper levels of his psyche.
– Carl Jung (1970, para. 105)

Introduction

I am alive because of a magic spell. As he wrote in his popular autobiography, *Life on the King Ranch*, when he was a small child my grandfather Frank Goodwyn became deathly ill with diphtheria. A local yardman, Don Federico, who was good friends with my grandfather and far his senior, however, knew it was something far more sinister, known as *ojo*, or the "eye." In the brush country in Texas at that time, the *ojo* was known to be an affliction that affects only children who have been admired by an older person who did not caress the child. According to folklore, no doctor could cure *ojo* and no spell could undo it. Only the one who caused it could remove it by saying the proper words and signs. When my grandfather became ill, Doctor Joseph Shelton was summoned by my great grandparents, and he made a heroic journey by handcar fifty miles from Kingsville to my grandfather's side. The case was serious—too much serum would kill him, and too little would allow the diphtheria to kill him. A higher dose was chosen. Don Federico, known to my grandfather as "Old Eeky," however, was sure he had caused the sickness, and though my great-grandparents thought it was superstitious foolishness, they let Old Eeky come to my grandfather's side after much insistence. Old Eeky crossed himself, made the proper signs and said the proper words, and as my grandfather puts it: "The *ojo* was removed. I was delirious a while, and for months after I got well, I couldn't climb the porch steps without wobbling. Mother and Dad said it was Dr. Shelton's serum that cured me, but Old Eeky knew it was the proper signs and words" (Goodwyn 1993 [1951]: 44).

Perhaps a few years ago, as a physician myself, I would have been strongly inclined to agree with my great-grandparents. But medical knowledge is expanding into areas previously unexplored, and as I will show in this book, there is room to allow for Old Eeky in our understanding of the effects of ritual, culture, and tradition on mind and body—two things once thought to be widely separated from such things.

Human beings are creatures of magic and ritual. Throughout history we have looked to the gods, saviors, spirits, ancestors, and mysterious powers to help us live our lives. The advent of modern science, despite many lofty statements to the contrary, has not changed much about this for the everyday human living his or her life. In many ways we are creatures of ritual, and we naturally place symbolic meaning on much of what we do. Some, as early as Freud (of the modern era), saw an interesting correspondence between the behavior of Obsessive Compulsive Disorder and the less pathological rituals and traditions of indigenous cultures. Carl Jung expanded on the idea of ritual and myth as understandable from a psychological perspective. Later psychologists have explored the idea of ritual as psychological action in greater detail and even use it in therapy, but in truth, the idea that ritual scholarship can inform the practice of psychotherapy is one that has not received the full attention it deserves. As we will see, ritual scholars have a lot to teach us about just how social and ritualistic the human soul really is, and I believe we can use this extensive knowledge to help inform our psychotherapeutic practices. As we will see, placebo effects, a concept I develop called "psychological resonance," and numerous cultural effects can be understood from a psychodynamic perspective and utilized in therapeutic efforts.

The Study of Ritual in Psychology and Anthropology

To do this, we have to first get a handle on what exactly a ritual is. Only then can we carefully attempt to apply ritual scholarship to the study of psychotherapy. It is well known that in most societies, when ethnographers inquire about the meaning behind a particular ritual, participants often do not have ready answers, or give cursory or dismissive answers, causing much frustration among anthropologists (Whitehouse 2004: 195). Thus the analysis of ritual is no simple matter and requires careful study from a variety of angles. Every culture known has its magical rituals designed to access the so-called "supernatural" realms in order to aid us in our daily lives, whether it be prayers to the gods, charms, herbal remedies, magic spells, or whatever (Brown 1991). All magico-religious practices are of course cultural expressions; each culture has its own set of rituals and/or spells, folk magic, or customs that they perform to aid in various life concerns. The important point about this, as I will show, is that these expressions are *non-random*. In other words, ritual charms may vary widely, but they are not completely arbitrary; they follow specific patterns related to universal psychological constructs and repeated situations. Ritual magic practice, like all magico-religious traditions, survives through transmission from generation to generation—even those that use a "sacred book" of some kind still hold true to a *culturally specific interpretation* of that book in a specific cultural context, and all "book" religions still have a considerable amount of folk practice surrounding them, oftentimes, interestingly, in direct contradiction to what the "experts" say the book says.

Psychology and anthropology are both about human behavior, but their approaches have traditionally been very different. In psychology, for example, traditionally the data gathered were from members of the scientist's own culture, on an individual basis, and the investigator was often a physician, like Freud or Jung. By contrast, anthropology goes beyond the parent culture to study a completely different culture, sometimes taking years to understand the foreign customs of another people. Perhaps because of these different approaches, psychology and anthropology have diverged from one another since the earliest days of their inception. Despite this, or even because of it, it is therefore all the more striking when both psychologists and anthropologists come to similar (though not identical) observations.

Two Disciplines, One Humanity

The relationship between anthropology and what is now called "depth" psychology—to differentiate it from the more experimentally derived cognitive psychology—has been a turbulent one throughout the histories of both disciplines. In particular, the thinking of Sigmund Freud and Carl Jung with anthropologists Claude Lévi-Strauss, Émile Durkheim, philosopher Lucien Lévy-Bruhl, and others has been observed to coincide as well as collide in many ways (Gras 1981; Greenwood 1990; Segal 2007; Staude 1976).

Freud, Jung, and Lévi-Strauss, for example, all proposed a universality and collectivity in human nature that hearkens back to a more archaic mode of thinking, but each differed in his characterization of that nature. Nevertheless, both disciplines have influenced each other from an early point. For example, Staude argues that "the importance of the psychoanalytic theory of the unconscious for the explanation of the origins and meaning of cultural phenomena was tremendous" (Staude 1976: 305). Staude argues that Jung drew heavily upon the work of Durkheim, Lévy-Bruhl, and many from the French sociological school (Staude 1976: 314).

Staude remarks that Jung in particular blended German philosophical traditions with the French sociological theory (Staude 1976: 334). Jung felt a natural connection with the Durkheimian school and adopted Durkheim's concept of "collective representations," a term he attributed to Lévy-Bruhl, who knew both Durkheim and Jung personally. Furthermore, Durkheim went to school with Pierre Janet, a psychologist who also had a significant influence on Jung's thinking (Greenwood 1990: 486; Haule 2011).

The parallels and interrelationships, intended and otherwise, do not stop with Durkheim and Jung only, despite decades of both disciplines continuing to drift apart. The work of anthropologist Claude Lévi-Strauss (1966) has been observed by several authors to have "a number of striking, if unintended, similarities" to the psychoanalytic models of the individual psyche:

> While Freud uncovered the personal unconscious and Jung the collective unconscious, Lévi-Strauss developed a conceptual model of the structures of

> the human mind that has room for both the Freudian and Jungian conceptions and a great deal more.
>
> (Staude 1976: 326)

Lévi-Strauss, like Jung, sought to understand the workings of the mind by understanding myth, identifying a common structure between the two. Lévi-Strauss tended to dismiss Jung, however, but later anthropologists have noticed that Lévi-Strauss misconstrued Jung and did not recognize the many similarities in their approaches, namely, their bipolarity, their formalistic models, and their dialectical approaches (Gras 1981: 471).

Comparing Depth Psychology and Symbolic Anthropology

To facilitate a more systematic and coherent integration of depth psychology and anthropology in the science of ritual, a good starting point is the acknowledgment that Jung's "collective unconscious" shares many affinities with Durkheim's *conscience collective* as well as Lévi-Strauss's "savage mind," and that these men appear to have influenced each other's thinking indirectly. But just as Durkheim and later anthropologists perhaps did not fully assimilate psychoanalytic theory into their theories of the individual psyche, the psychoanalytic models did not quite fully integrate the important contribution of symbolic anthropology. The essential overlap between these psychological and anthropological thinkers was that they all proposed a "collective element" of the mind that was influenced by and helped to create society (Staude 1976: 316).

It will be evident that models of the individual psyche and the social psyche are heavily overlapping and tightly interwoven, though neither depth psychology nor anthropology has fully integrated the two. The reason anthropologists paid more attention to Freud than Jung, despite Jung's closer affinity to them, is perhaps a distrust of Jung's more mystical, diffuse style of writing and thinking. The attitude toward Jung adopted by many social scientists can be summarized by the comments of psychologist Jean Piaget:

> Jung has an amazing capacity for construction, but a certain contempt for logic and rational activity . . . he adopts an anti-rationalist attitude, and the surprising comparisons of which he has the secret cannot fail sometimes to disturb the critical reader.
>
> (Piaget 1951: 196)

This attitude toward Jung remained typical until the later twentieth century, as Staude commented in the mid-1970s: "when structural anthropology has begun seeking to determine universals about human cognition, a re-evaluation of Jung's theories may be possible . . . Jung's psychological theory dovetails quite easily with a functionalist approach in sociology and anthropology" (Staude 1976: 319). The sociology of Durkheim and the psychology of Jung therefore present respectively individual and social approaches to religion in particular and their systems both contain close structural similarities noted by only a few scholars thus far (Guala 1970; Mestrovic 1985, 1988). The resurgent interest in universals, however, has brought the individual models of Freud, Jung, and many other depth psychologists since back into anthropological discussions. We will return to the challenging subject of universals in both depth psychology and anthropology later.

Staude's observations about the overlap between depth psychology and anthropology in 1976 have since been expanded upon. Mestrovic (1985, 1988) further outlined Freud's frequent references to Durkheim and his school of thinking, and recognized the role of the unconscious in Durkheim's theorizing. Later scholars have observed that Jung's model of the unconscious, which expands Freud's to include the collective as well as personal unconscious, has not been adequately processed in light of Durkheim's (and later anthropologists') thought and vice versa, as observed by anthropologist Susan F. Greenwood:

> Jung is well known for his work on the unconscious, but few scholars have acknowledged the presence of the unconscious within Durkheim's work . . . Likewise, the sociological implications of Jung's work have been neglected by psychologists . . . in general social scientists remain unaware of Jung's relevance in understanding Durkheim's explanation of religion, as manifested by the collective consciousness.
>
> (Greenwood 1990: 488)

Greenwood's observation of the blocks between the two disciplines continues to be apt today. Nevertheless, both approaches appear to grapple with similar issues. For example, the fact that Durkheim wrote that his "collective representations" were "partially autonomous realities with . . . the power to attract and repel each other" (1915: 31) can be compared to Jung's statement concerning the "archetype": "When a situation occurs which corresponds to a given archetype, that archetype becomes activated and a compulsiveness appears, which, like an instinctual drive, gains its way against all reason and will" (1959b: para. 99). Durkheim and Jung both wrote that the most important psychic phenomena were partially autonomous, unconscious, and had the ability to impress upon consciousness a variety of affects (Greenwood 1990: 490).

Greenwood makes a call for a "transpersonal" sociology of religion, noting the numerous similarities in Durkheim's and Jung's formulations. She argues that both Durkheim and Jung were describing *the same process*, that is, both theorists felt the human personality was strongly affected by some kind of "collective element" that developed largely unconsciously (Greenwood 1990: 491–492). Despite Greenwood's call to action, however, some difficulties need to be addressed in the endeavor to create "depth sociology," many of them conceptual in nature. Take for example the fact that Jung relied heavily on Lévy-Bruhl's thinking to develop his midway theory of individual and social psychology. How are we to proceed given the various criticisms of Lévy-Bruhl's more controversial ideas, such as "primitive mentality"? Many anthropologists since Lévy-Bruhl have denied that people of so-called "primitive" cultures (i.e. traditional cultures) think fundamentally or qualitatively differently from moderns, and some of these thinkers criticize Jung as well for apparently going along with Lévy-Bruhl (Evans-Pritchard 1937; Lévi-Strauss 1955, 1966; Radin 1957) in this regard. Thus, we cannot completely trust Jung or Lévy-Bruhl in building a depth sociology, but must re-evaluate both disciplines, restructuring aspects that do not work.

The Need for a Coherent Model

Lévy-Bruhl's ideas—particularly that of *participation*—will be discussed at length later. It is important to point out here that even today, Lévy-Bruhl's ideas continue to be debated among anthropologists, with new insights continuing to be discussed (Geertz 1973; Greenwood 2009) and as such it is unclear what aspects of Lévy-Bruhl's formulation should be reworked. Furthermore, what aspects of Jung's or Freud's theories should be reworked to create a more coherent model? How do we compare psychology and anthropology in a way that eliminates false dichotomies of mind/culture and nature/nurture? How do we compare the two in a way that eliminates the misrepresentations that have plagued both depth psychology and anthropology in relation to each other?

We can see that depth psychology and anthropology never have been entirely distinct disciplines, but the blunt comparison of the works of Freud, Jung, Lévy-Bruhl, Durkheim, and so forth results in a number of difficulties. These difficulties are perhaps due to the lack of an underlying coherent model of their interaction, based upon more recent knowledge gained from the study of evolutionary biology, comparative ethology, and social psychology. It is the aim of the present work, then, to propose such a model. Thinking along these lines is of course not new. In his influential *The Interpretation of Cultures*, American anthropologist Clifford Geertz analyzes the relationship between biology, psychology, and sociology, and clarifies what is now widely accepted within anthropology, that the debates about whether biology determines culture, or vice versa, were poorly conceived in principle. Minds and cultures do not predict each other, but continually interact with each other and influence each other. He showed this by calling into question the usual assumption regarding the study of behavior:

> As one analyzes man, one peels off layer after layer, each such layer being complete and irreducible in itself, revealing another, quite different sort of layer underneath. Strip off the motley forms of culture and one finds the structural and functional regularities of social organization. Peel off these in turn and one finds the underlying psychological factors . . . Peel off psychological factors and one is left with the biological foundations—anatomical, physiological, neurological—of the whole edifice of human life . . . [However] Despite first appearances, there is no serious attempt here to apply the concepts and theories of biology, psychology, or even sociology to the analysis

> of culture . . . but merely a placing of supposed facts from the cultural and subcultural levels side by side . . . There is no theoretical integration here at all but mere correlation, and that intuitive, of separate findings.
>
> (Geertz 1973: 37–43)

Many previous theories of culture implicitly assumed that there was some kind of foundational "human nature" upon which an external culture operated, and the interaction of the two produced the varieties of human behavior, thus implicitly assuming a dichotomy of nature and nurture that has been difficult to overcome. Freud and Jung both fall into this category, as did several of the early anthropologists; later psychologists refer rarely to anthropology at all. But Geertz highlights the problems with any model that views biology, psychology, and culture as distinct "layers": such a model glosses over the dense interaction between them and does not fully account for the particulars of the interactions in any case. As growing evidence continues to suggest (Brown 1991; Deacon 1998; Goodwyn 2012; Panksepp 1998; Pyysiäinen 2009; Rappaport 1999; Whitehouse and Laidlaw 2007), cultures and individual human minds have co-evolved and have continually interacted throughout our history as a species. Geertz argued that such facts make any discussion of a culture-independent human nature very problematic, and took this as evidence that the continued search for cultural universals—a subject which occupied Freud and even more so Jung, not to mention early anthropologists—was ill-advised. Geertz's influential ideas encouraged anthropologists toward a near-complete lack of interest in universals (Brown 1991), but a closer reading shows that this was perhaps not Geertz's intention. We will return to the study of universals and its implications for both psychology and anthropology later.

Thickly Describing Minds and Cultures

Developing minds do not create culture, nor does culture create developing minds; in fact, a more realistic view recognizes that developing minds both partially contribute to and are partially determined by cultures. Recognition of this complex situation encouraged Geertz to emphasize what he called "thick description" (a concept he borrowed from Ryle 1949), which focuses more on the interpretation rather than explanation of culture. Thick description of behavior emphasizes complete contextualization and nuanced interpretation over generalization and mechanical causation. His example (and Ryle's) is the human eye-blink—a mechanical-causal explanation of a human eye-blink would describe the muscle contraction and neurobiological mechanisms of this behavior. But there is far more to it when contextualized in human interaction; a blink can be a non-verbal sign of solidarity among two people. It can also be parodied as a type of sarcastic communication. It can also be *feigned* solidarity between two people and a kind of deception. All these nuances require a "thick description" of the context, the history, and the particular circumstance of the interacting parties in order to obtain a full interpretation of the phenomenon in question.

Whatever the particulars of the depth psychology school in question, depth psychology operates in precisely the same manner, and though there are now efforts underway to connect depth psychological approaches to neurobiology (Solms and Turnbull 2002), in general the practice of depth psychotherapy (Beinenfeld 2005; Gabbard 2010; Stein 2010; Wolf 2002) involves the same process of "thick description" in regard to the individual (Beinenfeld 2005; Tasman *et al.* 2003: 461–487). Such depth psychological theories, like those of symbolic anthropology, are not necessarily predictive in the empirical sense, but interpretive:

> The aim is to draw large conclusions from small, but very densely textured facts; to support broad assertions about the role of culture in the construction of collective life by engaging them exactly with complex specifics.
>
> (Geertz 1973: 28)

One has only to replace the word "collective" with "individual" in the above sentence to have the essential aim of depth psychological theory made identical (Tasman *et al.* 2003: 3–62). The methods of the two fields of depth psychology and symbolic anthropology therefore share similar approaches, regardless of what school of thought one uses. However, depth psychology and interpretive/symbolic anthropology naturally both utilize different data sets and different settings. They are not, however, unrelated to one another, since as we have already discussed, such thickly described individuals will act in a complex, interrelated manner to produce a thickly described culture, and in a manner so tightly interwoven as to give the lie to the artificial nature of the boundaries between them.

Blinders on Both Sides

Generally speaking, anthropology uses data about cultures and large-scale behavior patterns. Interpretations are based on theories of structures, anti-structures, functions, and so on within a culture. Depth psychology analyzes the detailed inner workings of an individual mind in all its internal complexities. Studying both kinds of literature, however, reveals the limitations of each approach. Where early psychologists such as Jung often misused the anthropological theories of their day (Segal 2007), there are also examples of anthropologists misreading Freud, Jung, and many others. Geertz (1973), for example, notes the various shortcomings of Freud's interpretations of culture, and Jung's work in general has been overlooked by anthropologists for some time (Greenwood 1990, 2009). Not only have psychoanalysts made overly simplifying assumptions about cultures, anthropologists, too, have often made simplifying assumptions about human mental activity, or would benefit from the insight of depth psychology.

Anthropologist Roy Rappaport (1999), whom I will discuss at length later, for example, in his discussion of ritual as self-communication, argues that rituals access aspects of the mind that are normally inaccessible to awareness, making them "auto-communicative" (1999: 51). Similarly, his discussions of the non-discursive aspects of ritual and the emotional and physiological systems it engages (1999: 99), the psychological balancing effect of ritual (1999: 103–104), the internal conflict brought on by excessive alternatives (1999: 165), the effects of altered conscious states (1999: 201), the proposed physiological effects of ritual belief (1999: 319), the concept of the *numinous* (1999: 374–381) which occupied Jung especially in his writings, and the dissociation of the psyche (1999: 384), describe phenomena in a comparatively cursory manner that would benefit from the insight of a neurobiologically informed depth psychology (such as Brüne 2008; Goodwyn 2012; McNamara 2009; Panksepp 2004; Solms and Turnbull 2002; Stein 1997; Van der Hart *et al.* 2006). However, it is only such an informed *depth* psychology that could do justice to the fully interpretive approach, and precisely because of the emphasis of thick description in both disciplines. Other, purely biological, evolutionary, or neural approaches would likely be prohibitively reductive—not that reductionism is inherently bad: Isaac Newton, for example, was able to reduce all physical motion to a handful of simple laws. But human ritual behavior is another matter entirely due to its immense complexity. I therefore adopt a cautious stance with respect to reductive analyses in this volume. One fine day, perhaps, we may be able to reduce human behavior to a set of equations—for now, however, I will only rarely assume that I have explained ritual phenomena "with zero remainder."

Further examples of the overlap between anthropology and psychology include Rappaport's assertion that the clear, "digital" messages of ritual can override or suppress the vague, ambiguous, and "analog" messages of a person's unconscious biological and/or mental state (1999: 140). Such statements would benefit from the literature on ritual in psychotherapy (cf. Orlandini 2009; Jungian literature on the psychology of ritual-like behavior is extensive—see Haule 2011, for examples; see also Van der Hart *et al.* 2006), in which such proposed processes have been discussed as they occurred in real time, while in psychodynamic treatment.

Geertz's discussion of the emotional effect of one's "explanatory apparatus" in ascribing meaning to life's experiences (1973: 100), in which a failure to explain life's vicissitudes leads to "deep disquiet", would benefit from the discussion of case material in which such disquiet could be thickly described, which could not only confirm or modify Geertz's hypothesis, but enrich it. Furthermore, his exploration of the emotional effects and praxis of more basic instincts in the Rangda and Barong ritual or Balinese cockfighting depend upon Freudian concepts of eros vs. thanatos, and id vs. superego, respectively, thus calling for a more intensive examination of these interpretations in light of more recent depth psychological thought. Geertz is sensitive enough to recognize this difficulty, and even outlines the psychological lacunae in his own theorizing when he states: "There is a good deal of talk about emotions 'finding a symbolic outlet' or 'becoming attached to appropriate symbols'—but very little idea of how the trick is really done" (1973: 207). The present volume attempts to look at such "tricks" and offers some proposed models for how they are done, the goal being to apply such "tricks" to the consulting room.

Elsewhere Geertz recognizes the individual psychology that is implicit in much anthropological thinking: "Anthropology is only apparently the study of customs, beliefs, or institutions. Fundamentally it is the study of thought" (Geertz 1973: 352, criticizing Lévi-Strauss). Lévi-Strauss is of course another example of an anthropologist who leaned heavily in the direction of psychology to explain his theory of myth, though he did not fully engage with psychodynamic literature of his time. In Chapter 2 I will explore one possible way to bring the psychological and anthropological frameworks together.

Chapter 2

A Dynamic Interdisciplinary Approach to Ritual and Psychotherapy

The pursuit of meaning is at the heart of human activity.
– Verdery (2009: 304)

One can see from the foregoing that anthropological theory and depth psychology both have lacunae with respect to each other, and that a careful dialogue between them might yield the kind of interdisciplinary approach we are looking for. Anthropology needs the insights of depth psychology to provide justification for the assumptions made in the areas of the emotional function of ritual, myth, social functioning, and communication for the individual. Depth psychology, by contrast, needs the insights of anthropology to cover its weak or vague characterizations of what is universal and what is particular in human behavior.

Universals

We have seen how anthropology can benefit from depth psychology. Now we shall explore how depth psychology can gain from anthropological inquiry. This is because psychologists have traditionally used the data from cross-cultural similarities to bolster their statements about how human nature and individual minds work. The hunt for universals was an occupation with early anthropologists, but in the middle of the twentieth century it fell out of favor. Geertz's influence was strongly felt here, in his criticism of the overemphasis on universals at the expense of the particulars needed to generate a thick description of human culture.

But universals have experienced a resurgence of interest, particularly in light of the investigations of evolutionary psychologists (cf. Buss 2005, Brüne 2008), and cognitive anthropologists (McCauley and Lawson 2002; Pyysiäinen 2009; Whitehouse and Laidlaw 2007), whom we will discuss later. A revisitation and perhaps reworking of Jung's theory of the collective unconscious and the "archetypes," in particular, due to its "midway" status between individual and social psychology (and its similarity with Durkheim's *conscience collective*), is a productive area to mine.

Anthropology, according to anthropologist Donald Brown (1991: 6), has traditionally fallen victim to three main assumptions that have precluded the study of universals: first, that culture is a distinct phenomenon that cannot be reduced to psychology or biology; second, that culture is the primary determinant of human behavior; and third, that culture is largely arbitrary. These assumptions, taken at face value, would seem to preclude any integration with psychology whatsoever, in that they rigidly and excessively reduce psychology to anthropology. Despite the obvious applicability of depth psychology to anthropology, and vice versa, Brown observes that anthropologists have traditionally been skeptical and even hostile toward psychology, particularly psychodynamic theory (1991: 38). This situation, however, need not continue.

Cultural Universals and Jung's "Archetypes"

Universals were especially important for Jung, as his theory of "archetypes" depended heavily upon his observations of the widespread distribution of various recurrent religious motifs. Jung linked his theorizing on archetypes to recurrent motifs—ideas that one can find in unrelated cultures all over the world and across time. To explain this uniformity, he posited that the unconscious human mind contained instinctual processes that did not contain innate stories so much as nudge the psyche to create stories of similar theme and structure in the presence of typical life situations. Archetypes manifest themselves in their ability to organize images and concepts in all human beings (Jung 1919: para. 440).

Jung theorized that archetypes work by "activating" in the presence of appropriate stimuli. He furthermore argued that archetypes are context-sensitive, requiring the proper environmental stimulation before "activating" and emerging into consciousness creatively (Jung and Meyer-Grass 2008: 162). Thus we see even here that a closer reading of Jung reveals a more subtle integration of individual and cultural contents, as opposed to a simple dichotomy of distinct minds and cultures distantly interacting. Unfortunately Jung was not systematic enough to emphasize this point throughout his writings.

The study of universals in anthropology, however, does not necessitate a return to a dualistic model of a culture-free "human nature," upon which an arbitrary culture is superimposed. It does not require a reduction of culture to psychology or biology either. What it does, in the context of a densely interactive and overlapping model of depth sociology, is in effect to rework the concept of human nature itself. Here, human nature is seen as a capacity that includes and operates *within, through, and from* culture that is not separate from biology and psychology but tightly interwoven within it. Put another way, the human mind is biologically prepared to receive and heavily process specific cultural information, and the interaction of both leads to self-organizing universals in the psyche. The kind of interactionism I advocate for here is strongly supported by much recent work in evolutionary psychology (Buss 2005) as well as work in many other fields

(Goodwyn, 2012). It is this fact that informs the present volume in what I am calling the dynamic interdisciplinary study of ritual and psychotherapy.

Donald Brown defines several types of universal. *Absolute* universals are behaviors that are present in all societies so far characterized, without exception. Examples of these include concepts of luck and precedent, body adornment, division of labor, romantic love, ethnocentrism, emotion-specific facial expressions, fear of snakes, specific kinds of tools such as cutters, pounders, piercers, and containers. *Near* universals are those which appear with very few exceptions—e.g. fire use, domestic dog keeping, and the use of the colors red, white, and black in rituals. *Conditional* universals include if–then statements such as: if a society expresses a preference for handedness, it will always be the right hand. *Statistical* universals are ones that are not universal but appear so often in unrelated societies that they far exceed chance, such as how in a large number of unrelated languages, the term representing the pupil of the eye is a word meaning "little person" (Brown 1991, 1999, 2004). Brown, however, notes that the anthropological study of universals has been shoddy and sporadic, lacking any sort of central, unifying theory. By contrast, he argues, psychologists have been much more systematic in such exploration, but they have always been open to the criticism that they lacked the anthropological data they needed to really back up their ideas (Brown 2004: 50).

Three causes for universals are identified by Brown. First is the diffusion of ancient cultural traits—an example being fire use and tools. These were developed at a very early time in human history due to their utility and were passed on to all cultures—note that even diffusion, however, must align well with universal human tendencies in order to survive (more on this factor—what I call "psychological resonance"—below).

The second cause is cultural reflection, which likely indicates universal experiences such as the differentiation of kin terminology. The third comprises, for Brown, "those universals whose causes lie more or less directly in the nature of the human mind, or that are features of the human mind" (Brown 2004: 50). Of the latter, Brown comments:

> Recalling what was said earlier about disciplinary differences, it should be noted that those sociocultural anthropologists who are most qualified to document universals are *not as a rule well qualified to explain them, [since they] are neither psychologists nor biologists* . . . Anthropologists usually define culture in terms that distinguish it from nature . . . Other definitions of culture correctly acknowledge a continuous intermixing *with* nature.
>
> (Brown 2004: 51–52, emphasis added)

The present work seeks to assist in this explanation, at least in regard to the subject of ritual biology, psychology, and anthropology. Compare this newer anthropological data with Jung's early speculations on human nature; building on the known universals in his time, of which many more now are known, Jung described his "collective unconscious" and its "archetypes":

> the instincts are not vague and indefinite by nature, but are specifically formed motive forces which, long before there is any consciousness, and in spite of any degree of consciousness later on, pursue their inherent goals. Consequently they form very close analogies to the archetypes, so close, in fact, that there is good reason for supposing that the archetypes are the unconscious images of the instincts themselves, in other words, that they are *patterns of instinctual behaviour*. The hypothesis of the collective unconscious is, therefore, no more daring than to assume there are instincts . . . [archetypes] are not in the form of images filled with content, but at first only as *forms without content*, representing merely the possibility of a certain type of perception and action.
>
> (Jung 1959b: paras. 91–99, emphasis original)

This basic definition of the archetype has undergone near-endless elaboration and mystification, some by Jung himself, but if we eschew such excesses and return to the kernel of Jung's idea here, and acknowledge the dense interactivity of individual minds and cultures, we can see a new concept emerging that incorporates mind and culture simultaneously. We will return to a discussion of the archetype later when we discuss the cognitive science of religion and ritual.

In any case, such instinctual processes would be universal biological and psychological content-free *tendencies* of emotion, perception, and conception. In other words, they are all forms of prepared, focused learning tendencies or attentional biases. These would from early development on interact continuously with the surrounding environment to create not an infinite variety of cultural forms, but rather a constrained plenitude of forms, some of them more likely to arise than others in any given culture. These tendencies are not simply unicorns postulated by Jung, either. Cognitive anthropologists (McCauley and Lawson 2002; Pyysiäinen 2009; Whitehouse and Laidlaw 2007), completely independent of Jungian theory, document numerous such tendencies (and characterize them in greater detail), and postulate similarly to Jung that they encourage the formation of recurrent cultural forms (see Goodwyn, 2013). Though they make no reference to Jung, their data are relevant to his initial hypothesis—it is merely an accident of disciplinary subdivision that Jungians themselves (typically more involved in clinical case study) did not undertake such empirical endeavors. In any case, in the spirit of interdisciplinary comparison, we can now see that such data are relevant to a reworking of depth psychology and anthropology with respect to each other.

The aforementioned tendencies are not merely due to individual universal psychological factors, but those factors *in the full context of* a surrounding culture that has built itself upon countless generations of continual feedback. Out of this interaction, it makes sense that certain forms would recur regardless of particular cultural lineage to produce statistical, conditional, near, or absolute universals, depending on the intensity of *both* the individual tendencies in question, *and* the regularity of the cultural stimuli in question.

With this model, we achieve a new level of clarity, insofar as we can begin to see what contributes to these tendencies' formation. To understand these *recurrent psychocultural forms*, then, is to understand not only recurrent cultural problems dealt with by all peoples, but provide an independent measure of the intensity of the tendencies responsible for the form in question, as the varying degrees of universality ranging from statistical to absolute give us a partial measure of their instinctual insistence. Each culture known becomes, then, a "natural experiment" in which such individual human tendencies do not *cause* such-and-such a form, but contribute, at varying levels of urgency, to the dense vortex of continual interaction of individual with environment and culture.

Applications in the Psychology of Religion and Ritual: The Collective Element

In general, the goal of "depth sociology" should be to achieve a more complete description and understanding of the individual *in context* with his/her society, allowing a fuller description of each individual as well as each culture. For the psychology of religion and ritual, this goal requires a model for how the individual psyche influences and contributes to the formation of recurrent psychocultural religious forms, and vice versa. That is, depth psychologists searching for a field in which to explore the rationale and details behind comparing individual dream content and ubiquitous mythic motifs will be able to find it in such a model, since its recurrence is suggestive of a constant intrapsychic and psychocultural dynamic for an individual in his/her cultural context. And anthropologists, seeking to explore precisely how constants of the human individual psyche may contribute to a religious structure, or how a particular structure interacts with each individual psyche (reflecting the approaches of both Jung and Durkheim, respectively), will be better equipped to do so, and in a manner which avoids false dichotomies of mind and culture.

The foregoing analysis suggests several conclusions which will be utilized in this book. As we have seen, since the days of the early anthropologists and psychoanalysts, individual and cultural systems have been largely viewed in isolation, with vague, incomplete, or sometimes simply inaccurate references to the other. This tendency has persisted to varying degrees. When psychoanalysts reference anthropological data, if they do so at all, the data are often distorted, dismissed, misused, or incomplete (Bruner 1998; Orlandini 2009; Segal 2007; Staude 1976). At the same time, when anthropologists refer to psychological principles as part of their theories, it is often in a way that is vague, cursory, or oversimplified (Brown 2004; Gras 1981; Haule 2011; Staude 1976); this is unfortunate since both subjects so obviously influence one another, with neither deserving of causal primacy. Neither individual psychology nor cultural forms and structures are solely responsible for one another, and neither can lay claim to the status of a first principle. Rather, both interact with each other in a given human lifetime from the earliest stages.

The Collective Element of Mind-Culture

With the recognition that what goes on in an individual psyche is a complex interplay of cultural symbols and imagery, combined with innate organizing processes that guide and direct learning and conceptualization, it is clear that—just as Jung and Durkheim proposed, albeit in different terms—there is a collective element within each individual psyche that orders the life experience of a person who in turn feeds into this same collective element. Thus neither culture nor the individual psyche can be seen as dependent upon the other in any simple way, and the collective element—whether one calls it the collective unconscious, the objective psyche, the *conscience collective*, or whatever—is a critical element of the behavior of both individuals and cultures, and this is particularly true of ritual, as we will see in the following chapters.

An initial example will be offered to illustrate how particular subjects and problems in the psychology of religion might be approached under this paradigm. In the 1970s, anthropologist Victor Turner offered a sociological analysis of the Mexican Revolution of 1810, during which a major social upheaval erupted and overturned the then-dominant regime. Referring to Freud's concept of "primary process," which is the raw, emotional, largely unconscious substratum of the mind, he describes how this individual psychological concept can be seen to have played out in the revolution due to its collective nature, likening the overthrow of political authority at the social level to the instinctive drives of the unconscious overthrowing repressive psychological defenses. This process, he argued, would be richly symbolic in expression due to its relationship with primary process as described by Freud (Turner 1974: 110). Later he went on to state:

> What seems to happen is that when a major public dramatic process gets under way, people, whether consciously, preconsciously, or unconsciously, take on roles which carry with them, if not precisely recorded scripts, deeply engraved tendencies to act and speak in suprapersonal or "representative" ways appropriate to . . . [for example] a certain central myth of the death or victory of a hero or heroes . . . Another way of putting it would be that "collective representations" had displaced "individual representation". The Christ myth is here the model, not in a cognitive and bloodless way, but in an existential and bloody way.
>
> (Turner 1974: 123)

Here we see Turner interpreting the Mexican Revolution in terms of the mobilization of collective representations (or, in depth psychology, archetypal images), making the point that humans are very much cultural as well as individual beings, with both aspects of their psyche playing out simultaneously. As an anthropologist, he writes from the perspective of large-scale movements, but he bases his explanation on Freudian ideas of primary process and includes a great deal of psychoanalytic speculation on the individual psychological contributions to these movements. Jung would have agreed with the idea of primary process, but would have likely gone further by conceptualizing this in terms of the mobilization of an archetypal narrative "emerging from the collective unconscious"—in this case, the passion, death, and rebirth of the Christ (Jung 1919, 1954, 1959a, 1959b, 1970). Jung often spoke of the way in which archetypal images emerge spontaneously at times of strong affect and/or strife and sometimes come to organize and/or dominate the individual psyche(s). He furthermore documented many examples from his practice of archetypal images emerging during times of stress, dysfunction, or social transition in individuals. He often noted the particularly "religious" nature of the dreams and ideas that came about during these moments (numerous examples in Jung 1984, 1997; Jung and Meyer-Grass 2008).

The Jungian and Durkheimian interpretations are, when freed of false dichotomies, complementary, but force the attention on either the perspective of the individual as acted upon by the surrounding culture (anthropological), or of the culture as acted upon by individuals (psychoanalytic). A synthetic, interactive perspective, following Greenwood, has both individual behavior and cultural forms acted upon by a collective element that is comprised of universal human tendencies—raw biological/instinctual predispositions toward certain kinds of action and conception embodied by the human universals discussed earlier—that have been nurtured by individuals over generations of feedback. This collective element will be experienced as "external" to the individual's personal element or "ego," because it did not create either the biological universals or the generationally maintained cultural forms that combine with them in early development. Thus this collective element impresses upon the personal element with great emotional power, bringing recurrent motifs or powerfully present cultural forms to bear upon it at a deep, emotional level.

The collective element acts on individuals early in development and affects individuals and cultures through its mythic narrative power during times of strife and revolution as a biocultural behavioral motivator. Individuals will react to this with varying levels of insight as to its influence on them. In the above example, the collective element would be composed of the human "primary processes," or biological–emotional internal conflicts that strive for the self, as well as other primary drives that strive for acceptance within a group (Freud's id–superego conflict, or Jung's analysis of the various complexes that vie for conscious control—both theories have been expanded and modified by more recent depth psychologists) combined with a collection of vivid symbols (themselves highly recurrent throughout history and across cultures) known to everyone, absorbed at an early age, and capable of profound interactions with those primary processes—in this case the peaceful mother-earth Brown Virgin of Guadalupe and the paradoxical hero-martyr of Christ.

The potency of the collective element is partly due to its both "Jungian" or depth psychological and "Durkheimian" or sociological (usually at least partially) unconscious origin. For our purposes, the collective unconscious and the *conscience collective*, preferring neither, are combined into the term "collective element." Blending them in this manner resolves the false nature–nurture dichotomy that has plagued both disciplines for so long. This collective element moves us like gods (and in fact will be experienced by the individual in often godlike imagery). And once various political pressures reach a critical point in a culture, the collective element then reacts similarly in many people, affecting individuals and societies at the same time to result in a transformation/revolution through its effects on key individuals that are at nexus points of power, such as the heroes of Hidalgo's insurrection—crucial members of the Mexican Revolution. As these key players act out their parts, the rest of the society dynamically both observes and contributes to the archetypal narratives apotheosized in the collective element, sometimes creating new variants to feed back into it for later eras. We will return to this model of the psyche in the last section of this book, but before we do that we must explore the biological and cognitive contributors to the collective element in greater detail, so we can discuss the whole model in terms of its impact on the way we will examine ritual in regard to psychotherapy.

Deepening the Roots with Biology and Cognitive Science

In order to integrate the foregoing model of psychology and anthropology with the biological and cognitive sciences, we have to recognize that simple models of linear causality will not suffice. In other words, as Geertz (1973) has already observed, we cannot simply assume a layered approach in which biology "causes" psychological functions, which in turn cause anthropological structures/functions. A more realistic approach that recognizes the inherent dynamic complexity of all these disciplines is the "circular causality" approach discussed by theoretical neuroscientist and philosopher Walter J. Freeman (1999). Freeman incorporates neuroscience in a manner which connects the normally reductive and linear observations of biology and cognitive neuroscience with concepts much more germane to both depth psychology and anthropology—intentionality and will. Without going into too much detail, for the present work it is recognized that in the human mental state in ritual, numerous factors interact with one another in a dynamic fashion, rather than in the linear fashion challenged by Geertz. In this model, basic neurobiological responses from the brain constantly interact with the environment: "Circular causality expresses the interrelations between levels in a hierarchy: a top-down macroscopic state simultaneously influences microscopic particles that bottom-up create and sustain the macroscopic state" (Freeman 1999: 146).

This basic model provides the primary structure for the dynamic interdisciplinary analysis of ritual (and of course can be applied to other interdisciplinary subjects as well): innate biological tendencies will interact and incorporate environmental states such as cultural expressions, symbols, and norms, as well as the history of prior states in a continual process of feedback adjustment. As Freeman observes, the maintenance of this outlook is crucial to understand the social sciences (among other sciences). It is Freeman's considerations that strongly advise against a hasty reduction of ritual to any particular cause (1999: 168). Thus, as we explore the cognitive and biological factors that play into the study of ritual, we should keep in mind that both are interactive players in a grand self-organizing system in the human mind: biology influences and is influenced by psychology, which influences and is influenced by culture. All combine to create the collective and personal elements of the human psyche. This formulation highlights a point Freeman discusses at length: that as the self develops, the dichotomy between subjective and objective becomes blurry and less useful for analysis. Here that is modeled by the fact that the collective element becomes a part of each person, and these two elements interact in complex ways. This will become apparent as we continue.

Balancing Biological, Psychological, and Cultural Perspectives in the Study of Ritual

As we explore the dynamic interdisciplinary approach to ritual and its applications, we should keep in mind that these various disciplines often have different frames of reference to the study of ritual, use different data, and ask different questions. That makes the multidisciplinary work tricky, but not impossible, providing that we are careful to recognize these differences. For example, biological theories often emphasize evolutionary origins, discuss ritual function in terms of adaptive benefits for the organism or species, whether collective or individual, and describe efficacy in terms of biological effects of a particular behavior, whatever it may be. The biological approach, which includes evolutionary biology, often focuses on both the ultimate as well as the proximate causes for various behaviors. That is, the function of religion or ritual can be explored for both its immediate effects and its causes in terms of neurochemical or physiological changes, or it can be understood from the point of view of adaptive behavior as compared to other animals.

Cognitive theories of ritual also discuss origins from biology and evolution, but are more specifically concerned with cognitive mental structures, and how they function in everyday development, learning, and functioning—they therefore tend to be more proximal than ultimate. What rituals do will be discussed in terms of how a particular behavior or cognition helps to clarify thinking, improve functioning in a proximal sense, improve social cooperation, and so on.

On top of the important discussion of causes, however, are the discussions of interpretation, which is where both psychodynamic and anthropological theories factor in. Psychodynamic theories discuss the origin of ritual in fundamental psychodynamic structures such as id, ego, superego, archetype, object relations, complexes, and so on. We have crossed the threshold now into interpretive science, where complexities must be dealt with from the perspective of mentality, intentionality, and complex webs of cultural meanings. Dynamic theories emphasize the role of the day-to-day, still more immediate function of intrapsychic interplay, whether it be the praxis of primitive drives, dealing with concrete intrapsychic conflicts and helping to resolve them, expressions of archetypal themes, mediating internal conflict, and so on.

Cultural theories, however, only touch on such issues. Rather, they emphasize the origin of rituals in terms of their stabilizing effects on societies, or the ways in which they solidify certain social interactions. Systems under study are much more complex and nuanced, and functions and effects are described in terms of group dynamics and social interchange. Only rarely, as in the example of biogenetic structuralism, are the other fields brought into discussion. Thus we have moved from biological, evolutionary principles all the way to large-scale effects of the interplay between individuals and societies. The way these various disciplines work, however, is not in isolation in any individual; all continuously play a part in constructing the individual's phenomenal world. Biological adaptations will need to be present to form cognitive structures, and interact with environments to generate various intrapsychic dynamics that will present across a lifetime, and will be in continual feedback with the environment and the culture, creating a dense interactionism:

Biology ← → Psychology ← → Culture

This web of interaction that, together, influences behavior, feeds into later biological function, psychological orientation, and local cultural dynamics.

Part II

A Dynamic Interdisciplinary Approach

In the following chapters, we will discuss what rituals do from a biological perspective, centering the discussion on biogenetic structuralism, neuroscience, and placebo studies. In Chapter 4 we will explore the cognitive science of religion and ritual and the ways recurrent symbols are created and maintained across many generations and/or are independently invented cross-culturally. We will see why this occurs and propose an explanation for why such symbols find their way into the collective element, and how rituals play into this. After that we will examine depth psychological theories of ritual and look at the ways rituals have been observed by therapists and clinicians to make profound impressions on individual minds. Finally, we will survey the various anthropological theories of ritual which have emerged in the last century or so and note the numerous points of intersection between them and the previous three branches. From there we will discuss how the study of ritual may be utilized in psychiatric and psychological practice.

Chapter 3

The Biological Branch

Mind/Body Interactions

The great error of our day in the treatment of the human body [is that] physicians separate the soul and the body.
– Plato

It will become apparent later when we review the field of ritual studies that our society is ritually "impoverished," meaning that compared to other cultures, we do not engage in much ritual activity. The reasons for this are complex and we'll get to them, but for now suffice it to say that generally ritual is not felt to be very useful or "effective," consisting of only so much pretense and "play acting." Though this trend is slowly changing, we can still see that, within the mainstream post-Protestant, post-Enlightenment Western approach to life that is quite dominant today, ritual behavior is not felt to be important. Contrast this to many traditional societies around the globe, in which certain rituals are simply *not optional.* Thus, in our society it is something of a surprise that rituals have so many potent effects at so many levels. To many other societies, however, this would be no surprise at all.

The Biology of Ritual

The field of biogenetic structuralism is a synthesis of neurobiological, anthropological, and phenomenological approaches to human nature that presages and overlaps with my dynamic interdisciplinary approach here. With Walter Freeman (1999), biogenetic structuralist Charles Laughlin (1990) points out that neurobiologically the mind does not passively record the world as it is, but anticipates certain kinds of sensory information that it selectively seeks out to help structure its "cognized world," or world of mentally structured phenomenal experience, and this very fact blurs the boundary of mind/body, culture/nature, and, I add, self/other. As we will see, rituals emphasize this blurred quality through several distinct mechanisms, making things "blurrier" and therefore enhancing the intense feeling of connectedness that often accompanies it, though the things connected vary greatly depending on the ritual. We will see that ritual incorporates all the mental associations, including conceptual, imaginary, affective, arousing, metabolic, and physical-motor connections, that elaborate the meaning of ritual objects, concepts, and participants.

Laughlin explains that ritual is so important to human functioning because of its enhanced effects on the highly symbolic nature of thinking in general (Laughlin 1990: 5). Biogenetic structuralists therefore argue that the brain plays a fundamental part in ritual experience through its capacity to *co-create* a *cognized and highly symbolic* world—that is, one in which the mind participates through its various biological mechanisms. In ritual, this cognized world is different than the everyday world, since it is

> thoroughly symbolic in nature. The symbolic function amounts to the relationship between a sensory object and neurocognitive, neuroendocrinal, neuroimmunological, or other somatic processes intent upon this object . . . [it] is the means by which the whole network of models mediating the meaning of an object is neuro-dynamically associated with that object.
>
> (Laughlin 1990: 20)

That ritual involves an intensely symbolic mode of thinking is discussed in great detail by the cognitive science of ritual, discussed later, as well as by depth psychologists and anthropologists; here we note that this mode of thought now has a firm biological underpinning according to biological science, and we are beginning to see how intense ritual activity can alter physiological function. Psychoneuroimmunologists, for example, suggest that concentration on certain kinds of vivid imagery (used often in ritual performance) may produce enhanced immunological activity at specific body regions (Ader 1980; Ganong 1986; Laughlin 1990: 30), encourage the elimination of pain and anxiety, or balance the autonomic nervous system functions in various ways, as can dancing, drumming, chanting, using entheogens, fasting, sleep deprivation, or physical ordeals. It should not be surprising, then, that ritual is an absolute universal. All of these techniques will be discussed in the following chapters.

Laughlin also points out that the reverse process, where biological activity can trigger certain kinds of dream imagery, can occur (1990: 30), a process I explore in much greater detail in *The Neurobiology of the Gods* (Goodwyn 2012). Laughlin argues that symbolically rich rituals (which is most of them) may furthermore intensify right-brain processing to produce an "alternative reality" rich in intuitive, vivid sensory and emotional experience (1990: 30–31)—types of experience that we are constantly trying to access in psychotherapy, and that are particularly difficult to access due to the typically low-ritual, abstract, and verbal nature of most psychotherapy modes.

Laughlin also observes that rituals use myths—sacred narratives—in a specific way, not as merely an "expression" of the myth, but by providing a way for ritual performers to *participate* in the myth as lived experience through metaphor. The importance of narrative will be discussed in full when we review the psychodynamic effects of ritual; here it is important to note its biological connection. A function of myth according to Laughlin is to provide an explanation for the origin of the cosmos and for society, to explain life and death and answer the "why" questions. Such myths are "grounded and vivified" (1990: 23) by ritual, bringing the cognized symbols to life. Myth also provides a cosmology that helps to interpret experience—this is crucial for human functioning, as we will also explore in more detail when we discuss the depth psychology of ritual. Interpretation imparts meaning to the events of life, and without it, we are left without any meaning. What, however, is the evidence that ritual activity (or even mental activity in general) can affect physiology? Such evidence can be found in abundant studies of the placebo effect.

Placebo Effects: Altering Biology and Physiology with Minds Engaged in Ritual

Meaning is perhaps the most crucial element of what is known as the placebo effect—the effect in which our physiology is shaped by medical interventions that do not have anything to do with biochemistry or other mechanisms of healing known to medical science. The most relevant data available to understand how ritual actions can affect physiology (such as what may have happened to my grandfather), hinted at by Laughlin, are therefore in the growing field of placebo studies. The placebo effect is a long-known effect in medical science, where the patient responds to treatment that does not have a specifically identified biochemical or surgical mechanism. In other words, a person who feels relief from back pain by the administration of a sugar pill is experiencing the placebo effect. Put another way, it is not the chemical in the pill that relieves the pain, it is the meaning of seeking medical attention, finding a physician, getting an explanation of her/his pain, and administering a physical object into his/her body which relieves the pain.

Often dismissed as a nuisance phenomenon, an example of "quackery," or a confounder of research trials, the placebo response is actually highly relevant to the questions posed by the present work because placebo studies examine exactly the kinds of physiological responses to actions that interest us; ones associated with actions that are known not to have any directly measurable biochemical or surgical cause. The placebo effect therefore shows us how our bodies can be directly altered by social variables, mental images, cultural beliefs, and so forth. Thus, to understand the wider question of how ritual might affect biology, it is worth going into placebo responses in greater detail.

We are only now beginning to understand what factors go into placebo responses; however, the efficacy of many healing rituals has been touted throughout the ages, and it is likely that ancient humans used the placebo response to maximal effect simply through generations of trial-and-error. Placebo researchers Shapiro and Shapiro even go so far as to say "The history of medical treatment is essentially the history of the placebo effect" (Shapiro and Shapiro 1999: 13). In any case, we will explore many such examples throughout this volume.

Physician, psychoanalyst, and placebo researcher Richard Kradin highlights the cultural nature of placebo responses: "A distinguishing feature of psychosomatic disorders is their ability to change with the times—a feature shared by the placebo response" (Kradin 2008: 59). Kradin observes that placebo responses are universal, and that there are no specific personality traits that distinguish placebo responders from non-responders—only the context of the interaction created by the caregivers seems to matter (Kradin 2008: 85). The placebo effect has emerged in some literature as a legitimate subject of study in itself (Kradin 2008), and as will be seen, placebo effect studies provide us with many examples of ways in which symbolic experiences can affect brain and body physiology, and in some cases there are solid clues as to the precise mechanism of how this works.

What Systems Can Be Influenced by Placebo Effects?

Anthropologists Thompson *et al.* (2009) argue that "direct embodied experience" may be the most important part of placebo responses, and they argue that the placebo response may be an evolutionarily adaptive trait, and Kradin agrees on this count (Kradin 2008: 117). According to placebo researcher and neurobiologist Fabrizio Benedetti, the placebo effect is a potent psychobiological phenomenon where the body and brain anticipate and participate in clinical improvement. This phenomenon, furthermore, is generated by psychosocial context (Benedetti 2009: viii). Koshi and Short continue by arguing that the placebo effect is a highly significant kind of psychosocial interaction between patient and physician (two socially constructed roles), and does not equal quackery: "Studies mentioned here showed that meaning can have considerable physiologic action . . . Therefore, placebo is not the equivalent of 'no therapy'" (Koshi and Short 2007: 13).

Placebo effects, to date, have been observed in a variety of mental and physical disorders, including irritable bowel syndrome (Vase *et al.* 2005), depression (Khan *et al.* 2007; Leuchter *et al.* 2002; Vallance 2007), pain (Colloca and Benedetti 2005), Parkinson's disease (Colloca *et al.* 2004; McRae *et al.* 2004; Oken 2008), coughs and asthma (Benedetti 2009: 188–189), dyspepsia, ulcerative colitis, Crohn's disease (Benedetti 2009: 195), multiple sclerosis, epilepsy, dementia (Oken 2008), arthritis, ulcers, hypertension, warts, and cancer (Kradin 2008). One famous study showed that for chronic knee pain a "sham" procedure was effective and showed persistent alleviation of symptoms—equal in effectiveness to common knee surgery (Moseley *et al.* 2002). In a large meta-analysis of depression therapies, Sapirstein and Kirsch (1998) concluded that 73 percent of therapeutic responses to antidepressant medication were due to psychological factors surrounding the administration of antidepressant medication and other non-specific factors, as opposed to 27 percent due to the drug itself. For a psychiatrist, this means that I have to treat *nine* patients successfully with antidepressant medication before I can be reasonably certain that at least one of them improved due to the drug itself and not placebo effects. Placebo interventions have been shown to cause measurable change in brain physiology in brain imaging studies (Vallance 2007) that are distinct from those associated with medication (Leuchter *et al.* 2002). Placebo response to depression has also been shown

(Khan *et al.* 2007) to be long-lasting rather than temporary, as is the common misconception.

Medical anthropologist Daniel Moerman (2002) reports that sham medical procedures for chest pain, lumbar disc herniation, knee surgery, and Ménière's disease often show similar responses to actual procedures. Notice that there is really very little difference between a "sham procedure" and a "magic ritual." In some cases these sham procedures produce improvements in symptoms that last for years. Other studies have shown placebo effects to be highly significant and inducible via *symbolically meaningful* visual, auditory, and olfactory stimuli as well as *ritually*. All had conscious as well as unconscious effects (Koshi and Short 2007). These, as we will see, are correlated with psychologically resonant principles and agree with many of the observations of anthropologists. Interestingly, the placebo effect is not unique to humans—it has been observed in other animals (Ader and Cohen 1982).

Most ailments can improve with placebo—or "non-specific"—interventions, and these appear to depend greatly on the subject's state of mind. Shapiro and Shapiro (1997) suggest that modern treatments—in first world nations, that is—do not maximize the potential for placebo enhancement of treatment, and furthermore placebo response appears to be state-related rather than trait-related.[1] These observations agree with anthropological observations that modern Western culture is essentially ritually impoverished. Other factors include the subject's state of suggestibility and expectation of cure (Bandura 1997; De Pascalis *et al.* 2002; Price *et al.* 1999), number of visits during a treatment course (Thomas 1987), and the perceived *meaning* of the symptoms (Brody and Brody 2000). More frequent administration of a medication, larger pills, newer pills, and even the *color* of a pill can enhance or diminish placebo responses, as does the physician's optimism/pessimism, reputation and personality, and what the patient is told about the treatment and by whom (Moerman 2002). One dramatic case observed a euglycemic patient with multiple personalities in which one of the alter-egos was an insulin-dependent diabetic. This study (Rossi and Cheek 1992) provides fascinating evidence of how the mind can profoundly affect brain and body. Medical anthropologist Moerman (2002) argues that the placebo response should be reconceptualized as a "meaning response," citing a large array of studies.

Mind/body researcher Richard Kradin observes that many aspects of the doctor–patient relationship can promote wellbeing, including gaze attunement, touch, meaning, and imagery (2008: 147; see also Colloca *et al.* 2008; Oken 2008). Kradin also argues that placebo and nocebo response are types of Jungian complexes (Kradin 2004), recalling that Jung (1919) suggested complexes were *mediated by internal images*. This, he states, is strong evidence that mental images can actually induce physiological responses. This is plausible because we know that mental images are in fact linked to most responses in the nervous system (Kradin 2008: 186).

Kradin has thus already connected the biological and depth psychological aspects of such responses. Elsewhere he observes that the data on the placebo response argue for a comprehensive self-regulation system, which of course was presaged by Jung (Kradin 2008: 190) in his theoretical construct of the Self (Jung 1959a), which is a kind of homeostatic aspect of the mind that works toward healing of psychological trauma and greater functioning in life and society. Finally, Kradin's research points to a system that has both innate and early developmentally acquired factors, is non-linear in response, is strongly correlated with unconscious mind–body physiology, and can be invoked in therapy (2008: 197). These statements by placebo researchers will be very important when we discuss various healing rituals in Chapter 8.

Placebo Mechanisms: The Biological Ritual Connection

How does all this help us understand what rituals can do? The answer is that placebo responses are essentially ritual responses. The mechanism of the placebo effect is currently under investigation, but so far has been shown to be related to not only universal human brain systems (Kradin 2008; Benedetti *et al.* 2005; Lidstone and Stoessl 2007; McNamara 2009; Mayberg *et al.* 2002; Oken 2008), but those brain systems interacting in *socially significant* settings.

How does this happen? We are only beginning to understand the answer to that question; however, medical science now has established firm links between the brain (and hence, via correlation, the mind) and the immune system, the cardiovascular system, the respiratory system, the gastrointestinal system, and the skin (Viamontes and Nemeroff 2010). In the immune system, for example, the brain (Viamontes and Nemeroff, 2010) has specific receptors for the molecular signals known as cytokines that are produced by immune cells. In other words, when an infection is occurring, the immune cells release a variety of cytokines, and the brain senses what is going on. Through these sensory responses, the brain "listens" to the immune system and the inflammatory responses, and can respond accordingly with its own modification of those same responses (Viamontes and Nemeroff 2010: 371). Viamontes and Nemeroff summarize:

> The brain continuously receives, integrates, and interprets many streams of information. As the information and its subjective "meaning" are neurally represented, dedicated neuronal circuits respond to perceived risks and opportunities by altering internal physiology . . . The clinical effects of mental processes on physiology are profound.
>
> (Viamontes and Nemeroff 2010: 379)

Since medical science is where much of the relevant data on the biological responses to rituals comes from, we will explore the details of the biological responses to rituals in Chapter 8 when we discuss healing rituals. For now, we can see that the concepts of *meaning* and *mental image* have significant biological correlates and contributors. As we will see, ritual, through its use of *belief*, *social setting*, *symbols*, *sensory imagery*, and *empathic connection*, affects and is affected by the biological systems involved in the ritual. Thus we can see that, among many other things, rituals can affect our basic biology and physiological responses, and these responses can be very long lasting.

Conclusions

Thus, our first principle is established: in mental health settings, placebo study and biogenetic structuralism have shown empirically that meaning, mental image, dance, embodied ritual action, belief, social role, sacred symbol, physical touch, eye-gaze, and empathic human connection can all combine to affect our various biological systems, including not only the brain but the immune system, the gastrointestinal system, the skin, the heart, and the lungs. It is not so far-fetched, then, to consider what effect Old Eeky's "signs and words" might have had (in combination with the serum) on my grandfather's young physiology. It is these responses that we want to utilize in mental health practice to alleviate suffering. But what are the details, so we can incorporate them into mental health practice? Having established that ritual symbols and actions can heal, the next question we need to answer is the nature of these symbols and actions.

In the following chapters we will explore these questions, so we will be better able to understand how to create healing symbols for use in mental health practice. In the next chapter, we will focus on imagery in particular and its relation to narrative, language, and symbol, using a concept I develop called "psychological resonance."

Note

1. The opposite of the placebo, or "nocebo", effect has also been demonstrated in a variety of settings. Furthermore there does not appear to be a single placebo effect but many (Benedetti *et al.* 2005, 2007).

Chapter 4

The Cognitive Branch

Cognitive Anthropology and Psychological Resonance

Human fortunes are too intertwined for any one person to narrate his life alone.
– Frank Goodwyn (1993)

So we have seen that image and meaning, as well as belief, symbol, ritual action, and social connection, have been shown to have directly measurable effects on human physiology. This shows us in clear terms that rituals can affect our brains and bodies in profound, long-lasting ways. One of the main ways this is accomplished, we saw in the last chapter, is through imagery. But what kinds of images and meanings contribute to such responses? Are some images more effective than others? In this chapter we will look in greater detail at how *imagery* is used ritually and what contributes to memorable and efficacious rituals.

Psychological Resonance: The Cognitive Science of Ritual

Cognitive science contributes to the understanding of ritual largely in its elucidation of the way the human mind universally tends to construct the images, themes, and narratives that are used in ritual. Hence, it is here that we will learn what kinds of images are more likely to be used in ritual, and also what rituals do to our cognitive structures. Cognitive science, however, is distinct from the study of the biological systems likely involved in ritual. Cognitive science is also distinct from the study of the internal conflicts, defenses, or projections that use such images as conduits for their praxis (discussed in Chapter 5). In any case, before getting into the cognitive psychology of rituals, I need to establish an important concept I call *psychological resonance* that pertains to the ideas and images that influence ritual (and many other kinds of) thinking across numerous cultures worldwide (Goodwyn 2013).

We begin by noting that around the world and throughout history, the same kinds of mythic, symbolic, and ritual ideas continue to crop up time and again (ARAS 2010; Cirlot 1971; Eliade 1954, 1958; Leach and Fried 1984; Lehner 1956; Propp 1968; Stevens 1998; Thompson 1960; Tresidder 2005; Üther 2004; also Jung 1956). The cognitive science of religion, folklore, and ritual all explore such recurrent symbolism (Barrett 2007: 179). As we will see, such symbols are recurrent for a number of reasons which facilitate their use in ritual and so may be partly responsible for ritual efficacy.

What we are interested in here can be summed up in the following question: what makes one ritual more likely than another to be repeated across generations? In other words, given ritual A and B, why should ritual A be remembered and performed instead of ritual B? Are they both equally likely? Of course we already know the answer to that question is "no, they're not." So what is the difference?

The way to answer this question rests with the concept of cultural transmission: even though images, symbols, and ritual actions are culturally transmitted, "cultural transmission" is not a mere carbon-copying of stories, rituals, and belief systems across generations, but a complex process that is influenced by universal psychological principles. Cognitive scientists of ritual Robert McCauley and E. Thomas Lawson explain that transmission actually tends to transform ideas rather than replicate them faithfully, and this transformation is along certain predictable lines as a result of our universal mental structure (McCauley and Lawson 2002: 41).

The result is recurrent ideas, as discussed by cognitive anthropologist Harvey Whitehouse:

> Certain systematic biases in the way we humans think persist despite all our efforts to transcend them . . . Cognitively optimal concepts are ones that the human mind is naturally well-equipped to process and remember, or that readily trigger exceptionally salient or attention-grabbing inferences, *in the absence of any special training or inducement to learn such concepts.* Even when people have mastered a body of difficult-to-acquire concepts . . . they never outgrow their susceptibility to more natural ways of thinking.
>
> (Whitehouse 2004: 189, emphasis original)

Anthropologist Dan Sperber elaborates:

> [the cross-cultural resemblance] among cultural items is to be explained to some important extent by the fact that transformations tend to be biased in the direction of attractor positions in the space of possibilities.
>
> (Sperber 1996: 108)

McCauley and Lawson add that because of these systematic biases, some cultural representations will be more likely to persist across generations than others. Thus, much like rainfall into a canyon will ultimately wind up in a limited number of troughs no matter where it starts from, after generations of transmission, images, stories, and ritual acts will wind up falling into similar patterns all over the world regardless of their origin. Put another way, the fact that cultural transmission is highly divergent is easy to demonstrate—cultures, languages, and practices vary considerably across the globe. But at the same time, in some ways it is also *convergent*, since only a fraction of cultural material will be retained with each generation. Thus despite the near infinite variations of stories, images, and rituals, only the most powerful, memorable, and deeply moving ones will survive cultural transmission and not be forgotten. The most convergent will even survive despite efforts at eradication (for examples, see Goodwyn, 2013). What is left will be ritual themes that are automatically more likely to be more potent psychosomatically, and the most memorable and powerful themes will be the ones that recur throughout the globe despite large differences in time and space.

This is why recurrent motifs can be thought of as "attractor points": because, over repeated transmissions, deviations from such points will self-correct (McCauley and Lawson 2002: 42), and stories and rituals dispersed over large regions will tend to converge onto those that strike the human soul to its deepest core and resist the constant cultural variation that occurs from day to day. Cognitive anthropologists argue that our unconscious, universal mental processes are what shape this convergent transmission of accumulated storytelling and ritual forms. Recurrent motifs are therefore recurrent because they are "easy to think," are hard to forget, and move us emotionally and physically, connecting deeply with our universal emotional systems. Studying recurrent motifs therefore provides us with clues to the most powerful forces of the collective element of the human mind—what Jung would likely call "archetypal."

Recurrent ritual themes include beliefs in the efficacy of certain ritual actions over others, the order they "should" occur in, various constraints on ritual roles, common points of variability in forms, and so on. These commonalities are not the result of teaching or diffusion, but simply a matter of universal human tendencies facing similar situations, over time finding similar answers by way of the complex, concentrating process of cultural transmission. Over many generations, even the most isolated cultures gradually use similar universal cognitive mechanisms to maximize the effectiveness of their rituals (McCauley and Lawson 2002: 48). As we will see, this fact allows us to co-create rituals with patients in mental health settings, because everyone possesses these basic intuitions: only it takes a trained eye to find the convergent, recurrent elements amid the mass of chaotic material presented by the average patient.

Examples of Recurrent Motifs

As we explore what mental factors help to explain the phenomenon of recurrent motifs, we must venture into the study of oral folklore for the most relevant data. Oral folklore by its very nature is dependent upon the biological constraints of human memory, affect, and cognition, and thus highlights the process of cultural transmission that we are arguing is so relevant to the study of ritual. Interestingly, folklorists have noted that many recurrent motifs can be surprisingly specific. For example, the first two major episodes of the eighth-century Anglo-Saxon poem *Beowulf* (where the hero faces the monster Grendel and his mother) have been shown to parallel folktales and motifs in many other regions, and comprise both types 301 ("the Three Princesses") and 650A ("Strong John") of the Aarne–Thompson folktale type index—of which *Beowulf* is one example among 600 of type 301 alone so far that have been documented (Thompson 1960; Üther 2004). In these tales, a bear-like hero of unusual strength defeats a monster who is raiding a king's palace, which in defeat flees wounded, followed by the hero's descent into a watery underworld where he finds a magic sword and defeats more monsters there, but is left there by his treacherous companions, only for him to find his way out by various means (Garmonsway *et al.* 1971). Parallels to *Beowulf* have been found in areas such as Scotland, Ireland, Iceland, Wales, and Scandinavia, which is perhaps not surprising given their proximity to Anglo-Saxon England. But there are also parallels in Africa, Armenia, Burma, China, Finland, France, Hungary, India, Italy, Japan, Mexico, Poland, Polynesia, Russia, Sicily, Spain, Turkey, and the Americas (reviewed in Fulk *et al.* 2009: xxxvi–xliii; see also Ashliman 1987). The fight between Beowulf and the dragon also has countless parallels worldwide.[1]

As mentioned, with each retelling of a tale, subtractions and additions occur, but only some of these will "stick" and successfully become a part of a folk narrative. Gradually stories acquire "cognitively optimal" or "attractor state" elements, so that any story can, through the process of accretion, achieve the status of great legend, myth, or folktale. This seems to have occurred in the case of King Arthur, for example, according to historian Geoffrey Ashe (2003).

Further evidence comes from historian of folklore, Max Lüthi:

> The stability of fairytale transmission over centuries, which constantly provides grounds for amazement, is only partially ascribable to literary influence (which was for a long time underestimated but presently tends to be overestimated). The listener's demand for the familiar, for what was felt to be valid, was also a factor; and the demands imposed by narrative and mnemonic technique on narrators, as well as their artistic sense, conspired to maintain what was successful in terms of rhythm and sound. The narrator commits himself voluntarily to a formulation which seems to him to be optimal.
>
> (Lüthi 1984: 69)

Lüthi does not reference cognitive science in his 1984 work; however, more recent folklorists do (for example, Zipes 2006).

Attractor Points in the Narrative Field

To better understand cultural transmission, and to avoid the false dichotomy that oversimplifies it into either diffusion or independent invention, and the false nature–nurture and psychology–culture dichotomies implied within it, it is helpful to think of all the possible narratives as existing together on a field, but with a "terrain" corresponding to the likelihood of such a narrative being transmitted. Troughs correspond to high likelihood, acting like gravity wells on narratives over time. These gravity wells, or attractor points, represent stories that align well with the reliably emergent patterns in the human mind, and so stories will, over time, tend toward those positions. Since stories are constrained by the limitations of human memory, attention, visuo-cognitive ability, and emotional tone, eventually similar *themed* stories will emerge despite large distances in time and space. Such limitations, however, cannot operate in a vacuum and require an ambient culture to operate on. It requires storytellers, ritual-makers, religious men and women, and participants to make stories, rituals, and images.

But the things they make up will only be *guided* by universal human cognitive tendencies—as we are dealing with human beings, there will always be an element of freedom, arbitrariness, or perhaps even randomness to what is created. The end result, however, will either "stick" with the universal aspects of emotion, thinking, and memory—clearly part of the collective element discussed in Part I—or they will not. Over time, those created things that are the "stickiest" will remain because they have been discovered to be the most impressive to the most amount of people. These "resonant" or "sticky" elements are the ones most likely used in ritual to effect desired changes.

Thus we see that, like so many aspects of human experience, nature and nurture do not oppose one another but operate in concert to make our phenomenal or (to use the biogenetic structuralist term) *cognized* world. Moreover, those resonant images, stories, and rituals will tend to have the curious property that even though they have been created and modified by individual humans at various points, the criteria by which they survive generations are not. Such resonant expressions are therefore neither entirely created nor entirely given, but a combination of both. As such, they fit perfectly into the blended dynamic interdisciplinary model, and can be thought of poetically as "utterances" of the collective element of the psyche.

Psychological Resonance

But what are the qualities of these "sticky" stories, images, and rituals? What do they look like? Cognitive scientists Laidlaw and Whitehouse (2007), basing their argument on decades of cognitive science research, summarize that:

> People cannot be taught to believe just any old thing, no matter how hard you try to drum or beat propositions into them. They will only end up believing things that *resonate* with their implicit assumptions about the world—and the more implicit assumptions a proposition is supported by, the greater its chances of being believed. Those implicit assumptions cannot be taught . . . they are "instinctive", in the sense that they are the sorts of beliefs that children rapidly and uniformly acquire.
>
> (Laidlaw and Whitehouse 2007: 22, emphasis mine)

In Goodwyn (2013), I propose a definition I think may prove useful for theory and empirical research in the psychology of religion and folklore: *Psychological*

Resonance is defined as *a characteristic quality that can be applied to any image or narrative, that describes its mental "stickiness," its tendency to spontaneously emerge, and/or its intergenerational staying power.* For the present study, the more resonant a story or image is, the more likely it will be efficacious in ritual. This is because the most resonant expressions have either withstood the test of dozens if not hundreds of generations of cultural transmission, or they are so "sticky" and easy to think that they are independently invented all over the world.

Formally, I define highly "resonant" expressions as those which are:

1. Highly resilient across generations of transmission, especially oral transmission.
2. Resistant to cultural efforts at eradication.
3. Spontaneously and independently emergent cross-culturally despite large distances in time or space.

In other words, resonant stories and expressions are easy to think, easy to remember/hard to forget, and that is why they are recurrent motifs. Note that we still have not discussed what such an expression will look like. We are only defining psychologically resonant expressions as those which satisfy the above criteria (from studies in folklore or cross-cultural symbolism). This part of the definition is why we must be aware of folklore studies, historical analyses, and cross-cultural symbolism, as these things demonstrate *empirically* whether or not something is psychologically resonant. What is not included in this definition is *why* they are so—that is where the proposed cognitive model comes in.

Thus, rituals will more often than not be *psychologically resonant* expressions themselves. Because of this tendency they will also *use* psychologically resonant stories and images.

The Proposed Criteria for Psychological Resonance

So what are the characteristics of psychologically resonant expressions? To answer this question, we must remember that whether or not something is *resonant* depends upon whether it has been shown to survive many cultural transmissions (like myths, folktales, and so on), *or* has been found cross-culturally (like most recurrent motifs). It is a separate question, however, as to *why* something is so resonant. Based on the above considerations (reviewed in more depth in Goodwyn 2013), and more I review below, I propose that the most resonant expressions are likely to have some or all of the following:

1. Minimal counter-intuitiveness (Barrett 2007), meaning that they have only a few unusual or strange elements and so stand out, rather than have too many or too few counter-intuitive elements. Examples: talking animals, flying carpets, dragons, glowing swords.

2. Emotional evocativeness (Panksepp 1998). Examples: stories involving basic human attachments, or evoking basic emotional responses such as fear, anger, lust, and so on.
3. Sensual vividness, with a tendency toward extremes. Examples: castles of gold, mountains of crystal, brilliant lights, absolute darkness, and so on.
4. Indeterminacy in time and space. Examples: "long ago in a far-away land"—evocative of an oceanic feeling.
5. Biasing toward middle-level categories. Examples: "sword," rather than "weapon" (too abstract) or "quillioned pattern-weld blade with Brighthampton scabbard and cross" (overdetailed)
6. Low complexity of characters and motivations. Examples: the most beautiful in the land, the king, animal gods, the thief, the beggar.
7. Rhythmic and prosodic/musical elements. Examples: "magic mirror, on the wall."
8. Simple plots with reversals and/or irony. Examples: nothing is as it seems, plot twists, the slow animal beats the fast animal, and so on.
9. Apparent interconnection of events. Examples: things always occurring "just in the nick of time," and so on.

Non-resonant expressions will be: overly counter-intuitive or overly mundane, emotionally detached or frustrating, sensually vague or abstract, specific in time and space, contain over-specific or over-general categories, be internally complex or ambiguous, will lack any rhythmic or poetic qualities, will lack a clear plot, will lack reversals and interconnection. I argue that the most potent rituals will contain stories and images with the above elements. We will see from several fields of inquiry that this is true.

Support from Folklore Studies

This definition of resonance receives some support from the work of folklorist Max Lüthi (1982, 1984), who theorizes (along with cognitive scientists) that folktales have similar characteristics because of the oral transmission process and the psychological aspects of teller and audience. Like the cognitive anthropologists, he explains that the process of storytelling shapes folktales into similar patterns that *self-correct* deviations. The qualities described by Lüthi are similar to the ones identified by cognitive science, and include:

1. Objects and settings that tend to be described in vivid, static terms, like gold, crystal, metal, and so on, and/or in basic colors like black, white, red, or blue.
2. Characters which are "depthless", meaning they are simple types that act with very little reference to internal dynamics or psychological conflict, and they are often in extreme social positions (king, prince, demon, god, and so on).
3. Stories that often have extreme opposites in imagery, duplicate or triple events in a rhythmic pattern, and have simple plots (task/fulfill, lack/gain, and so on).

4. Environments that are also general, but simple and easy to visualize, with castles, lakes, forests, mountains, and caves, and frequently are of a uniform substance (glass mountain, brass city, and so on).
5. Heroes who are isolated through various means (the youngest, the oddball, the "stupid one," the most beautiful in the land, and so on).

These qualities match up somewhat with the predictions of psychological resonance qualities given above, including minimally counter-intuitive elements (such as forests of iron trees or talking animals), emotional extremes in plot, lack of excessive complexity (what Lüthi describes as "depthless" characters), easily visualized and simple environments and objects, indeterminacy in time and space, and rhythmic quality.

To provide an example, Lüthi observed that Wilhelm Grimm, when writing down the famous folktales he had collected (along with his brother Jacob Grimm), changed the tales from the above characteristics for various reasons (reviewed by Zipes 2003). Despite Grimm's changes, however, when these folktales were later recorded by storytellers in Europe continuing the tradition, the changes did not endure: "when the Grimms' folktales returned to the folk, they tended to become purified and in many ways have again approached the abstract style that was weakened by Wilhelm Grimm" (Lüthi 1982: 110). His example: in Grimm's version of *Rapunzel*, the prince becomes "overwhelmed with grief and despair" when he finds Rapunzel gone, and jumps from the tower. This is a deviation because normally misty descriptions of internal emotions are avoided in folktales. Thus, Grimm actually *reduced* the psychological resonance of *Rapunzel* by this change. Folktale characters *act*, rather than feel. However, this deviation corrects itself in subsequent tradition: "in oral tradition it corrects itself . . . In two later narratives derived independently . . . the passage is corrected" (Lüthi 1982: 111) and the witch simply throws him from the tower. Thus, over time, the process of repeated storytelling caused *Rapunzel* to revert back to its originally more resonant form.

This and other examples led Lüthi to conclude that "one may indeed say that in the oral tradition of the folk, the folktale style passes through a process of self-correction" (Lüthi 1982: 111).[2] This agrees with the above predictions, where stories and mental images drift toward structures that are psychologically resonant attractor states. Future, more rigorous studies of this prediction should be carried out, in order to test resonance criteria more systematically.[3]

These, I suggest, are the characteristics that will apply to the most resonant ritual expressions. That is, rituals that contain not only resonant images and stories, but resonant processes will be the most powerful and most likely to evoke a physiological change.

Symbolic Physical Actions: Acting Out the Myth

We have talked about the nature of the stories and images used in a ritual and we propose that resonant stories and images will likely be the most effective at achieving a particular effect. We will see examples from actual rituals in subsequent chapters to confirm this suspicion. But remember that rituals are not thought out but *performed* with bodies and physical objects. Thus we have only touched on part of the story so far. Another part is the *embodied action* of ritual.

As cognitive scientist Gilbert Lewis observes: "For a religion to be alive (and not just entombed in texts), it must be practiced. It exists in knowledge and practice. It must be present in particular people's experience" (Lewis 2004: 167; Sørensen 2007a: 13). Rituals contain both action as well as a type of thought associated with it. For example, as pointed out by Sørensen (2007a), the importance of symbolism, metaphor, and metonymy in ritual spells has been highlighted by Stanley Tambiah, who argues that rituals obtain their ends due to their very enactment (Tambiah 1968, 1985, 1991).

Furthermore, ritual acts have a symbolic quality to them. This is not to say that participants are required to think of what they're doing as "symbolic" in the usual Western sense; that is, as a merely personal mental exercise. Rather, the symbolism involved is that the objects, words, and movements are real, but non-literal representations of deeper, mysterious, but very real entities. In other words, when a stone is placed in the crook of a tree in a ritual manner to allow a hunter to return home before the sun goes down, the participant does not ever think that the stone is *literally* the sun, rather that they are somehow symbolically "connected" in an ill-defined manner. Ritual is thus a symbolic action even when it is felt to have very real effects.

Example: The Spoken Word in Ritual

To show that ritual is not merely thought but in fact symbolically *enacted*, we will examine the way ritual handles the spoken word. According to cognitive scientists, ritual spells and formulas are not merely ideas but also often contain special kinds of speech acts that negate the semantic meaning of what is said in favor of a more indexical, symbolic meaning of what is said. Put another way, it uses language in non-verbal ways. This seemingly paradoxical situation, in which ritual uses language in non-linguistic ways, is achieved via the way ritual speech "deliberately exploit[s] nonsensical or archaic word-forms" (Sørensen, 2007a: 68; see also Tambiah 1968, 1985) and this de-emphasizes their straightforward semantic qualities and highlights the non-verbal qualities of such utterances, such as their special, deliberate intonation, prosody, and iteration. Incantations are notable because they are deliberately restricted in form and made distinct from everyday language through the mechanisms of altered words, grammar, comprehensibility, prosody, linearity, and syntax. This has the effect of de-emphasizing the verbal content of the speech and transforming the uttered incantation into a ritual action due to its obfuscation of direct semantic meaning. This effect is usually accomplished via archaisms, ungrammatical forms, nonsense words, special prosody, redundancy, and repetition. Such techniques have the added benefit of indirectly connecting the ritual to the past, which gives a timelessness to the utterances, which are often seen as the language of angels, gods, spirits, and so on. From the biological perspective, Richard Kradin observes that prosody—the volume, tone, and rhythm of a verbalization—"evokes responses primarily from the right brain and strongly influences the limbic system" (Kradin 2008: 220). Much like music, then, ritual language speaks wordlessly to our more universal emotional selves.

One way to achieve this is by the common method of using dead or foreign languages, or at least languages that *sound* dead or foreign (we will see many examples of this in Chapters 7 and 8). Nonsense words emphasize the indexical nature of the words by completely obscuring any semantic content, highlighting the indexical and iconic nature of what is spoken, and delineating it clearly as "magical" utterance. This technique also differentiates practitioners by highlighting experts who have taken the time to learn the magical language needed. They also limit access to magical abilities by such requirements and therefore make them more "powerful" through the idea that effort = power. Repetition and non-standard syntax erase the semantic meanings of words and emphasize iconic and indexical aspects of speech through repetition fatigue and/or changed expectations of meaning. These linguistic effects also emphasize the mysteriousness of the sacred domain to which they refer. In short, ritual language is a special kind of language that is biased away from semantic meaning toward non-verbal expression.

The Word as Creative Act

Even more specifically, in all forms of magic we see the idea that verbalizing something makes it so—thus the word in ritual is transformed from the representation of an idea to a physical act of creation. Religious scholar Åke Hultkrantz observes this in his analysis of American Indian rituals:

> The abstract notion of creation from nothing or, more correctly, through the holy word, is naturally explained if we adduce the parallel with the magic power of the medicine man to evoke, bind and destroy through the word . . . it is in the medicine man, the religiously gifted one, that the highest forms of religious conceptions among primitive peoples are crystallized.
>
> (Hultkrantz 1979: 21)

Proof of the universality (and hence emotional/psychological resonance) of creative, enactive, non-verbal language in ritual is Hultkrantz's observation that while in a trance, medicine men ranging from California to the Arctic speak a private language that originated from the guardian spirit or the gods. Unsurprisingly, such trance languages consist of archaic words and phrases (Hultkrantz 1979: 101). Such secret societies often made war medicine, such as standing on a hill near a battle singing magic songs and pointing to the enemies. Further demonstrating the universality of this practice, we find the same practice among the Druids described by Romans encountering the Celtic war bands (Ross 1999).

Sørensen argues generally that by ritualizing, participants de-emphasize culturally specific meanings and causal relationships of agents and objects in favor of essentialist and schematic properties. In other words, ritualizing biases the expression toward the culturally enriched, collective psyche. The more iconic or indexical the meaning, and the less semantic the meaning, the more effective the ritual will be felt to be (Sørensen 2007a: 178–179). In other words, the more symbolic and non-literal the acts and words spoken are taken to be, the more effective they will be. An example of the way ritual language utilizes the exotic and non-semantic can be seen in the way Egyptian hieroglyphs were used by European magicians for centuries. Sørensen explains:

> Egyptian hieroglyphs played an important role as a "magical" alphabet with occult powers in Renaissance Europe. This role was diminished substantially as the hieroglyph's everyday and profane linguistic function was revealed. The search for the exotic did not abate but moved on to India and Tibet and, more recently, pre-literate people are ascribed secret knowledge and magical abilities. This . . . is not a Western phenomenon . . . [but] illustrates a general tendency of ascribing strong, morally dubious magical powers to neighbouring people and their rituals.
>
> (Sørensen 2007a: 179)

From depth psychology, Jung also mentions this phenomenon—that is, the way in which people tend to think of foreign languages and customs as exotic, mysterious, and containing greater occult power—in his dream seminar discussions (cf. Jung and Meyer-Grass 2008). The common thread here is the appeal to the unknown—the unknown people and their unknown ways allows for their language to acquire intuitive, symbolic meanings because the ritual participants are not distracted by literal and semantic meanings they would find more difficult to ignore if they used their own language.

The loosening of cognitive associations facilitated by ritual thinking and language allows symbols and actions to be underspecified in meaning, forcing such symbols to rely on cognitive intuitions that are universally emergent. Thus, participants do not need to have a full explanation of how a ritual works to feel intuitively that it *could* work, through an unspecified, but intuitively "correct" flow of action. This provides the practitioner, through the mechanisms of conceptual metaphor (Lakoff and Johnson 1999) with a means to manipulate forces that are otherwise mysterious or unknowable.

To summarize, we have seen that metaphorical thinking and language is crucial to what rituals do. Specifically, it is iconic and indexical signs that operate in ritual. This is probably because metaphor is the mechanism we use cognitively to connect something nebulous and vague to something easily comprehended and concrete (Goodwyn 2012; Lakoff and Johnson 1999, 2003). Put another way, metaphor "is, at its simplest, a way of proceeding from the known to the unknown" (Nisbet 1969: 4).

Anthropologist Victor Turner, whom we will discuss in detail in Chapter 6, adds that other cultures also recognize this mechanism of ritual action, reporting a corresponding definition of ritual symbol among the Ndembu. He concludes that "Metaphor is, in fact, metamorphic, transformative" (Turner 1974: 25). Thus this idea of metaphor is not merely an academic idea of the West, but a more universal human experience. In Chapter 9, we will discuss another mechanism of magical ritual—contagion—that was introduced first by James Frazer and elaborated on by other scholars of ritual.

Transformations across Time: Imagistic and Doctrinal Modes

We have so far seen from cognitive science that ritual uses recurrent, convergent, and *resonant* images and stories. It also is primarily a symbolic, performative act. So does that mean that once a culture comes to build a ritual it stays that way forever? Obviously the answer to that question is no. Rituals change over time, and as it turns out, the particular ways rituals change follow recognizable patterns, according to cognitive anthropologists. Recognizing the ways rituals change over time, as we will see, reveals interesting information about the collective and personal elements of the psyche discussed earlier.

Cognitive anthropologists Harvey Whitehouse and James Laidlaw (Whitehouse 2002; Whitehouse and Laidlaw 2004) classify two modes of expression in religion—that of the "imagistic" and the "doctrinal." Imagistic expression is emotional, involves personal mystical/ecstatic experience, and uses vivid symbolism, but all of this emerges in a disorganized, chaotic manner. Though often very emotional and powerful, it is not particularly stable over time. The doctrinal mode, by contrast, is more concerned with dogma, structure, organized belief and/or practice, and conservatism. It is highly organized and stable across time. Whitehouse and Laidlaw observe that across the board most religions feature both of these modes to varying degrees and in varying combinations, but often there is a progression from an imagistic mode in new cults and "revivals" to solidification into a doctrinal mode over time. This is illustrated by the rise of Buddhism from Hinduism, of Protestantism from Catholicism, of Evangelical Protestantism from older forms of Protestantism, of countless millennial cults from traditional religious systems all over the globe, and so on. Where the doctrinal mode offers stability and longevity, it is often rebelled against due to its stultifying "tedium effect," which leads to new bursts of imagistic mode activity. Thus Whitehouse and Laidlaw argue that religions have an internal tension between two opposing forces. Interestingly, Jung argued (1954) that the human psyche has a tendency to operate in the same manner, in a process he called *enantiodromia*, or the continual returning of opposites.

If a given religion can withstand such surges of imagistic activity without splintering off into a separate cult (as can be seen in the emergence of new religion, a "revival," and so on), sometimes it can achieve a balance. Several theorists have examined these modes with respect to specific cultures, such as Peel (2004), who has looked at differing modes in West Africa and in various forms of Evangelical Christianity (Malley 2004), practiced all over the globe, which combine the two modes in one degree or another. Shankland (2004) has further observations concerning the two tendencies in Islamic modes of practice. Whitehouse and these other theorists suggest that doctrinal modes are always on guard against the more primal, emotional, and iconistic encroachments by the imagistic mode (cf. Bayly 2004). These considerations are important for ritual because ritual activities in the two modes are radically different. Leo Howe summarizes:

> Briefly, doctrinal religion, transmitted through frequent and highly repetitive sermonizing, can spread rapidly, building up large, anonymous, imagined communities that tend to have hierarchical structures bent on disciplining their members. They are often unemotional, and are therefore prone to the tedium effect, which causes members to drift away or revert to more ecstatic rites. Imagistic religion, by contrast, relies on nonverbal, infrequent, highly arousing, sometimes violent rituals that create specific episodic memories that bind together the small number of participants in very cohesive, face-to-face groups, leading to an elaboration of local differences rather than extensive homogeneity. While conceiving of these modes as ideal types, in reality they are only tendencies and often aspects of both can be found in any particular religious tradition.
>
> (Howe 2004: 135–136)

As we will see when we study the anthropology of ritual, these modes can be observed to vary with large-scale cultural variables such as grid and group, discussed in Chapter 6. For now, it is interesting that scholars note that there is often a class effect here; common folk of widely distributed regions, who adhere to the putatively dominant doctrinal religion (normally Christian, Buddhist, or Islamic), often have strongly imagistic elements that the priestly class is continually complaining about (Whitehouse and Laidlaw 2004). This effect has also been observed throughout European history as well, which will become more evident when we discuss European folk rituals of various types. Generally, it has been observed that "Without a centrally integrated religious system, people tend toward imagistic practice" (Lewis 2004: 156). Moreover, the imagistic mode is usually seen as existing prior to the doctrinal mode (Whitehouse and Laidlaw 2004).

What these observations suggest about the psychology of ritual will be evident later. For now, suffice it to say that the imagistic mode is obviously the more psychologically resonant of the two, which is why religious practice tends effortlessly toward it over time without the continual effortful pressure of a doctrinal religion to halt the gravitational slide. Put another way, the collective element of the psyche is continually trying to inject vivid, emotional, but idiosyncratic and "intuitive" resonant elements into a particular ritual practice that the doctrinal mode, which is more closely allied with the personal element since it requires directly concentrated effort, must deal with one way or another. As we will see, when we are thinking about the use of ritual in psychotherapy, we should consider the balance of imagistic vs. doctrinal modes—imagistic ritual modes tend to be personal, quirky, vivid, emotional, and moving. Doctrinal modes tend to be solidifying, concentrating, and stabilizing, but can sometimes feel empty, unemotional, or meaningless.

For our purposes, this tension between the automatic, emotional, but chaotic, boundary-blurring, and messy imagistic style of ritualizing and the stabilizing, structure-forming, and yet occasionally desiccating and rigid doctrinal style of ritualizing will play out in therapy as a tension between the collective and personal elements of the psyche. But before we get into that, we need to understand the concept of "participation" in ritual to show how these two elements can be brought together.

Participation

In the field of ritual study, the concept of *participation* has been a subject of study for over a century; we will see how this concept involves both sorts of ritual modes. Initially proposed by philosopher-anthropologist Lucien Lévy-Bruhl (1985), participation continues to be discussed and elaborated on by more recent cognitive scientists such as Jesper Sørensen (2007a: 25) and anthropologists such as Susan Greenwood (2009). Participation has been discussed by depth psychologists, particularly Jungian analysts, for some time. Briefly, Lévy-Bruhl argued that *participation* (sometimes also called *participation mystique*) is a mental state in which a ritual participant feels at one with either the other participants, the gods, the ritual objects, the ancestors, or some combination thereof. There is a biological perspective also: the idea of the interpenetration of minds finds interesting support from anthropologist Maurice Bloch, who argues that it has a biological and cognitive foundation (in the working of mirror neurons) that is found cross-culturally, *especially in ritual*:

> it is in ritual that the conscious and culturally encoded awareness of lack of boundedness between persons is clearest . . . even more than is the case for non-social animals, and differently than is the case for other social animals, the boundaries between individuals are, at best, partial. This fact . . . is fuzzily available to our consciousness. It is this awareness that becomes a recurrent element in a great variety of representations in different cultures, representations which we must not forget are different kinds of phenomena from the simply psychological.
>
> (Bloch 2004: 76–78)

Richard Kradin notes this effect as well. For example, certain brain cells (in the anterior cingulate gyrus) are activated when a subject watches another subject get poked by a needle (Iacoboni *et al.* 2005). This is but one example of many so-called "mirror neurons" (a concept that has perhaps been overextended in the literature), in which we appear to mimic the neurobiological experience of others through observation. Kradin argues that, regardless of what one thinks of mirror neurons, human brains do interact with one another and this correlates with empathic connections. These connections tend to dissolve the barrier between self and other and cause us to experience one another vicariously (Kradin 2008: 219).

Thus all three disciplines appear to have converged on this idea of participation as important in ritual as a mode of interconnection of the participants, and how shared imagery can affect the physiology of the recipients of healing rituals. Thus the concept of participation has biological, cognitive, psychodynamic, and cultural components and is a key aspect of ritual. We will return to the concept of participation throughout this volume and how it forms a part of both kinds of ritual modes.

Example: Participation in the Explanatory Myth

Here I will provide some examples of the concepts we have been discussing thus far. As we discussed earlier, psychologically resonant stories—being mentally "sticky" and resilient across many cultural transmissions, and/or tending to be independently invented cross-culturally—have a way of attaching themselves to rituals naturally. In both imagistic and doctrinal modes, resonant ideas are used in symbolic ways to carry out embodied, enacted rituals.

Sørensen (2007b), for example, reviews a number of ritual examples where profane objects, actors, and actions are blended with mythic ideas in order to make them ritually effective. Trobriand Islanders, for example, say that magic ritual objects gain their power by coming from the primordial ancestors who brought them with them from "underground," i.e. from the great mystery outside human understanding. Other cultures describe magic as coming from a culture hero. In many cultures, spells are seen as replicas of the spells given to humans in mythic times, and magicians receive their magical powers from the ancestors. The magician in this case is the only one allowed to use magic and must obey certain taboos—negative methods of emphasis. In all these cases, notice the references to the timeless, to the infinite, and to the mysterious. These are ways in which participants use symbolic action and vivid resonant narratives and images in order to not simply observe but *participate* in and therefore *become a part of* the mysterious source of All, with the Divine, with the past, and with each other.

Sørensen also discusses the Zande rituals described by Evans-Pritchard (1937) in which the focus is on magical objects, which receive their efficacy from myths about the special essence of those objects. Notably, there is a correlation between the perceived danger in collecting the ingredients for a spell and their power; the stronger the magic, the more dangerous it is to collect it, as it will be guarded by snakes and ghosts. We will see this theme repeated when we discuss tenth-century Anglo-Saxon magic and Norse magic in Chapters 7 and 8.

Many more examples are detailed by Sørensen, who shows these tendencies are not simply practiced outside the West in "primitive" cultures but are part of religious traditions in the West, such as the Eucharist (Sørensen 2007b: 86–87). In any case, Sørensen (2007a: 180–181) argues that the more resistant concepts are to precise semantic interpretation the more magically efficacious they will be. Over time, however, practitioners will tend to explain actions by cultural models and structures and place them into established conceptual networks, and this appears to diminish the magical agency if the symbolic interpretation penetrates into rituals. Thus we see how initially imagistic modes, through effortful acts of interpretation and dogmatization, become doctrinal. New rituals will therefore appear as either transformation/appropriation of existing rituals into new contexts or as ascriptions of agency facilitating the production of new rules—a type of "founder effect." This shows how rituals vacillate between the imagistic and doctrinal modes.

Ritual Interplay and Change over Time

One final question cognitive science investigates is how the modes of ritual develop over time: what mental process guides the change from imagistic to doctrinal and back? The answer has to do with the effect of ritual on *memory*. As we have already seen, cultural transmission is less about direct replication of mental representations and more about expressions settling into cognitively optimal positions that make the most sense to our innate mental architecture (McCauley and Lawson 2002: 44–45). Rituals follow these rules of transmission also, but are more specific in that they also gravitate toward *rituals that optimize memory*:

> Extensive experimental research has revealed the ability of mental images to organize memories, to distinguish specific episodes, and to serve as mnemonic cues—especially for spatially and dynamically related materials . . . Thus, it should come as no surprise that religious systems and ritual systems, in particular, have evolved so as to exploit variables that facilitate memory.
>
> (McCauley and Lawson 2002: 73, 85)

Rituals that are remembered are rituals that will endure; only those that are remembered will endure and survive cultural transmission. Most importantly for this section, *such rituals will be able to organize the thoughts and memory of the participants*. Memorable rituals also continue their effects as long as they are remembered due to their effect on a person's personal narrative—which is a part of their very identity. Both imagistic and doctrinal modes of ritual exploit memory in different ways—that's why they both can survive despite their differences.

McCauley and Lawson argue that rituals gravitate toward two different types, both of which optimize memory: those that use high levels of sensory pageantry and those that are repeated frequently. These are inversely proportional to each other in general. That is, rituals of high repetition will be typically low in sensory pageantry and vice versa. Logically, rituals that should only be performed a few times—like initiations, funerals, inductions, coronations, and so on—will *need* high levels of pageantry to be memorable. They will need to be *resonant*. They endure because the resonant sensory pageantry is impressive to human memory despite their low frequency. Rituals that involve low frequency and low pageantry, they add, *can* still be sustained despite their low frequency by other support systems such as literacy (which preserves doctrines in writing and circumvents the limitations of memory) and/or long periods of memorization of sacred narratives, such as that performed by the Nambudiri, an oral culture whose Brahmin initiates spend hundreds of hours memorizing the Vedas. These are exceptions, however, and require immense effort to sustain them.

Thus, low-sensory pageantry can typically only be remembered via high frequency of repetition. Frequently performed, high pageantry rituals—another unusual case—are often found in splinter groups and millennial movements (McCauley and Lawson 2002: 181–192), but this level of stimulation comes with a cost: the high level of emotional activation eventually runs into problems such as habituation, the increasingly greater expenditure of resources (law of diminishing returns), and the risk of sensory overload and exhaustion.

Thus within any ritual system, two opposing forces appear to operate: excessive pageantry and sensory overload can cause a system to crash, whereas tedium can cause splinter groups, innovation, and religious rebellion. So of the four types identified by McCauley and Lawson, only the high pageantry/low frequency types and the low pageantry/high frequency types tend to endure. The other two combinations are unusual and normally do not survive, and this is due (again) to universal cognitive processes.

Summary

The cognitive science of ritual has revealed a number of factors we need to understand if we are to utilize ritual in mental health settings. We have seen that rituals typically vary inversely in their sensory pageantry and frequency. High levels of sensory pageantry are used because it is memorable and ideal for use in rituals that should not be performed often (lest we encounter overload, exhaustion, or desensitization effects—discussed later). They stick in memory due to their psychological resonance (using mythic, recurrent themes, and so on). By contrast, rituals that are to be performed often, like purifications, daily rites, votives, and so on, are low pageantry/high frequency, and they stick in memory due to rote repetition. In both cases the ritual affects the psyche through its effects on memory, which influences our sense of identity.

Cultural systems vary in the degree to which they tolerate *imagistic* modes of ritual expression. Imagistic modes tend to be personal, intensely emotional, and idiosyncratic, but can be chaotic and fractionating. By contrast, doctrinal modes tend to be dispassionate, reassuring, and stabilizing, but can be stultifying and rigid. Both modes, and both kinds of ritual (pageantry/frequency), utilize the concept of *participation*, where the practitioner uses indexical metaphorical images, stories, and ritual acts to blur the boundaries of the self and make themselves a part of something greater, whether it be the social group, nature, their ancestors, the glories of the past, God, the spirits, or the universe.

These patterns hold across all ritual systems and are simply due to stable, universally emergent properties of the human mind, and they have been demonstrated by years of cross-cultural cognitive science research, though much research remains to be done. For our purposes, however, these general themes provide a number of clues as to how we can best incorporate ritual study into psychological theory and treatment. In the next chapter we look at why rituals can affect mental health from *within* psychodynamic theory.

Notes

1. Another motif found in *Beowulf*, of the divine child Scyld Scefing being set adrift in the waters, has wide parallels in the Japanese myth of the child of Izanagi and Izanami, and the Old Testament story of Moses.
2. He also says that "the fairytale takes on the shimmer of the perfect, the indestructible, the timeless, the absolute, and with it that of the transcending, even of the transcendent" (Lüthi 1984: 13).
3. Consider Lüthi's comment: "That the same listener wishes to hear the same fairytale several times—completely in contrast to the case, say, of the joke—shows that it sets in motion a pattern of internal experience, sets off a sequence of tension and relief of tension . . . similar in effect to that of a musical work, whose interest is also not exhausted by a single hearing and which one needs to hear time and again, since the effect is deepened through repeated listening" (Lüthi 1984: 73).

Chapter 5

The Psychodynamic Branch

Image, Projection, Narrative, Meaningful Coincidence, and Dissociation

It is surprising how often the term "sacred" may be translated as "set apart" or "on one side" in various societies.
– Victor Turner (1974: 241)

We have seen that rituals can affect our physiology. But how does this work? What are the mechanisms that enact this change? So far we have found hints in the cognitive science of ritual: we learned why rituals use resonant narratives, why and how they are metaphorical, why they differentiate into the imagistic–doctrinal tension, and why they are remembered. We also touched upon the concept of participation. It was here that we first got a clue as to how rituals can change our mental and physical makeup: the participant is, through all these various modes and methods, connecting herself/himself with something deeper/greater. But how does participation work? What exactly does ritual do to the structure of the mind? How does it do it?

To understand this, we begin first with a discussion of the way ritual affects the individual self using psychodynamic theory. Then, in the next chapter we will examine the way ritual affects our group selves—that is, the part of us that is defined by our surrounding culture. To start we will continue the discussion of the role of mental images in ritual, as images play a very important part in depth psychology as well as in the cognitive and biological study of ritual. Next, there are a number of largely unconscious but very common behaviors observed constantly in psychotherapy that are likely playing a major role in ritual: these are *projection* and *projective identification*, both of which relate to the concept of participation. Third, ritual is a major way in which we construct a self-*narrative*, which is very important in depth psychology. The fourth mechanism of ritual action is that of *meaningful coincidence*, or as Jung put it, "synchronicity." Meaningful coincidence is relevant to the study of ritual because rituals likely put us in a frame of mind in which we experience a greater sense of meaningful coincidence. Finally, we will discuss the psychodynamic phenomenon of *dissociation* in relation to ritual (also noted by anthropologists), and how rituals likely affect this basic property of the mind.

The use of psychotherapy-based psychodynamic theory in the study of ritual is justified primarily by the common observation that psychotherapy itself is a very ritualistic process, and so engages all the mechanisms thus far studied, including placebo and cognitive structures (particularly the so-called archetypal images). Quoting Lévi-Strauss (1966), for example, medical anthropologist Daniel Moerman observes that successful psychotherapy is very ritual-like and has key features of rituals worldwide, including the doctor (or folk healer/shaman) making a myth of the patient's pain and making sense of "the inchoate, the anomalous, the unapproachable" (Moerman 2002: 96). The ritual transforms the meanings that a patient has about his/her life into a different myth—this touches on the narrative aspect of ritual discussed below. Psychotherapy, therefore, is a kind of ritual we use in modern society. As we will see throughout this volume, however, psychotherapy is (in its present form) somewhat ritually impoverished. Thus the study of ritual can help a dynamic interdisciplinary psychiatry develop new tools to enrich it with ritual awareness.

Mental Images

We have discussed the importance of images in our discussion of both the placebo effect and of the cognitive science of ritual. Mental images can affect physiology, and there is good reason to believe that the most effective ones will be resonant images due to their "stickiness," their seeming emergence from "outside" (i.e. spontaneous images from the collective element or through cultural transmission), their vividness, and their emotionality. In cognitive science we saw how images link with memory and basic universal thought-structuring human tendencies, but how do images get so tightly linked with emotions? How does this work? Physician, psychoanalyst, and placebo researcher Richard Kradin, whom we referred to in the first chapter, has proposed an explanation. According to Kradin, images become linked to emotions early in development (Kradin 2008: 145), in such a way that emotional attachments with important others (like parents) are encoded first with images rather than words, making them more potent regulators of mind and body:

> somatosensory schemas are inextricably linked to affect; these in turn are integrated with images as the visual system matures. Finally, cortical centers of the left brain intervene. By that time, a complex associative map of somatic sensation, affect, and image, has already been established . . . From this perspective, the idea that mind and body are distinct is patently absurd . . . As a result, well-being can be promoted by, for example, touch, gaze attunement, imagery, and meaning.
>
> (Kradin 2008: 146–147)

Jungian analyst Donald Kalsched, in working with victims of severe trauma, has observed that patients often spontaneously come up with imaginary characters to help them cope and survive—little green men, angels, the "little girl," the grandfather, and others (Kalsched 1996). This has been corroborated by my own therapy patients as well as leading researchers in the psychodynamic treatment of trauma (Van der Hart *et al.* 2006). Here we see images not only linking with potent emotions, but interacting in a complex manner with patients to facilitate healing *as if they were separate human personalities*. The connection, therefore, between these mental images and gods or spirits as agents in rituals is fairly clear. As we study rituals in the next part, we will observe how potent images and characters—often from mythology or religion—are used to facilitate change. Here we see how such a mechanism may actually work.

Images, states Kradin, are not merely airy fantasies, but tightly correlated with physiology and linked to most responses by the central nervous system (Kradin 2008: 186). Let's explore an example from psychiatric practice. Orlandini (2009) documents a case in which a severely traumatized woman, haunted by gruesome dreams and very troublesome symptoms, was having a difficult time grieving her five miscarriages—a situation known as "complicated grief," which we will explore in more depth in Chapter 10. During the course of therapy, the patient and therapist decided that the patient needed to enact a ritual of some kind to symbolically allow the children to "pass into the next world." Notably, before her final miscarriage, the patient dreamed that her deceased grandmother was telling her that she needed to give her baby to her, and that she would raise them as she would in the afterlife. The next day she miscarried. Together, the patient and therapist created a ritual based not only on the patient's spontaneous intuitions and dreams, but also on universal patterns in rituals documented by anthropologists. It involved creating a symbolic representation of her children, along with a letter written to them expressing her love for them and her grief at losing them, and after a specified time, she (with her boyfriend), buried the "children." After this event a long-standing recurrent and terrifying dream completely stopped, along with several troublesome symptoms. From my own practice, I have seen this operate as well.

Already here we can see several of the principles we have discussed in action. This ritual involved going to a grassy hill to bury the notes; the patient was accompanied by her boyfriend, and it was highly emotional and symbolic. It is a high pageantry, low frequency ritual because the goal was to only do it once. It contained resonant, imagistic elements in that it drew from her own dreams, but there were also doctrinal elements as well which likely stemmed from both the patient's and therapist's investment in classical psychodynamic theory and the ritual process of psychotherapy itself. It also, like all ritual, benefited from the very *physicality* of the process of writing, digging, burying, and verbalizing, engaging her entire body and not just part of her mind in the process of grieving and helping her children "pass on," which in turn allowed her to transition from complicated grief to a healthier integrated grief. Through the ritual, she was able to physically and symbolically participate in connecting with the otherworld, her children, and her grandmother. The remission of symptoms confirmed the success of the ritual action.

Kradin discusses further psychoanalytic case reports of ways in which psychological pain and physical pain interrelate, and many theorists (reviewed in Kradin 2011) see psychosomatic symptoms as a failure of symbol formation—i.e. the inability of a patient to put physical symptoms into a coherent psychological framework. Such suffering continues unless symbol formation is facilitated by ritual and *narrativization.* Notably, these clinicians observe that patients who remain unable to psychologize (i.e. transform into a narrative of personal meaning) their symptoms stay resistant to treatment. In this context, by "symbols" we mean concrete images/objects that are iconic and indexical signs of more abstract, difficult to verbalize, and frequently highly emotional ideas. Manipulating them in a ritual manner is a way of accessing deep emotional issues in a very physical, embodied way that cannot be duplicated by mere verbal discourse. This is due to all the mechanisms we have discussed thus far, and many more we have yet to review.

Arthur Kleinman (1989), in *The Illness Narratives*, notes that psychiatry shares many features of ritual healing by "transforming experience." Demons are named and the healer creates a dramatic story of the subject's suffering, and then through the use of symbols, allows them to symbolically exorcize those demons. Jungian dream analysts often spot "initiation" characteristics in dreams, as if the dreamer was spontaneously attempting to create a ritual which the dreamer could go through in order to solidify the needed change. Initiations are specific kinds of life-transition rituals utilized by cultures worldwide; thus they are resonant ideas, often containing recurrent elements. We will return to the subject of initiatory rituals in Chapter 9.

Anthropologist Victor Turner (discussed further in Chapter 6) observes that ritual symbols and images tend to connect the opposing poles of the concrete, emotional, and physical with the sublime, the ideal, and the spiritual:

> physiological phenomena (blood, sexual organs, coitus, birth, death, catabolism, and so on) and normative values of moral facts (kindness to children, reciprocity, generosity to kinsmen, respect for elders, obedience to political authorities, and the like) . . . the drama of ritual action—the singing, dancing, feasting, wearing of bizarre dress, body painting, use of alcohol or hallucinogens, and so on, causes an exchange between these poles in which the biological referents are ennobled and the normative referents are charged with emotional significance.
>
> (Turner 1974: 55)

For Turner, then, ritual is a connecting act; it brings many separated things together. Support for Turner's essentially biological and psychological interpretation abounds throughout this volume. Anthropologists Thompson *et al.* situate this deeply connective process in the performative aspect of ritual: "We suggest that the efficacy of mental practice resides in its performativity—that is, *doing* (even in the mind's eye) *makes it so*" (Thompson *et al.* 2009: 134). Thus, resonant mental images of the highest value connect tightly with deep emotional and body processes by way of ritual bodily enactment, and this is one potential mechanism by which rituals effect mind/body change.

Projection and Projective Identification

As we have already seen from biological and cognitive perspectives, it is clear that humans do not live as isolated, completely self-contained units floating about in the cosmos like particles in a gas. We interact with each other constantly, and there are a number of ways in which brains and minds become bound together in a tight network. In psychodynamic research and clinical practice, these processes are looked at in fine detail in the workings of an individual mind, and there are a number of psychodynamic processes (Gabbard 2010; Stein 2010; Beinenfeld 2005; Tasman *et al.* 2003) that impinge on our understanding of what rituals do that have been observed by this research.

A basic working hypothesis from this perspective is that a ritual, when properly done, may invoke changes in a person's unconscious attitudes, behaviors, and/or affects, which, upon interaction with others, produce subsequent changes in others in reaction. As any psychotherapist can tell you, humans generally struggle with introspection, but we are much better at attributing external causes to problems and conflicts that are actually *internal.* One way we do this, universally recognized by psychotherapists of all stripes, is through *projection* (e.g. Tasman *et al.* 2003: 464–485), in which internal conflicts are attributed to external causes and entities. In the classical psychodynamic understanding, projection is employed most often when the internal conflict is too intense to entertain as internal, or when one consciously or otherwise cannot accept the feeling one has and so the psyche projects it onto someone or something else so as to avoid being associated with it.

I argue, however, that while this is no doubt true, this understanding of projection may be too limited. I suggest that projection not only serves such emotional needs, but is also a natural consequence of normal human cognitive tendencies as discussed earlier. In other words, the natural tendency to project internal conflicts and dynamics onto external objects and entities likely occurs not only because of the above cause, but because of psychological resonance and normal symbolic thought processing. As I have discussed at length in my previous book *The Neurobiology of the Gods*, vague, difficult, abstract, and challenging concepts are often symbolically equated with concrete visuo-spatial objects because these are easier to understand or imagine ("love is a journey," "I'm feeling down in the dumps," "I'm flying high as a kite," and so on). Projection of an internal problem, a conflict, or an emotional issue therefore not only serves as a defense mechanism to avoid internal strife, but it is simply easier to think. That is, treating the difficult, vague, or abstract workings of life experience as if they were external objects and personalities requires less cognitive effort—hence the reason we speak of moods going "up and down" as if a mood were an object bouncing up and down. In the psychodynamic case of projection, what is missing is the insight that one is literally attributing such conflicts to someone else when in fact they are one's own. We will see what this process has to do with ritual in a moment.

A more complex dynamic is known as *projective identification.* A large body of work that has emerged since the concept was introduced by psychoanalyst Melanie Klein (Christopher *et al.* 2001; Segal 1964; Tasman *et al.* 2003: 473–474), but briefly, projective identification occurs when a person projects an emotional internal issue onto someone else, who then as a reaction internalizes this projection and identifies with it. Psychoanalysts observe that a person's behavior tends to evoke the emotional response in the other and becomes a sort of self-fulfilling prophecy; for example, a person who feels angry that they have been victimized in the past may project the victimization onto someone else so as to be "rid" of it. If that person begins to behave in a vulnerable or victimized manner due to a strong projection, the projector may react angrily toward that person (or may be nurturing, but even then it is themselves they are nurturing and not the other person). These sorts of pathological dynamics, along with others involving projective identification, have been observed in many couples (Young-Eisendrath and Dawson 1997), and in therapy in general.

Projective identification of strong negative images of other people, often associated with some kind of trauma, can be so potent that it actually *invokes* a negative response in others that corresponds to that projection. Another example would be a patient who feels no one will support them in a time of need, then acts and behaves in exasperating ways toward the therapist, so much so that the therapist becomes annoyed with the patient and finally makes an insensitive comment or action. This behavior is rarely conscious, but the upshot is that once the therapist gets fed up with them and expresses even mild annoyance, the patient responds as if he "knew it," which further reinforces his negative beliefs. Projective identification most often occurs in ideas that are charged with a great deal of emotion; the parts of the self that are most likely to be projected are often intolerably angry, fearful, or lustful, but they can also be high ideals and principles that may feel too godlike to accept in oneself and so they are projected onto others and worshipped, sometimes clumsily. The power of projective identification is that it makes the internal complex real by inducing another to embody it—in the pathological case it allows the projector to avoid whatever it is she/he is projecting. But I argue that pathological projective identification is a subset of an otherwise normal means of trying to understand the world, and this more functional projective identification operates in ritual. In these non-pathological cases, it can concretize and materialize something only dimly understood or verbalizable. As pointed out by psychotherapists, projective identification can be a very important emotional and non-verbal kind of communication that may serve to heal and get help with otherwise intolerable emotions. As we can begin to see, this intense emotional action will play out in rituals and help us to understand the strong emotional pull of some rituals in the imagistic mode especially.

In ritual I believe projection and especially projective identification occurs on a large scale, especially since some rituals (particularly in traditional societies) can involve the entire community. Internal dynamics such as intense emotion and godlike ideals are projected onto ritual objects and practitioners; this is likely facilitated by the very non-verbal and non-semantic emphasis of ritual. As we will see in our discussion of the anthropology of ritual, in particular the work of Victor Turner, we will find many connections between this psychological concept and the observations of the anthropologist. From a psychodynamic perspective, therefore, rituals may facilitate projections and projective identifications—for better or for worse—and so connect people together on a visceral, unconscious level. This is because they resonate with these psychodynamic principles; i.e. magic spells are always directed at an external object of some kind, rather than internally directed. Magic rituals and magical thinking in general typically project vague, emotional ideals onto concrete external objects and ideas—the depression that has afflicted a loved one is caused not by internal dynamic conflicts and complexes, which we still conceptualize as affecting "the ego" as if from outside (only in this case it is outside the ego but still within the larger psyche), but because a demon has possessed them, or an evil sorcerer has inflicted a curse upon them, and so on. Gods, whose images consist in part of ineffable and powerful emotional impressions, are nevertheless usually seen as existing "out there" somewhere, rather than as integral parts of our subjective awareness.

Thus a spell aimed at healing an illness, scaring off a nasty neighbor, or invoking amorous feelings in someone may (if effective) bring about such changes because it activates *internal* changes in the practitioner that, through projective identification, evoke the desired effect to some measure. A practitioner, confident in his love spell, may approach the desired person in a way that is entirely different, perhaps more seductive, affable, and so on (and often enough in a manner he is not aware of) which causes an entirely different reaction in the target. The likely reason much of this appears "magical" is because it is unconscious.

Projective identification, like all defenses, is a tough nut to crack in therapy, mainly because it is so complicated and involves a level of introspection most people are not that great at. But the point of bringing it up here is that an effective ritual or series of rituals, likely in a context of very high intensity affect and vivid imagery and embedded in a firmly established cultural tradition, may potentially through the above mechanisms cause subtle unconscious effects in the participants. This will subsequently cause changes in the feedback loops between them and others, but the recipient of the ritual is much more likely to notice changes in others because of the externalizing bias of the human mind. The result is that the spell is given credit for the change, and imagined to somehow extend and exert occult forces upon them. Interestingly, in a sense this is actually a correct assessment of the effect of the ritual, provided we substitute the word "occult" with "extremely complex and very difficult to observe directly." We will continue to explore the concept of projective identification as we look through the examples of Part III.

Narrative

The earlier biological and cognitive discussion of ritual has touched on the issue of narrative; here we develop it further. Anthropologists Thompson *et al.* (2009) emphasize the importance of narrative in healing rituals, such that with his health-care provider, a patient will construct his illness experience with his symptoms and change can occur through examination of this story:

> Anthropologists have documented many examples in which determining the "right" explanation for the patient's suffering is an extensive process involving consultations with a number of providers . . . illustrating that what constitutes an effective therapeutic relationship may be more a practitioner's ability to provide an acceptable explanation for the patient's suffering than a "good" interpersonal relationship.
>
> (Thompson *et al.* 2009: 126)

From the biological perspective, Richard Kradin recommends that to maximize placebo improvement, physicians should construct a narrative for the illness, including its "cause," its meaning, and implications for recovery. Humphrey (2002) argues that the placebo response is *amplified* by conviction in the religious (and hence symbolic) descriptions of their symptoms, whereas neuroscientist Patrick McNamara (2009), whom we will discuss later in this chapter, points out many similarities between placebo and ritual responses. Others argue similarly that the process of administering any sort of treatment—inert or not—is embedded in learned expectancies and symbolic meaning (Koshi and Short 2007: 10). Narrative is an expression of meaning and ritual constructs meaning in a special non-verbal manner.

Physician Howard Brody (1997), like Kradin, proposes that doctors should work with patients in constructing the story of their illness, its cause, current meaning, and implications for recovery. Anthropologists Thompson *et al.* (2009) emphasize not merely the consciously entertained symbolic meaning or understanding of ritual healing, but the direct sensory, implicit, embodied experience of the process. Pennebaker (1990) has shown that people who simply write down their feelings and personal history need less in the way of mental health treatment and have overall better health as measured in a variety of ways. The best results, in fact, were in those who told the best stories—most coherent, organized, and persuasive. Thus we can see the power of verbalizing the inner world and constructing a meaningful narrative.

Daniel Moerman emphasizes the biological basis of narrative meaning, stating that it is "not simply some wooly fantasy from the fringe, some airy pipedream, or otherworldly spiritism. Human biology is comprised of neurons, neurotransmitters and synapses; but it is also comprised of meaning, experience, knowledge and practice" (Moerman 2002: 109). In a variety of studies, it has been shown that a patient's own assessment of their health condition was a better predictor of their overall longevity than any of the "objective" assessments of their health (Moerman 2002: 119), indicating that self-rated health has a unique (if unexplainable) effect on mortality. Such a self-assessment is part of a person's self-narrative—this apparently has a measurable effect on our physiology.

Howard Brody offers his mechanism for the placebo effect as a "meaning response," and suggests that a good healer more often will provide a satisfying explanation of illness, demonstrate care and concern, and hold out a promise of future mastery and control over the illness. Furthermore, "he offers the patient either an explanation of what is happening, or perhaps some mumbo-jumbo which sounds like an explanation and which the patient finds reassuring" (Brody 1999: 80). The primary method is to tell stories about the illness—this is done cross-culturally, as we will see, and these stories often touch upon larger issues such as the nature of mortality, the origins of evil, and so on, in a way that connects the patient's problems with universal conflicts. Note also that stories are moving whether or not they are true in a literal sense (dreams and fictional stories are a good example of this). As psychologist Jerome Bruner puts it: "A[n essential] feature of narrative is that it can be 'real', or 'imaginary' without loss of its power as a story" (Bruner 1998: 44). Thus, narrative is an integral part of what it means to be human and this is both utilized and added to by the physical, emotional, and non-verbal contribution of ritual.

Mythic narrative-making, argues religious scholar Mircea Eliade (1954: 98–99), makes suffering tolerable because it gives it meaning, thus elevating it from the absurd and meaningless:

> almost everywhere we come upon the archaic concept . . . according to which suffering is to be imputed to the divine will, whether as directly intervening to produce it or as permitting other forces, demonic or divine, to provoke it . . . there is nothing that does not, in one way or another, find its explanation and justification in the transcendent, in the divine economy.
>
> (Eliade 1954: 100)

The escape from the absurd and the meaningless is a powerful tool for those suffering from such things—not only in psychiatric illness do we see this, but in all forms of functional disturbance. Narrative is one mechanism humanity has discovered to counterbalance the abyss of meaninglessness and emptiness.

Narrative, argues Bruner (1998), is a way of framing complex, ambiguous data and regulating the affective response to such chaos, as well as aiding memory construction and reconstruction—which we have already seen is critical in ritual. Narrative frames social constructs and relationships also and is a key element of mental functioning. Bruner argues, and summarizes thinking along this plane, that a major part of mental function is storytelling—we continually tell stories about ourselves to ourselves and to others, and this process connects us with disparate parts of ourselves and with others. This narrating self inherently "not only recounts but justifies" (Bruner 1998: 121) and so provides meaning and purpose to our experience, and rituals provide concrete events with which to build narrative. Rituals provide the building blocks for narrative, for better or for worse, and add a further dimension by their *physical enactment*. In other words, on a certain level we *become* what the ritual enacts. Thus, psychotherapy already utilizes the naturally self-stabilizing power of narrative. What incorporating ritual does is take it to a deeper level through the physical enactment of the narrative, and through the ability of the ritual to connect the participant to something larger—what we called participation. Through the action of ritual, subjects reconstruct their narrative and connect it with mythic narratives, with the narrative of others such as family and/or loved ones, with their past, the dead, or what have you. It brings them, through physically enacted symbolic action, out of isolation and into the world of resonant narrative.

Meaningful Coincidence

Ritual does more than consolidate a person's story, however. It can prepare them for meaningful events in the future. This happens through the phenomenon of meaningful coincidence, which is another mechanism that is related to narrative and by which rituals produce psychological changes in their recipients. This is because the vague/symbolic/metaphorical nature of the narratives and themes of rituals is highly conducive to invoking the feeling of meaningful coincidence in people's lives. Thus, whereas the previous mechanism involved rituals invoking mind/body changes, related to changes in specific neurobiological regions, the mechanism of meaningful coincidence, or what Jung called "synchronicity" (Jung 1952), causes alterations in the perception of external events in a patient's life.

The basic pattern might be that a person seeks an increase in fortune or perhaps to spark a love interest. Upon performing a ritual in the proper context and involving all the right elements, she notices not long after that a significant event occurs in her life denoting financial or romantic success. She finds in this coincidence of events an intense feeling of *meaning*, which she attributes to the success of the ritual. Skeptics of course respond that the spell did not likely cause the event, but that is actually a separate issue from whether or not the event is perceived to be "meaningful." Meaning is perceived subjectively, regardless of cause/effect, because it is an emotional response, and so if rituals affect subjective impressions, which I argue that they do, then meaning is altered by ritual as well. Thus it is relevant to examine the particulars of meaningful coincidence detection as a subjective perception in itself, regardless of causal arguments.

Finding patterns and attributing meaning to events is a natural subjective human impulse. Practically *any* meaning is preferable to *meaninglessness*. Thus our meaning-making impulses help us survive our environments. But it is a capacity that is shaped by a number of factors. There are certain conditions under which we as humans tend to increase our pattern-seeking/meaning-finding behavior (Beitman 2009; Coleman *et al.* 2009):

1. Under sensory deprivation conditions—these conditions improve our ability to make out faces, find intent, or see patterns in ambiguous environments.
2. When isolated or lonely—probably a variation on the first circumstance, but with the emotional coloring of social separation and the discomfort that involves.
3. Under conditions in which we feel a loss of control—this tendency can be useful in therapy since depression and anxiety are often accompanied by feelings of loss of control.
4. People with high religious and spiritual tendencies (itself influenced by genetics) are more likely to find patterns in the environment.
5. Certain drugs increase or decrease this capacity as well.

Note that many rituals exploit all five of these conditions. For example, among the Charrua of Uruguay, men seeking passage into adulthood and a guardian spirit will seek a lonely hill with a stone mound on it and then torture themselves via fasting and self-mutilation until they see the spirit. This practice is also found among North American tribes (Hultkrantz 1979: 71). There are examples of similar practices among tribes from the Americas, as well as the ancient Greeks, Vikings, and Celts. We will discuss more examples in Chapter 10. In these circumstances, the practitioner is sensorily deprived, is isolated, feels a loss of control through various mechanisms including self-torture or being literally bound, and often entheogens are imbibed such as fly agaric, alcohol, high-potency tobacco, and peyote, among others. The very act of embarking on such a journey suggests strong religious belief as well—these examples are perfectly designed to maximize the likelihood of a greatly enhanced sense of meaningful coincidence.

Note that there are some important functions to meaningful coincidence detection. When we do find a pattern amidst the chaos of input, fear centers in the brain are relieved (Beitman 2009; Coleman *et al.* 2009). Anxiety is reduced, and subjects report greater wellbeing.

Meaning-Making Biases

There are also a number of so-called biases that help determine whether someone will attribute meaning to a set of coincidences or not, and factors that help shape the *kind* of meaning we will attribute to a coincidence as well:

1. Confirmation bias—this is the tendency to come to conclusions that support views of the world we already have.
2. Egocentric bias—the tendency to attribute personal coincidences as more important, more uncanny, and more meaningful than similar coincidences occurring to others which are more likely to be downplayed as chance.
3. Hindsight bias—the tendency to attribute more meaning to a coincidence after more information is acquired later. A chance meeting with someone who later dies, for example, might make us think the meeting was more than chance.

4. Availability bias—the tendency to attribute meaning to a coincidence when it is related to things you have been thinking about a lot recently (particularly if they are very emotional).

(Adapted from Beitman 2009)

Most of these biases operate using unconscious brain processing, and are emotionally driven (though we always have the option of denying them consciously). Other biases include the allowance of "near misses" as still meaningful, or the tendency to attribute meaning to things that have a relatively high chance of co-occurring randomly. These "biases" (I prefer the less pejorative term "heuristics") I am pointing out not to argue that such thinking is delusional; rather it highlights an important aspect of human thought. Biases are of course, in themselves, neither good nor bad; in fact, they serve important functions. Confirmation bias prevents us from changing our minds constantly in the face of confusing and contradictory information. Egocentric bias keeps us from disengaging from life because it is "meaningless" to us—a state which shares common features with depression. Hindsight bias keeps us from viewing our lives as a collection of unrelated incidents from which nothing can be learned. Availability bias keeps us attuned to emotional events, and since emotions are our primary motivators and have a long evolutionary history, they have a good track record despite their potential problems.

These biases serve important functions, and researchers studying the reports of meaningful coincidences have yielded some interesting results (reviewed in Beitman 2009). For example, people who report high frequencies of meaningful coincidences appear more likely to take advantage of normal coincidences when they occur—in other words, the tendency itself leads to meaningful coincidences occurring more often. They also point to the fact that though statistically speaking, just by the sheer number of combinations involved, "incredible" coincidences are fairly frequent (perhaps this is because life is incredible!), they provide meaning only to those who take notice of them and do not dismiss them. Furthermore, subjects who reported more coincidences tended to report more spiritual experiences. The reports of meaningful coincidences were also correlated with a number of personality traits: subjects who were more extroverted, religiously committed, had faith in "intuition," had high "vitality" (a measure of how intensely they engaged with life), actively sought meaning or felt life was inherently meaningful all reported meaningful coincidences more often.

As we will see, the specifics of rituals have a number of characteristics that predispose them to the invocation of meaningful coincidence in their practitioners, whether or not the ritual is carried out by oneself (which is likely to be accompanied by a sense of empowerment, mystery, and interconnection), or by an expert practitioner on a group. In particular, they will change a person's outlook to involve a less negative worldview, perhaps alleviate the terror of powerlessness to some degree and provide hope, unconsciously predispose them to take advantage of normal coincidences, increase a sense of meaning and wonder, and increase the sense of vitality and engagement in life. From a biological perspective, note that these latter two have been correlated with higher dopamine levels and increased SEEKING activity in the brain (Goodwyn 2012). This latter conclusion needs to be empirically tested, both in subjective post-ritual report and in brain activity if possible, and represents one of many predictions the model I am developing here makes that could be potentially tested with empirical research.

Meaningful coincidences can form powerful building blocks for narrative construction, and for the above reasons these can be very positive. Speaking as a clinician, however, the detection of meaningful coincidence can operate in the opposite direction as well, where people feel events, God, life, or whatever is "stacked against" them. Often people suffering from depression have extremely negative worldviews related to their personal experiences. This state of affairs, however, is often shifted around through the ritual of psychotherapy, and so it uses this natural tendency to reverse the negative meaningful coincidence effect and create a positive one.

When the meaning is positive, it can have a profound effect on one's life. Daniel Moerman equates the sense of meaning in the various events of life with overall healing (Moerman 2002: 98–99). So meaningful coincidence is an important part of narrative construction that can be very convincing because it feels as if it impinges upon us from outside, connecting us with the gods, with the mysterious, with the overall scheme of the universe; again, connecting us with the world. Thus it appears meaningful coincidence is another form of *participation*, which we have seen can be a powerful influence on the mind. Furthermore, ritual, through its various mechanisms, has evolved cross-culturally to exploit this universal human tendency to find meaning. The foregoing therefore shows us why focusing attention on meaningful coincidence plays a part in effecting mental change. Up to this point, however, only Jungian therapy looks for ways to foster a sense of meaningful coincidence. Here, though, we can see why this approach should receive a wider currency in therapy.

Dissociation and Decentering

Another thing rituals do is related to what psychodynamic theorists call dissociation. Elsewhere in this volume, anthropologist Roy Rappaport is quoted as speculating on one of the functions of ritual:

> given the extent to which in solitary rituals various parts of the psyche ordinarily inaccessible to each other may be brought into touch, and given the extent to which the emotions of participants may respond to the stimuli of their own ritual acts, it is reasonable to take ritual to be auto-communicative.
>
> (Rappaport 1999: 51)

We will study Rappaport's theory of ritual in the next chapter. For now, however, we should note that psychologists have described the phenomenon of dissociation since Pierre Janet (Ellenberger 1970) coined the term in the late nineteenth century, and in more recent years dissociation has gained a resurgence of interest, research, and empirical support as an important psychodynamic mechanism of (mal-)functioning (Scaer 2001; Van der Hart *et al.* 2006; Van der Kolk *et al.* 1996). Jung developed the concept of dissociation in his complex theory (1919), which we will discuss in more detail with respect to ritual and Patrick McNamara's neurobiological–psychodynamic theory of what rituals do.

For the moment, dissociation is the tendency of the mind to break off into fragments—particularly in response to trauma (Briere 2006). This natural tendency of the mind to operate at some level of dissociation is the basis for several types of psychotherapy in which the purpose is to bring the disparate parts of the psyche together and foster a sense of unity within the self (Stein 2010; Van der Hart *et al.* 2006). As we will see, it is likely that psychotherapy is but one ritual among many that humanity has discovered to achieve this purpose, and but one function among many that rituals have.

Patrick McNamara's Formulation of the Self

In *The Neuroscience of Religious Experience*, neuroscientist Patrick McNamara defines a set of neurobiological structures/processes that he labels "the Executive Self" or simply "the Self." This structure, McNamara points out, is implicated in a variety of experiences deemed religious, both in normal religious behavior and in pathological religious behavior such as fanaticism, religious delusions, hallucinations, or "harmful" spirit possession. The Self is a construct that according to McNamara evolved to bring order to the chaotic interplay of various unconscious circuits or impulses, and in his review he noticed that there is a considerable overlap in brain regions associated with the Self.

A strong Self, it is argued, is essential for good functioning, and is composed of autobiographical memory (the importance of which we have already noted), emotional/evaluative systems, agency, bodily awareness, empathy, and a sense of unity in consciousness. McNamara's assertion here is in agreement with psychotherapists on this point. McNamara then reviews clinical data and research on the neurobiology of the Self from many perspectives, and so connects psychodynamic ideas with biological data. He describes pathological Self constructs that arise in the setting of schizophrenia, multiple personality disorder, bipolar disorder, temporal lobe epilepsy, obsessive-compulsive disorder, or stroke, and concludes that the experience of the executive Self is associated with the activities of the limbic, orbitofrontal and right-sided temporal areas and the right-sided dorsolateral prefrontal cortex, and that it is primarily with these areas that religious activity, both harmful and helpful, is most correlated. Thus McNamara blends the biological perspective with the psychodynamic perspective and dovetails nicely with the themes we are developing here.

In reviewing a large database of neuroscientific studies of religious rituals, McNamara concludes that religious practices of all kinds converge on consistent associations with Self circuits, which he specifies as the orbital, dorsomedial prefrontal cortex, right dorsolateral prefrontal cortex, ascending serotonergic systems, mesocortical dopamine system, amygdala/hippocampi, and the right anterior temporal lobes. He notes that all of these sites are interconnected and found time and again to be altered in brain activity in the context of various spiritual and mystical ecstatic states that are common, if not universal, in ritual activity. Since these are implicated in religious processes, McNamara argues, the function of religious activity must be related to the functions of the Self.

The Divided Self, Ideal Selves, Alternate Selves, and their Interaction

Thus far we have looked at how ritual makes unique and powerful use of psychodynamic principles already well known to clinical practice and combines them in a special way to effect change. These principles include the use of mental images, projection/projective identification, narrative, and meaningful coincidence. In this section we will see how ritual may alter the structure of the personal element of the psyche through its effect on dissociativity.

What we are calling here the "personal element" of the psyche is also known by other names such as (classically) the "ego," the "conscious ego," or in neuroscience "the Self" (capitalized by convention). Building on representational theories of the Self concept as well as the Self concept coming from narrative psychodynamic theory, McNamara proposes that the "current Self" structure exists in the psyche within a matrix of "possible Selves," which are imaginary narratives about the Self in the future. These possible Selves compete with one another; some of these Selves will develop into "Ideal Selves," which I find analogous to archetypal images (Stein 2010) of the collective element. He notes the considerable empirical backing for this construct of the Self and proceeds to situate it within a neurobiological framework. McNamara draws not on Jung but on William James, whom Jung nonetheless greatly respected, and he seems to have come to many of the same conclusions about the executive Self that Jung did concerning what he called the "conscious ego," as we will see. In particular, the "Self/possible Self" interaction appears to be cognate with the conscious ego complex (or archetypal image) from Jungian psychology.

Of central concern is the notion of the inherently divided psyche, and McNamara poses (building on Haig 2006) a very plausible genetic explanation as to why we inherit a mind full of conflicting impulses and desires that tends to dissociate over time (McNamara 2009: 34–35). Using this framework, and providing many more examples, he produces a model of the Self born into conflict:

> the default state of most organisms, including human beings, is internal conflict. We are a conglomeration of conflicting sets of genes, all of which are in competition with one another to pass copies of themselves down the generations. They build physiologic systems that assist them in that process, and

> among these systems are systems of the brain . . . By far the greatest source of conflict around alternative courses of action arises out of conflicting internal desires that in turn are rooted in evolutionary genetic conflicts.
>
> (McNamara 2009: 38–39)

Upon this chaotic foundation arises the executive Self, which McNamara argues is both a biological adaptation and a cultural achievement (two concepts that are interdependent anyway, cf. Goodwyn 2010—this assertion also agrees with the discussion in Chapters 1 and 2) that can help to provide a more coherent framework for decision-making and behavioral strategy construction. The purpose and mechanism behind religious rituals, he argues, is to assist in the process of building up a strong, centralized executive Self—in many psychodynamic theories this would be analogous to an ego-strengthening exercise. The way ritual does this is by reducing the discrepancy between ideal Selves and the current Self through a process McNamara calls "decentering."

Decentering the Self

Decentering is described as taking the current Self "offline" and out of working memory: "it is a conscious form of imaginative mental processing that does not occur in working memory" (McNamara 2009: 45). This brings up Jung's concept of active imagination, and the variety of ways in which ritual verbiage and action sidestep semantic meaning in favor of iconic, emotional, non-verbal, and indexical meaning. In this process, several key aspects of the Self are diminished, most notably *intent.* Recalling that a strong Self circuit functions to provide the organism with autobiographical memory, emotional/evaluative systems, agency, bodily awareness, theory of mind, and a sense of unity in consciousness, decentering actually weakens this whole structure, with the intention of breaking down the old functioning and allowing the internal conflicts to resolve themselves, through ritual, into a newer, more coherent, and less conflicted Self.

Decentering may be a natural rhythm of the psyche (seen, for example, in dreaming), but it is amplified and maximized in ritual. Here McNamara outlines just a few of the qualities of rituals we have discussed already, such as their hypnotic and rhythmic qualities. To this we may add the mechanisms we have already talked about. All of these mechanisms, according to McNamara, appear to decentralize the Self and allow a temporary state that is more chaotic, less controlled, and spontaneous:

> Decentering temporarily displaces or decouples the executive Self from its position of control over executive cognitive and motor functions to repair that sense of Self and then links it back with a greater range of cognitive systems than it was linked to before the decoupling was implemented . . . a Self controls the cognitive and behavioral repertoire of an individual when it controls attentional resources.
>
> (McNamara 2009: 45)

Already we are seeing the parallels between a decentered Self and the pageantry of the imagistic mode. Decentering reduces intentionality and diffuses attentional mechanisms. It is interesting to note here that psychotherapy literature describes in various schools the concept of "regression in service to the ego," in which the ego is dissolved into a more primordial state of raw impressions and emotions, the purpose being to restructure the ego into something stronger than before. Jungian therapy has the analogous process of "active imagination," which is engaging in imaginary dialogue with archetypal images (Jung 1954) for the same purpose of renewal and rejuvenation/restructuring. The similarity of these processes serves to underscore the basic ritual nature of psychotherapy which we have discussed already.

In this decentralized (or regressed) state, the decentered Self can transform through its interaction with the numerous possible Selves and/or Ideal Selves that also exist within the mind and allows for a transformation of the Self circuit. But there are dangers; for example, one potential consequence of a breakdown or malfunctioning of the decentering process is fanaticism, which McNamara argues is when the Self decenters and instead of searching for and merging with an Ideal Self, in which it binds with that Ideal Self, it instead binds with itself—old Self with old Self, and what he calls "narcissism" or fanaticism ensues—this is highly analogous to Jung's description of ego inflation (1954) and what other schools label pathological narcissism. Other potential "malfunctions" of this system include harmful spirit possession—in which the Self gets overtaken with primordial emotional systems, and which is analogous to the highly emotional "switches" of personality seen in various dissociative disorders (Van der Hart *et al.* 2006).

Ritual Transformation of Self

The ritually decentering Self can encounter and interact with other Selves or Ideal Selves—a process very much like dreaming—though the practitioner is awake. If successful, the ritual allows a binding of the Self with an Ideal Self to allow a transformation to a newer, more integrated, and coherent Self. This process can produce multiple positive effects. Quoting Pahnke (1967), McNamara reviews the observed effects of decentering and restructuring: a sense of unity, transcendence, positive mood, sense of the sacred, a feeling of insight, "paradoxicality" or the ability to respectfully hold opposing points of view, ineffability, and persisting positive changes in attitudes. He adds other effects based on his own research: an enhanced sense of personal power, enhanced empathic skills, enhanced control or appreciation of sexual behavior, enhanced appreciation of music, improved use of complex visual/metaphoric imagery, more sophisticated ability to use ritualization, and encounters with God or spirit beings: "Ritual allows for the entertaining of a very high conception of a possible Self—indeed, a saintly or even a godlike Self" (McNamara 2009: 53).

McNamara outlines his provisional model of how religious rituals can transform the Self through, first, a reduction in intentionality, followed by a "flood of images and affects that resolves into a process of attempts at meaning and then finally insight and gratitude/joy" (McNamara 2009: 143). Using the available neurobiological data on religious experiences, he identifies what brain regions and neurotransmitters might be active during these processes. This activity, McNamara argues, strengthens the Self through its interaction with the Ideal Selves and other Selves—in a manner much like a more controlled and positive type of psychosis—that interact with the current Self, to create a more unified Self.

Note that the Self is identified not as a "thing" but as a process, fragile and dynamic. During these transformations the Self "dies" and is renewed through interactions with other Selves and Ideal Selves in dreams and religious activities. McNamara is thorough in his analysis, working through philosophical issues as well as neurobiological and religious concepts. For example, in his examination of the parallels between his theory and Islamic Sufi mysticism, he observes:

> in most if not all of the other religious traditions, religious practices are focused on transformation of [the] base qualities to turn them into gold or a set of higher qualities. When enough such qualities have been transformed, you get a new Self . . . From an appetite-ridden, fearful, egocentric [Self], one is transformed via ascetical practice into a serene, free, autonomous, gift-bestowing, compassionate, and generous individual.
>
> (McNamara 2009: 153)

We will note that the rituals McNamara is probably referring to are of the high-sensory pageantry and "imagistic" variety, because of their vividness and use of altered mental states; this mode of ritual is the more "natural" or primary ritual mode, which may be correlated with the ability of such processes to produce intense and dramatic neurobiological changes, rather than reinforce the existing structure, which is what doctrinal mode rituality does. We will return to this process of transformation when we discuss transitional rituals in Chapter 10.

McNamara also points out that such processes are utilized in a variety of contexts, and not just to produce serene and benevolent Selves. Since the process of ritual transformation is so potent, it is unsurprising that it has been utilized for other pursuits. For example, since it functions to produce a more focused and unified Self, ritual transformation has been used for warfare, such as the Norse berserker-trance, wherein the less ferocious Self is set aside to be taken over by a nearly unstoppable combatant. Elsewhere he discusses the concept of spirit possession (a near universal cultural phenomenon) and the neurobiology behind it. Finally, another area McNamara ties together in relation to ritual transformation is the relationship between religious experiences and psychopathy—an area that clearly fascinated Jung in his early work and led him to very similar-sounding theories. In these sections, McNamara also compares religious rituals and various parallel pathological conditions such as dissociative identity disorder, possession, fanaticism, and many others, all of which he suggests are related to the normally adaptive process of religious thinking.

God Concepts in Decentering

Another interesting aspect of McNamara's formulation, and the one which has been observed in various psychodynamic models, is his account of the neurobiology that correlates with god concepts. He begins with some very psychodynamic statements about the psyche as a whole in relation to dreams:

> there may be several Minds or subpersonalities within a single person. The multiplicity of minds within a single person can even be seen in normal, healthy individuals when we dream.
>
> (McNamara 2009: 196)

Such comments remind us of Jung's theorizing on complexes and archetypal figures that emerge from the unconscious. McNamara is quick to point out, however, that dream characters "are not mere inventions of the dreamer. They are to some extent independent of the dreamer's will" (McNamara 2009: 197). This characteristic marks them as emergent from the collective rather than personal element. He goes on to point out that in his own research he has observed that some dream characters recur and remember previous interactions with the dreamer and act accordingly; thus

> dream characters (both the dreamer and other characters within a dream) appear to satisfy some of the most stringent criteria philosophers have produced for "personhood". It should not be surprising, therefore, to find that our ancestors treated dream characters as spirit persons and accorded special and sometimes divine status to characters in dreams.
>
> (McNamara 2009: 198)

These new data and McNamara's analysis appear to ally with many psychodynamic approaches that advise patients to attend carefully to dream material, in particular with the conceptualization of dream characters as autonomous personalities that should be dealt with as such rather than explained away or considered as abstract mechanistic processes. McNamara goes on to summarize some aspects of ritual that tie in to this theory of Selves and decentering, pointing out the aspects of ritual including the indexical or metonymic use of symbols, the atemporality and connection with the ancient past including history, tradition, and lineage, all of which are corroborated by many other scholars of ritual. He also notes that according to the studies he reviews, religious belief and behavior appear to improve self-regulatory functions and control impulsivity, and he argues that it is an evolutionary biocultural adaptation.

Summary

McNamara argues convincingly that religious behavior is an evolutionary adaptation, citing the universality, relative ease of acquisition, associated genetics, and biology and its function in strengthening the executive Self toward whatever end it may be focused on. His formulation of dream characters as autonomous personalities, related to possible Selves or Ideal Selves that can be encountered in ritual, ties together a number of concepts on the neuroscience of dreams, ritual, religious thinking, and personal development that all align well with much of the depth psychology formulation discussed so far, and in some cases, builds on it by using more recent data on brain functioning. It already incorporates the concept of narrative, but does not discuss the projective aspects of ritual, and in general McNamara looks primarily at ecstatic rituals involving altered states of consciousness. While this is an important aspect of ritual, and may occur to varying degrees in all rituals, there are other points to consider. The concept of projection in particular is important since it highlights how other people in a participant's life may have strong influences on a ritual. Participants may have projective identifications with loved ones, deceased relatives, and hated enemies (and vice versa) that all may play a part in their mind as the ritual unfolds. The concept of meaningful coincidence feeds into how "convincing" a ritual is and plays a large role in narrative construction and a continuous sense of *participation mystique*.

The mechanisms discussed in this chapter include imagery, narrative, projective identification, meaningful coincidence, and decentering. It is evident that ritual utilizes all of them in a unique manner to effect powerful changes in the individual psyche. The common theme is that ritual uses the collective element to temporarily dismantle the current ego/Self/personal element and restructure it—hopefully in a positive manner. Recalling previous chapters, it does this through the invocation of metaphorical, spontaneously created, or passed down (i.e. *resonant*) stories and images, and invokes a "top-down" flow of control through its use of physically enacted ritual action to cause empirically measurable changes in brain and body physiology. The degree to which any particular ritual does this, and hence just how drastic the dismantling and restructuring is, likely depends on how imagistic it is, and how much sensory pageantry is involved. Some rituals are "big" and life-altering, tearing down the old ego and building a new one. Others merely serve to reinforce and strengthen the current ego, bracing it against the vicissitudes of life and helping it to maintain the status quo. For this, more doctrinal and high-frequency rituals serve best.

So far we have focused a great deal on the individual. In the next chapter we will look at the final branch of our dynamic interdisciplinary theory: anthropological theories of ritual, which look at the whole person in cultural context. Finally, we will note the ways modern society is ritually impoverished and therefore missing out on this powerful activity.

Chapter 6

The Cultural Branch

Structure and Function

Symbols appear in widely diverse cultures due to the like working of men's minds under like conditions.
– Tylor (1878: 3)

Thus far we have explored the biological, cognitive, and depth psychological approaches to ritual. All of these aspects of ritual, however, are not typically the central focus for those who study ritual the most—anthropologists. Anthropologists are often the first to admit their lack of expertise in psychology or biology: "The interpretation of emotion presents . . . special problems for the anthropologist, because we are not well equipped to deal with inner states" (Metcalf and Huntington 1991: 43). What *are* well known and well characterized by anthropologists, nevertheless, are the many subtleties that occur in social settings between and within groups. Ritual is, above all, a social thing. Anthropologists Peter Metcalf and Robert Huntington, for example, despite their previous statement regarding the connection between ritual and emotion, observe that:

> Conventions condition feelings and provide a setting for them. Between ritual and emotion there is a subtle feedback, so that it is difficult at any moment to say whether the emotions are propelling the ritual or vice versa.
> (Metcalf and Huntington 1991: 203)

To the word "subtle" in the above quote, I would add "rapid and continuous." Religious scholar Jane Harrison as early as 1912 recognized the link between religion, emotion, and ritual by stating "Ritual is the utterance of an emotion, a thing felt, in *action*, myth in words or thoughts" (Harrison 1998: 72). Much later, in the 1990s, religious scholar H. S. Versnel advised interdisciplinary efforts by observing that everywhere

> in a great mass of myths, fairy tales, stories (and dreams) from all over the world—we can discern a more or less identical basic pattern, [and we have] the right if not the duty to try to find an explanation for this phenomenon.

> Perhaps this can be done without the help of recent ethological and biological insights, but it may be better to try to incorporate them.
>
> (Versnel 1998: 466)

These statements, although separated by a long time span, agree fully with the principles discussed in the first few chapters, such as psychological resonance and the cognitive, physiological, embodied, and emotional/psychodynamic aspects of ritual.

The Anthropological Study of Ritual

The study of ritual has a long history. In the late nineteenth century, Old Testament scholar Robertson Smith (1998), following Tylor's evolutionary framework, forwarded a theory that ritual was primary in the origin of all religion and society, theorizing that ritual existed for the sake of the preservation and welfare of society. Sir James Frazer, a student of Smith, elaborated on this framework and developed a model which depicted all religion as originating in an ancient ritual enacting the death and resurrection of a god-king of fertility. Sigmund Freud (1913), slightly earlier, had advanced an evolutionary theory that rituals served personal psychological needs to assuage the guilt involved in the killing of a father in the unspecified deep past. For Freud, ritual ultimately dealt with the same repressed incestuous drives that neurotic symptoms dealt with. Émile Durkheim (1915), while eschewing the evolutionary aspects of Smith and Tylor, later argued similarly that ritual served sociological needs.

For several decades in the twentieth century, these ideas on the primacy of ritual over myth/religion flowered into the "Myth and Ritual School" of thinking, well summarized by Segal (1998). At the same time, phenomenologists of religion looked not to a historical-diffusionist model, but saw religion and ritual as reflecting timeless universals of either the divine sacred or as within human consciousness. One of the primary theorists of these approaches was Mircea Eliade (1954, 1958), who saw myths and symbols as more primary than ritual, which was a secondary reworking of the first-experienced symbols and myths, and Carl Jung, whose work we have discussed already, developed allied views.

The Myth and Ritual School is no longer an important part of the study of ritual, however, as there is far too much discrediting evidence against it now. Myths and rituals are no longer seen as dependent upon one another, but as interacting with one another, sometimes feeding into each other, sometimes developing on their own independently (Bell 2009: 20–22). This is consistent with the findings of our first three branches discussing ritual—that is, myths are the psychologically resonant images and stories that are often associated with what is otherwise a performative, physical, and predominantly non-verbal kind of communication. They enrich each other, but neither is dependent upon the other as was once thought.

Anthropology was not directly related to this development in religious studies, and as the field began to develop on its own, the focus began to turn to the functions of ritual within society. Émile Durkheim's theory of ritual as serving social functions has endured in general (Bell 2009: 25), though there are many viewpoints explored in this volume that argue there is more to ritual than social function. Moreover, Durkheim's very psychological arguments concerning "effervescence" call for a psychologically informed analysis of ritual, explored throughout this volume, and his distinction between magic and religion has not withstood the test of time (e.g. Davies 2003; Sørensen 2007a); thus we will not concern ourselves with any such distinctions here. Durkheim's social-function theory was expanded by Alfred Radcliffe-Brown (2009 [1922]), who argued similarly to the myth-ritualists that belief was the effect of the ritual, though he acknowledged a more complex, interactionist relationship between myth and ritual than a simple either/or cause–effect. In any case, Radcliffe-Brown argued that rituals do not alleviate anxiety (which was the explanation given by Bronislaw Malinowski 1925) or intense mental states, rather that rituals *create* such mental states. Here we see an early form of our psychological/biological argument again, presaged by a sociologist.

E. E. Evans-Pritchard (1965) recognized the social function of ritual but saw Durkheim's reduction of religion to society and his description of "effervescence" as an oversimplification not supported by detailed fieldwork. Instead, he noted the variety of emotional responses to performed rituals, and concluded that the emotionality is of secondary importance to the more essential requirements and symbolic structure of the rituals themselves. They express certain realities about the practitioner's worldview and it is more important that they be carried out than that they produce any particular emotional effect. As we have seen, however, the relationship between emotionality and ritual is highly complex.

Rappaport (1999), whom we will discuss in more depth later, showed how ritual does not merely serve social functions but also concrete material functions as well, in his analysis of Maring pig-slaughtering rituals which occurred at precisely the time at which the pig population approached an unwieldy level. The ritual, argued Rappaport, benefited the community not only through its consolidation of social interactions, but also through its balancing effect on the very subsistence of the tribe. This effect was also observed by Marvin Harris (1977), in his "cultural materialism," who observed the way in which Hindu taboos against eating cows served a very important cultural preservation function in a powerful, religious, and emotional way that could not be duplicated by rational economic arguments.

Further nearing the biological level, Julian Huxley (1966) connected human ritual behavior with that of animal ritual behavior. He proposed that ritualization of activities provides structure to emotionally motivated behavior that has been subject to natural selection. From the biological perspective, it is important to note that affective neuroscientists have linked a number of our emotional systems to cross-species structures and functional complexes that are shared with many other animals (Goodwyn, 2012; Panksepp 1998, 2005), strengthening this idea. For Huxley, ritualization clarifies *communication* between animals regarding aggression, sexuality, social bonding, and other primary biological behaviors shared by humans and other animals. Ritual dance, art, play, and education all appear to share this communicative element in non-verbal ways.

Building on this framework is the "biogenetic structuralism" approach of Eugene d'Aquili and Charles Laughlin (1979; see also Laughlin 1990) which we encountered in Chapter 3. This approach emphasizes the way in which ritual serves social and material goals, and biogenetic structuralists make arguments for their adaptability and hence selected-for status. Rituals solve problems otherwise too challenging for simple reflexive behavior and represent a kind of "technology"—an idea I will expand upon later. Connecting biological to individual psychological development is the psychological theory of psychoanalyst Erik Erikson (1963), who proposed that the human lifespan encompasses eight successive stages that must be successfully navigated by each person in order to establish social and mental wellbeing. According to Erikson, ritualization is an important mechanism through which the individual traverses these stages. Critics of these approaches argue that ritual and religion herewith became reduced to purely societal and material matters, whereas supporters argued that these ideas contributed to the understanding of ritual as constrained by biological determinants but also creatively responsive to environmental situations (Bell 2009: 33).

Arnold van Gennep (1960), while influenced by Frazer and his universalizing approach, nevertheless disliked Frazer's tendency to take myths and rituals out of context to superimpose his diffusionist theory upon them. Van Gennep emphasized the transitional aspect of rituals in the way they, through various symbolic means, made concrete transitions of practitioners from one social category to another in order to help them adjust to their new roles, thus functioning for individual wellbeing as well as social wellbeing. We will be exploring van Gennep's work later.

Max Gluckman's (1962) analysis emphasized the way in which rituals express difficult social tensions through their enactments of social conflicts and "ritual rebellions." The more potential conflict exists in a particular society, whether due to lack of mechanical divisions of power hierarchy or whatever, the more highly ritualized will be the expressions of such structure, since the rituals serve to differentiate roles and defuse tensions (Bell 2009: 39). Victor Turner (1974) built on these two models to construct his own model which we will explore in more depth later, where he argues that rituals depict, enact, and give form to conflicts as well as the dominant value systems in a particular group. Rituals, argues Turner, dramatize the situation in a way no other activity can. For Turner,

> the symbol is the heart of this ritual mechanism; it is the irreducible unit of ritual activity . . . the human body is the source of symbols and systems of symbols, which are extended outward to organize and understand the social world. Among the most basic human symbols is the set of three colors

> composed of white, red, and black, representing the products of the human body: milk or semen, blood, and feces or decayed matter.
>
> (Bell 2009: 41)

I have made similar arguments in my survey of religious and dream symbolism (Goodwyn 2012).

Anthropologist Claude Lévi-Strauss (1966) also emphasized symbolic thought in great detail, arguing that the systems of symbols depicted in rituals are not reflections of social structure, as argued by Durkheim, but rather that humans create symbolic systems on social relationships in order to structure and organize them. "For Lévi-Strauss, social structure does not exist out there in the observable world of human interaction so much as it exists in the unconscious processes of human thought" (Bell 2009: 42). We have seen the often unrecognized similarities between Lévi-Strauss and Jung in Chapter 1. Lévi-Strauss argued that symbolic systems are always collections of binary oppositions, the most important of which is the contrast between nature and culture, "the most fundamental of the binary oppositions that organize human thought" (Bell 2009: 43). Elsewhere Lévi-Strauss argued that the grammar-like rules of human symbol making and mythologizing do not exist in culture but in the brain itself (Bell 2009: 63).

Cultural Effects on Biology and Psychology

In the previous three chapters, we have looked at the physiological, cognitive, and psychodynamic effects that likely contribute to and are affected by rituals. Now we will look at the cultural dimension. The amount of literature that has been devoted to the cultural effects of ritual is immense and so I cannot be exhaustive here. Nevertheless, as discussed in Chapter 1, there is much overlap in anthropological inquiry with depth psychology, and also cognitive and biological approaches to ritual. In particular, it has been noted that the cultural context can have profound effects on a person's biology and psychology. As already discussed, we cannot assume only one-way influence from biology to psychology to culture, but must assume a continuous, dense interactivity at all levels.

For example, placebo researcher Fabrizio Benedetti notes that when a medical treatment is administered, there is a complex matrix activated by a variety of social stimuli. This cascade of biochemical events interferes with any drug given and can change the response of the drug itself (Benedetti 2009: 252–253). This is of course no surprise to anthropologists, who have noted that all illnesses have significant cultural factors shaping them (Kleinman 1989). Furthermore, social context can affect *how* we experience what we normally think of as "purely biological" events. For example, placebo alcohol has been shown to increase sexual arousal, aggressive behavior, and alcohol craving (Wilson and Lawson 1976; Lang *et al.* 1975; Marlatt and Roshenow 1980), showing that our bodies react and communicate to others in response to cues which are entirely social in nature—put another way, culture is *expected* by our biology, and hence there can be no simple nature–nurture dichotomy. Other examples are the fact that hypodermic shots of placebo medication elicit stronger responses than pills, but only in the United States (Moerman 2002: 79–85); Moerman provides many other examples of culturally specific treatment response effects.

Brody and Waters (1980) argue that "diagnosis is treatment," meaning that a significant part of the healing encounter is the labeling of an illness by the physician/healer—a concept we encountered previously when discussing narrative. Such illnesses are always culturally defined to a significant degree (a fact difficult to see in one's own culture). Thus, from the biological branch, placebo researcher D. B. Morris writes:

> The placebo effect thus belongs to an encompassing cultural narrative in which humans project their own self-healing powers onto a doctor or shaman or priest, who triggers relief through certain arcane rituals and prescriptions. Despite the progress of modern biomedicine, it is a narrative that has not changed for thousands of years.
>
> (Morris 1999: 196)

Here we see the psychodynamic process of projection already being incorporated into the healing effects of cultural interaction and narrative. Biogenetic structuralists (Laughlin 1990) argue that the structured, repetitive, stereotyped activity of ritual coordinates the behavior of a group relative to some goal; it coordinates both within participants and between them. This applies even to solitary ritual performers since they are performing a set of actions that is still socially derived, thus coordinating them ideologically if not in time or space.

The psychodynamic concepts of meaningful coincidence, image, and narrative do not emerge independently of culture either, but grow from it. For example, Price *et al.* (2008) link placebo effects to meaningful coincidence, noting that the expectancy of benefit creates a positive feedback loop in which subjects selectively notice signs of improvement in their lives—linking cultural expectations, psychological biases, and placebo responses together. Elsewhere, Brody (1999: 229) argues that meaning-making comes through the co-construction of narrative between and within individuals. Regarding imagery, Morris notes that the culturally maintained chants and songs important to many Native American healing rituals are images of peaceful harmony (Morris 1999: 199). We will see many more examples of these in later chapters. As we continue we will see that just as rituals are themselves shaped by universal biological, cognitive, and psychological structures reacting to local environments, rituals can in turn affect physiology, cognition, and emotion. These latter effects have been primarily explored by anthropologists studying rituals.

Arnold van Gennep: Rituals as Rites of Passage

At the turn of the twentieth century, anthropologist Arnold van Gennep wrote an extremely influential work, *The Rites of Passage*, which continues to be relevant today. Van Gennep showed in his classic work that a great many rituals cross-culturally consist of a tripartite structure that is primarily focused on transitioning participants from one socially relevant, well-defined social role to another, equally relevant and well-defined role. Van Gennep's tripartite model argues that all such transitional rituals divide into *separation*, *transition*, and finally *incorporation* rites. Note at the outset that these are always high pageantry/low frequency rituals that often utilize imagistic modes of ritual behavior. During separation rites, the target of the rite is dramatically and symbolically separated from the previous group he was a part of before the ritual began. Then, the target participates in a ritual of transition wherein he is seen as in a *liminal* state of being neither in the initial nor final state. Many rites symbolize this state, and this part is often the most imagistic and decentering. After a set amount of time has passed in this state, the final rite of incorporation brings the target out of the neither/nor liminal state and invests him with his new, sharply defined social stature with various symbolic gestures.

Van Gennep theorized that this basic structure underlies most rituals, and his theory has held up well since it was first introduced at the beginning of the twentieth century. Elements highlighted by van Gennep are those which symbolize transitions and transformations of ritual participants—a subject we will explore in more depth in Chapter 10. He begins by showing, using examples from worldwide, how territorial markers such as portals, gates, rivers, and so on are used as concrete symbols of transitioning from one state to another:

> the door is the boundary between the foreign and domestic worlds in the case of an ordinary dwelling, between the profane and the sacred worlds in the case of a temple. Therefore to cross the threshold is to unite oneself with a new world. It is thus an important act in marriage, adoption, ordination, and funeral ceremonies.
>
> (Van Gennep 1960: 20)

Only the "main" portal, notes van Gennep, is seen to have this powerful quality, which is why in many cultures corpses, menstruating or pregnant women, or thieves (people who are "liminal" as we will see) are required to, or prefer to, leave through a side portal or secondary door. Thus the building is seen as a symbol of the important mental and social state in question. Pregnancy and childbirth both inspire many rites to protect women from evil spirits that involve separating them via physical seclusion, but also removal from normal work duties, various prohibitions and taboos often related to food and sex, and being placed in a transitional state for a variable amount of time following childbirth.

Childbirth and childhood hold their own rites of passage that also follow this basic structure, where the child must also undergo rites of separation from the mother, via various activities such as washing/rubbing, or being pulled through some kind of portal, touching earth, spring, tree, flower, forest (i.e. the realm of Nature and Her spirits), hair cutting, putting on clothes, circumcision, cutting the first tooth, and so on. Afterwards there is usually a given time period in which the child is considered in a liminal state until she/he is fully incorporated through naming, baptism, or another rite of incorporation, often by the father. Naming is particularly emphasized by van Gennep: "When a child is named, he is both individualized and incorporated into society" (1960: 62). Exposure to the sun, earth, or moon is also included as a rite of incorporation into the physical cosmos.

Rites of incorporation emphasize connection and bringing together. Examples include handclasps, common meals, drinking from a common cup, sacrificing animals, smoking a common pipe, sprinkling water from a single source, being covered together, sitting on the same seat, and so on. These actions symbolize the concept of social, mental, and emotional unity via concrete physical contact (van Gennep 1960: 28). Other examples of incorporation are handfasting, embracing, exchanging gifts, kisses, or spouses, spitting on one another, mixing blood, and exchanging sacred objects, in such a manner as to effect a contagious "mutual transference of personality" (van Gennep 1960: 30).

Marriage rites follow similar structures to birth rites and adulthood rites, and often involve mock abductions as markers of separation from prior familial networks (and not, as some investigators have thought, "survivals" of ancient practice or re-enactments of historical events). Other examples include changing clothes, emptying a pot of milk (significant in itself), cutting, breaking, or discarding something connected with youth, releasing/cutting/shaving hair/beard, removing jewelry, hymen perforation, changing food habits, giving gifts to childhood friends, ritually fighting or insulting childhood friends, destroying items related to one's family of origin, veiling, washing feet, bathing, being beaten or insulted, vomiting, name-changing, and/or being subject to new (sometimes permanent) taboos. There are rites that emphasize and highlight the change of the bride or bridegroom, manifesting the same tripartite structure for both parties, culminating in gift-giving and communal feasts—rites of incorporation—of the new couple into their new social environment. Other incorporation rites include tying clothes together, using objects belonging to one another, being wrapped together, drinking from the same container, drinking each other's blood, eating from the same container, rubbing or anointing with clay/blood, washing each other, entering a house together, and so on (van Gennep 1960: 131–132). The whole community often joins in these incorporation rites with feasts, dancing, gifts, visits, and so on, which non-verbally emphasize the union of two families rather than just two people.

In general, transition rites into adulthood or secret societies are more likely to involve the use of special languages, secret languages, along with a variety of taboo observances. Transitional periods are often those that entail a breakdown of typical social mores and gender proscriptions and involve cross-dressing, reversing or ignoring normal social hierarchical structures, and a rubric of "equality" and non-differentiation even while the initiators are obviously in charge of the proceedings. Rites of incorporation often involve temporary lifting of sexual rules and are more likely to involve orgiastic or bestiality rites as well (van Gennep

1960: 172–173). These characteristics of the liminal state reflect the largely *anti-structural* role we will explore later in this chapter.

Van Gennep and Ritual Psychology

Later commentators have noted that Van Gennep's study of initiatory rituals has yet to be explored from the framework of learning theory and also from the point of view of modern alienation and role confusion in today's society (Kimbali 1960: x–xiv). Van Gennep's pattern of passage from separation to liminality to reincorporation has been modified by Lincoln (1991) to include female transformation as enclosure, metamorphosis, and emergence—an obvious variation on Van Gennep's structure. Victor Turner has expanded Van Gennep's model to include a much wider conceptualization of liminality and pilgrimage-as-liminal state. As Kimbali (1960) observed, depth psychology is very much concerned with "initiation"-type symbolism in the individual, in particular in the Jungian approach to dream imagery (Jung and Meyer-Grass 2008). Since Van Gennep's analysis of ritual centers on rites of transition, we will postpone further discussion of these rituals until Chapter 10. For now note that Van Gennep's theory of ritual tells us that rituals transition people in highly symbolic, non-verbal, visceral, and vivid ways from one important social role or state and put them into another social role or state. This has obvious implications for a person's sense of *identity* as it pertains to the collection of their social roles. As we have discussed so far, this can have profound effects on the way a participant sees themselves and interacts unconsciously with others (psychodynamic), the way they structure and imagine their place in the world and society (cognitive), and even the way physiology and development (biological) manifest.

Roy Rappaport: The Function of Ritual

In his monumental *Ritual and Religion in the Making of Humanity*, anthropologist Roy Rappaport (1999) argues that ritual evolved as a cultural response to the fundamental challenges that arose with the evolution of language. His argument is complex and highly nuanced, and as such cannot be fully summarized here, but in general, he makes a convincing case that ritual is the foundational activity of all religious forms, and predates myth and all other forms of religious speculation or theology. His reasoning comes from not only the existence of ritual-like behavior (as non-verbal communication) in many other animal species, but also from the way in which rituals solve two of the primary problems that accompanied the emergence of language in human behavior.

Along with the capacity for language evolved a capacity for symbolic thought and an advanced mechanism for modeling possible situations, worlds, images, and narratives (Pinker 2007). The ability to convey such information, and so construct possible scenarios in detail and convey them to others of the species, conferred many advantages to our species in terms of adaptability to many environments.

This capacity has allowed cooperation, which is highly advantageous if one can achieve it in the animal kingdom (Wilson 2013), to reach heights never before seen in the natural world. Language capacity and symbolic thought therefore allowed for organized human activity to reach levels of complexity and coordination that are unparalleled.

But like all things in nature, this capacity came with a tradeoff, and the collection of changes which allowed this behavioral adaptability brought new problems. The first of these, Rappaport argues, is deception. While deception is observed in the animal world, it is elaborated to unprecedented levels in humans, so much that there may even be counter-adaptations to it in existence (Cosmides and Tooby 1992). Nevertheless, it is hardly controversial that along with the ability to share complex and detailed information with others comes the ability to share complex and detailed *mis*-information. And so, in one fell swoop, the cooperative benefit from language capacity brought with it the disintegrative capacity of deception—therefore, unaided, language capacity's benefits came with built-in drawbacks. Such is the nature of Nature, it seems. The second, not entirely distinct drawback of language capacity is "alternative," meaning the ability of language and complex symbolic thought to conceive of the world in a near infinite variety of possibilities. As Rappaport puts it:

> This enhanced flexibility has . . . an unavoidable but dangerous concomitant . . . No actual society is utopian. It may, therefore, be difficult for any society's members not to imagine orders in at least some respects preferable to those under which they do live and labor . . . The conception of the possible is always in some degree the enemy of the actual.
>
> (Rappaport 1999: 17)

The capacity to conceive near-endless alternatives to whatever is going on at the present moment has a disintegrative effect that parallels deception. Any ambiguities in life, therefore, will inspire nearly endless speculation about the alternative meanings that could be attributed to such ambiguities. One's present place in society, one's current developmental progress, the meaning of past, current, or future events or possibilities of events, are all grist for the endless mill. Thus, the two major disintegrative qualities of our enhanced (self- or other-) communicative behavior include deception and alternative. These two problems are not unique to language capacity, but were highly amplified by it. In the animal kingdom, for example, deceptive behavior is known to occur at various levels—this is refined if we consider only *intentionally* deceptive behavior, which nevertheless still exists in primates and possibly other species (Mech and Boitani 2007; Mitchell and Thompson 1986).

Ritual, argues Rappaport, significantly attenuates these two major problems, and as such is probably at least as old as language itself—in fact ritual behavior exists throughout the animal kingdom, in part because it solves the primitive forms of these problems in other animals. Thus ritual is probably older than language.

Rappaport (1999: 24) defines ritual as "the performance of more or less invariant sequences of formal acts and utterances not entirely encoded by the performers." With this definition, Rappaport goes on to show how it logically follows that such rituals establish convention, seal social contracts, construct conventional mores, frame time and eternity, represent a paradigm of creation, generate a concept of the sacred, evoke numinous feeling and an awareness of the divine, and construct orders of meaning which transcend semantic meaning. There are a number of qualities that make rituals *unique* in this regard, including their non-verbal yet communicative nature, their groundedness in physical action and performance of ritual act (as opposed to simply thinking or talking about an idea), their emotionality, and their participatory nature (as opposed to the audience-like nature of a ceremony, sport, or theatrical demonstration).

Rappaport observes that rituals are self-communicative acts from the perspective of the performers, but also communicate to the other performers and to the onlookers, and that this effect is enhanced by the strangeness and the "grotesque quality" of postures, gestures, and unusual language—qualities that are observed in animal rituals as well. The unusualness of the ritual is emphasized by exaggerated movements and acts, in order to set them apart from normal everyday movements and acts, both in animal rituals and (to a far greater level of elaboration) in human rituals (Rappaport 1999: 50). This heightens the symbolic quality of the ritual an as act that is non-instrumental and non-typical. Since rituals signify through physical acts and with physical, material objects, they attenuate the difficulties inherent in symbolic–linguistic capacity. This is because of the way they concretize and literalize the abstract concepts they represent, the way ritual self-referentially portrays the physical, emotional, and social states of the performers, and the participatory nature of the ritual act. As Rappaport puts it: "ritual relies heavily on indices that are virtually impervious to falsification and resistant to misinterpretation" (1999: 56).

For example, among the Tsembara Maring tribe in New Guinea, long periods of tribal war are concluded by an elaborate ritual known as the planting of the *rumbim* tree, after which all hostilities are ended. All members of the tribe participate in this ritual, and it occurs after a long preparation that can stretch into years. As Rappaport observes, participation in this ritual eliminates multiple ambiguities and opportunities for deception. As it requires actual physical participation by all members of the tribe, it represents a forced-choice resolution to the vast array of possible feelings each participant may have about this event, and resolves it into a strict either/or. In other words, when asked about whether or not one wishes to end hostilities, any individual might be able to give verbally ambiguous, double-talk, or otherwise deceptive answers. One might also be able to argue for any number of transitional states in the spectrum between "at war" and "not at war." The ritual eliminates all that because while it is possible to be verbally or cognitively ambivalent, it is *physically impossible* to both participate and not participate in the ritual. The ritual resolves this fluid state into a concrete state, and communicates this state not only to every other participant, but from each participant to him/herself. It also communicates in a firm, undeniable, and material way one's membership in the community performing the ritual and so brings the community together through its mechanisms.

Dancing—another widespread aspect of many rituals—also provides physical, non-verbal communications about otherwise ambiguous, abstract, and ineffable things (Rappaport 1999: 78); war dances in particular not only display the warrior's dedication to the act of warfare, they also display in firm, certain terms the participant's physical dexterity, endurance, and strength. It is no coincidence that women onlookers are often very interested in these displays, much like animals take interest in animal mating ritual displays—and for the same reason. They are often undeniable expressions of vitality and/or virility. The widespread use of ritual objects plays into this as well, according to Rappaport. Through their use of material object symbolism, such objects are used to "translate such important but incorporeal, complex and non-metrical aspects of social life as prestige, worthiness, honor, shame and influence into terms that are not only simple and metrical but also concrete" (Rappaport 1999: 85). Such displays can be seen in the exotic dress worn by warriors among the Maring, but also in many other cultures as well. In the tenth-century Anglo-Saxon poem *Beowulf*, for example, the anonymous poet often comments on the "fine war gear" of boar-crested helms, gold rings, exquisite swords and mail coats, not only belonging to the greatest warriors, but given to them by their kings. Such kings' accoutrements were therefore concrete, metric symbols of not only the kings' generosity in the heroic culture of the Anglo-Saxons, but of the warriors' worthiness. Within such a system, such symbols became resistant to deception and alternative as cultural symbols.

For Rappaport, rituals thus help simplify and define vague, incompletely observable, ambiguous, but highly important aspects of social life, and increase the clarity of communications about these qualities, not only to each other but self-referentially as well. Rituals "impose sharp, *unambiguous qualitative distinctions* upon *continuous ambiguous quantitative differences*" (Rappaport 1999: 95, original emphasis). Among these are social status, time, and even mental state. Even pledges are subject to this principle: this is because, while a ritual participant can certainly speak words she/he does not mean, she/he cannot deny that she/he has spoken them.

In the sense that rituals concretize and clarify, making digital data from analog data—or, in other words, taking ambiguous, chaotic data and enforcing an either/or state upon it—rituals are by their very nature *acts which create order from chaos.*

Ritual participants convey to others and themselves an acceptance of the relatively invariant canon or myth associated with the ritual in a way that cannot be falsified: "Whereas belief is vexed by ambivalence and clouded by ambiguity, acceptance [and performance/participation] is not" (Rappaport 1999: 122). Ritual gestures and movements have the effect of instantiating ideals into the physical substance of the body. The pain, pleasure, ecstasy, and so on, experienced in ritual will, because of their intense emotionality, tend to encode strong memory which can have a lasting effect on the psyche as a whole—we heard similar arguments made by the cognitive scientists studying ritual. In such cases, moreover, "notions so abstract that words can barely grasp them are represented by material signs" (Rappaport 1999: 149).

Even time itself is affected by ritual, giving it a character of permanence, signifying, through its structure and acts, the Eternal. It imposes recurrence upon non-recurrent processes. The length of a ritual can also serve to strengthen this effect, imposing a structure on the participants such that it creates that which it first simply asserts, possibly via alterations of consciousness. "The intensity of the ritual state is not a function of length alone but of such elements as tempo, unison, density of symbolic, iconic, and indexical representation, sensory loading, strangeness, drug ingestion, or pain, every one of which may, by itself, be affectively powerful and . . . even more so in concert" (Rappaport 1999: 202). All of these factors also emphasize distinctness from the surrounding culture and cohesion within the ritual performing group.

Taboos serve an important function also, in that they allow for the expression of personal feelings in a sanctified manner, allowing for disruptive distinctions to be expressed in a controlled and acceptable manner.

Implications of Rappaport's Theory for Ritual Psychology

Rappaport reaches a number of conclusions about ritual that impinge on what we have discussed already from the biological and psychological perspectives on what rituals do. For example, he points out that infrequent but lengthy rituals serve to bring people out of mundane time and draw them into divine time, common in many religious systems—evocatively called "dreamtime" by the Australian Pitjandjara people, recognized as a continuous present tense rather than past tense. Contrasting this effect of lengthy rituals, Rappaport states that frequent, short rituals bring divine time into mundane time. These two *connective* aspects of ritual, which unite the divine with the mundane, lead him to speculate:

> Whereas psychiatrists might view the numinous state as *dis*sociated, the experience is often reported to be what might better be characterized as *re*associated, for parts of the psyche ordinarily out of touch with each other may be united, or better, in light of ritual's recurrent nature *re*united.
>
> (Rappaport 1999: 220)

Elsewhere he states that in rituals:

> various parts of the psyche ordinarily inaccessible to each other may be brought into touch, and given the extent to which the emotions of participants may respond to the stimuli of their own ritual acts, it is reasonable to take ritual to be auto-communicative . . . [which is] of utmost importance even in public rituals.
>
> (Rappaport 1999: 51)

Such statements recall the concept of *participation* introduced by Lévy-Bruhl and discussed by biological, cognitive, and depth psychological work on ritual; in particular the work of Patrick McNamara corroborates Rappaport's conclusions, as do the dissociative models of depth psychologists; in particular, Jung's theory of the unifying function of therapy follows a similar model of intrapsychic connection, and later Janetian theorists such as Van der Hart *et al.* (2006) argue for a similar process resulting from psychotherapy, which as we have seen is a ritualistic process as well. Thus, this aspect in particular—the intrapsychic connective aspect of ritual, and the strengthening of the Self/ego/personal element via the collective/divine—is observed by all four branches of our inquiry.

The concept of projective identification may furthermore be operating on multiple levels during rituals in ways previously only explored in one-on-one psychotherapy. Rappaport observes that "in all rituals, both animal and human, the participants transmit information concerning their own current physical, psychic or social states to themselves and to other participants" (1999: 52). A ritual's "canonical" elements, i.e. the relatively invariant aspects of the ritual, signify agreement among participants on an eternal quality of the ritual. This represents a timeless aspect of the ritual act as repetition of an eternal ideal form. The unification process is carried out through coordination, formal repeated structure, and the unison actions of a ritual. This process allows the community to become like a single organism, even to the point of physical biological motion and rhythm. Thus we see how ritual not only binds together disparate parts of the individual psyche, but binds individual to individual into a more organic whole that may contribute to the oceanic feeling of interconnectedness and "magical consciousness" described by anthropologist Susan Greenwood, whom we will discuss later, and to the strong emotional "pull" of ritual often felt by participants. Here again we find dense agreement between Rappaport's theory and the cognitive branch.

The symbols in a ritual are, according to Rappaport, likely to be relatively simple ones that can be easily visualized and are of a "high taxonomic order". Here we see support for the principles of psychological resonance I outlined earlier: narratives and images used in rituals will more likely contain resonant themes. Such symbols are flexible and can accommodate many meanings, and are compact expressions of many complex ideas and beliefs. Furthermore such symbols tend to combine highly abstract divine expressions with potent, emotional, blood-and-guts sensuality, which connects the universally human, material, and biological with the cultural and the divine—the highest order of meaning. Often such symbols are so emotional, idealized, and symbolic as to be rendered "ineffable," an important quality of potent symbols discussed in my previous work (Goodwyn 2012). We have already discussed the symbolic—rather than literal—language and thought used in ritual and its cognitive components; this aspect of ritual did not go unnoticed by Rappaport either, who states:

> It is in the nature of language to make distinctions that not only serve as grounds for meaning, but for boundaries and barriers as well. It is, on the

> other hand, intrinsic to the chordlike or simultaneous dimension of liturgical representations, at once indexical, iconic, and symbolic, to unite and reunite, the psychic, social, natural or cosmic processes which language distinguishes and which the exigencies of life pull apart.
>
> (Rappaport 1999: 262)

Here Rappaport notes nuances perhaps missed by the other approaches discussed. Specifically, he acknowledges the fact that ritual communication is also recognized as being primarily and often deliberately non-verbal (Rappaport 1999: 323). This fact, observed by other branches of study reviewed thus far, is noted by Rappaport to have an especially *cohering* function, both intra- and inter-psychically.

Thus Rappaport, like so many others, highlights the participatory/connective aspect of ritual, as well as the (self-) communicative aspect, and the order/structure-creating aspects, both within the individual mind and within the greater social network. He envisions ritual as a cohering act along a number of independent lines, where ideals are united with behaviors in a continual way that opposes the entropic tendency of daily, non-ritual life (Rappaport 1999: 153). This important function of ritual that continually repairs a constantly degrading world will be encountered again when we examine later the differences in societies that are highly ritualized vs. those (like ours) in which ritual plays very little part.

For now, there is considerable agreement, then, between Rappaport's theory of ritual and the other branches of ritual theory we have already encountered, particularly on the way in which ritual creates mental states which then contribute to ritual and hence to social structures in a continual feedback process. There is also agreement on the way in which ritual can profoundly affect our intrapsychic state. But what are the factors that contribute to the *use* of ritual within a particular culture or subculture? As is abundantly clear, not all cultures utilize ritual to the same extent. What social factors influence the kinds of rituals used, and how do these factors play into the particular goal of any given ritual? Can ritualization be compensated for by other factors in societies that do not utilize ritual? Finally, what needs give rise to what sorts of rituals and ritual attitudes? All of these questions are crucial if we are to have a full understanding of ritual *in our society*, whether in mental health settings or elsewhere.

Mary Douglas: Grid and Group Correlates of Ritual

Apart from recognizing cross-cultural patterns in rituals, anthropologists such as Mary Douglas look at patterns of variation in cultural *attitudes* toward ritual. Such attitudes correlate with ritual practice and larger-scale social structure. While not dismissing the universal functions of ritual discussed above, Douglas ventures cross-culturally to show that cultural attitudes toward ritual practice, as well as general tendencies to use ritual in one way or another, do not emerge in a vacuum, but correlate with a variety of social conditions.

Douglas first defines a quality of a culture known as "grid." Grid is "the scope and coherent articulation of a system of classification as one social dimension in which any individual must find himself" (Douglas 1996: 62). Thus, grid represents the level of hierarchy, the level of specialization, and the elaboration of well-defined roles within a culture. The other quality Douglas defines is "group," which she states is the amount of social pressure exerted on someone from within a defined social context, ranging from very little (as in the case where group obligations are considered minimal or ill-defined), to a great deal, in which intergroup bonds are tightly bound up with strong, well-defined obligations to one another. As we will see, in a mental health setting we will want to know what these variables are for each patient because it will affect the kind of ritualizing they are used to.

Examples

Anthropologist Catherine Bell modifies Douglas's "grid and group" designation of cultures into four basic types (Bell 2009). The first type, "appease and appeal," is seen in Haitian Vodou, rural China, many varieties of Catholicism, and probably the ancient Anglo-Saxons and Norse (Turville-Petre 1964), possibly the Celts (Cunliffe 1997), and ancient Egyptians (Brandon 1998: 400–401). For this type, the world and everyday events are seen to be the results of a large array of spirits. Ritual exchange of gifts and counter-gifts creates a relationship complex between humans and the spirit world that must be maintained continuously if protection and good luck are to be ensured. This kind of society exemplifies high group but low grid qualities.

The second type, "cosmological ordering," is commonly found among the elite in large city-state or imperial cultures, and centers on ritual recreation of the perfect harmony between humans and the divine. The traditional Chinese state cult is a good example, along with the Aztec empire, traditional Japanese culture, traditional Navajo society, and to a lesser extent pre-modern German society (Bell 2009: 184). Maintaining the state and the hierarchy are the primary goals of this type of ritual practice. These cultures exemplify both high grid and high group qualities, and display a marked and high degree of ritualism throughout the culture.

The third type, "ethical-moral," is exemplified by Protestant Christianities, as well as many forms of Buddhism and Islam. Here the basic ritual practice involves continued reminders to behave in a moral manner, with emphasis placed on the individual rather than the group. Each person is seen as included under a broad set of principles and is responsible for her/his fate through right action. In this type, ritual is less important than the previous two forms, and becomes subordinate to a dedication to abstract principles and internal monitoring of mental states. This type of culture exemplifies high grid, low group qualities.

In the fourth type, "privatized," ritual is focused on the personal individual alone. New Age religions, Transcendental Meditation, the Rosicrucians, the

Mbuti pygmies of the Ituri Forest, the Basseri nomads, and many evangelical Christianities are examples of this style, in which personal spiritual attainment is the aim of ritual activity. Dogma and ethics become subordinate to an ethos of personal transformation, actualization, and individuation. I add that many schools of psychology fall under this type of ritual attitude. Practitioners of this type seek personal spiritual experience rather than express a desire to uphold theological final truths. These cultures exemplify both low grid and low group designation.

Douglas's formulation has been evaluated positively by subsequent anthropologists, and it appears that, though sometimes oversimplifying, especially in complex, multicultural societies, Douglas's system nevertheless is able to correlate the degree of ritualization with a number of other variables previously thought unrelated (Bell 2009: 44).

Several observations follow from Douglas's analysis of the way rituals and attitudes toward rituals *change* with varying social conditions. For example, as we saw in our discussion of the cognitive science of ritual, there are a number of factors that appear to play into the process of splinter-group formation, millennial movements, and revolutionary movements. First, she observes that millennial movements are often revolts against established symbolic systems, and one of the key features of these movements is to attack the established rituals of the order against which they are revolting. They often decry the meaningless of the old forms and proclaim them "empty." Douglas finds that these groups are almost always low grid and low group. She provides another example of the "rejecting the established order"-type group in university academic movements. Individuals in these groups appear to be responding to the local social situation of the university, which tends to treat people as rootless, interchangeable items. Members of such groups complain that the institutions are deaf to their needs and only value them for their instrumental isolated achievement. Those who do not meet the standard are discarded as "failed." By definition, this is a high grid/low group situation. The response in this case is normally to attack the old ritualism, but also to attack differentiation and definition itself. Such movements, argues Douglas, rarely better the situation, which we will discuss in more detail below. The point is that along with social change and social unrest comes a concomitant attack on the established ritual structures; this normally is associated with symbolism of universal equality and love, which both appear to oppose both grid and group. In these settings new rituals will emerge that reflect these newer value systems; we will look at their particulars momentarily.

Douglas's main observation is that, generally, ritualization and formal ritualized behavior are strongly correlated with group and (to a lesser extent) grid. This is likely due to a number of forces that grid and group apply to the individual psyche, and the way in which ritualized behavior may be able to respond to it. In other words, a person living in a high grid, high group society will feel different pressures than a person living in a low grid, low group culture, and their rituals will have different goals and aims, and do somewhat different things. Since we have seen already from all four branches ways in which rituals unite and cohere, it appears reasonable to assume that the ritualized behavior will serve to reinforce the current surrounding grid and group. Alternately, it may serve or be changed to serve a new dynamic that is emerging within a culture, such as the emotionally charged, structure-rejecting millennial movements observed cross-culturally in the face of massive cultural changes. It is difficult to say which is primary: cultural structure or ritual structure. Given the concerns of Chapter 1, it is most likely that both co-create each other.

Grid, Group, and Psychology

Evaluating the kind of situation a patient comes from will help therapists determine the level of ritualization and the kind of ritualization they may best respond to. The psychological factors that correlate with grid and group are highly relevant to what rituals do, since rituals do different things in response to those factors which vary with them. In the following summary, adapted from Douglas (1996) and Bell (2009: 45) we see how grid and group correspond to various attitudes and psychological structures. The notation is as follows: grid/group is signified by a pair of 'g's, with capital G representing high group or grid and lowercase g low group or grid, in order of group/grid. In other words, high group, low grid would be G/g. Below I summarize how grid and group correlate with four variables: the level of formal ritualism within a society or subculture, the attitude toward trance practices/altered states of consciousness, the well- or ill-defined nature of personal identity, and the beliefs surrounding the existence of suffering. Group and grid affect more than these, but these four are of foremost importance to us here.

Ritualism: G/G—high ritualism; rituals reflect and symbolize the pervasive classification system
G/g—high ritualism, but reflecting only the group identification and boundary
g/G—less ritualism; reflects individual desires and goals for success/achievement
g/g—low ritualism or rejecting of ritual, preferring spontaneous/idiosyncratic expression

By "ritualism" here I mean the attention paid to carefully worked out rituals, with *emphasis on proper execution rather than internal mental state*. This is an important distinction since people of different backgrounds will worry about different things. High ritualism, for instance, values proper execution over sincerely felt belief/emotion.

Trance: G/G—viewed as dangerous; tightly controlled and limited to experts
G/g—often viewed as dangerous; practitioners considered vulnerable to possession
g/G—not viewed as dangerous; used pragmatically
g/g—approved, welcomed; loss of self-control not feared

Note how the attitude toward internal mental state shifts along with ritualism defined above. As trance is a type of decentering, we can see here that high levels of grid and group are associated with less comfort with rapidly changing dynamics in general. Low levels, however, are comfortable with it, perhaps because these are settings in which identity is unstable anyway, as suggested by the next observation.

Personal identity: G/G—well-defined and deeply internalized group belonging and hierarchical roles
G/g—focused on group membership but not roles, which are confused or vague
g/G—fluid and adapting to rapidly changing local grid, associated with achievement
g/g—hazily defined, rejecting of roles, rejecting of "old society," low self/social control

Note here the relationship of group, in particular, to personal identity construction.

Suffering: G/G—mechanistic consequence of violation of formal rules, not a moral or personal issue
G/g—unjust, capricious and attributed to evil forces such as "the Devil"
g/G—a consequence of poor management of personal affairs, shaming, victim-blaming
g/g—love believed to overcome all misfortunes—no real explanatory framework

Some common patterns emerge from Douglas's analysis. First, attitudes toward ritualism appear to reflect the pervasive social structure. This is not to argue that social structure *causes* rituals to be constructed in such-and-such manner; however, based on the analysis of Chapter 1, it is more likely that cultures and subcultures with high grid and high group not only encourage a high level of ritualism and formalism, but that high levels of formalism and ritualism help to shape a culture into one of high grid and group. In any case, an individual's attitude toward ritualism will likely tell us the way in which they are structured psychologically in terms of their sense of what their roles are (grid) and to what social group they feel they belong to (group), if any. These variables will then reflect in the ritual expressions they are likely to be a part of and/or participate in.

Attitudes toward trance provide another clue to the relationship between culture and psyche. Trance states, from the biological perspective, allow free rein for alternative expressions of personality, whether they are called the "possible Selves" of McNamara's neuroscientific study of trance states, the complexes discussed by Jungian analysis, the "emotional personalities" emergent in dissociative states of Janetian psychotherapy, or simply the "disparate parts of the psyche" discussed by Rappaport. These alternatives would by their very nature be quite different from the current reigning self of an individual. Since roles and group affiliations are so important to G/G and G/g cultures, it makes sense that such alternative states would be seen as threatening, disruptive, and potentially "evil." In fact *group* appears more important than *grid* in this instance. In any case, from comparison with the data of the other branches, it appears that the fearless use of trance correlates with cultures in which group and grid affiliation are weak because there is nothing to be lost in the process of rearranging the self through such restructuring. Thus it is the internalized group and grid within the subject that is threatened by such states, which results in the fear and distrust of them. This relates to the next subject, personal identity.

It is evident from the table that the definition of personal identity appears to be strongly influenced by the surrounding grid and group. Cultures with high grid, by definition, inculcate through unspoken rules and formal structures a variety of roles into their members. Ritual is a large part of how this is accomplished. Similarly, cultures with high group inculcate a strong sense of group belonging through various symbols of pollution, purity, and boundary. These are all accomplished, argues Douglas, through ritual communication, and because of this method such characteristics become a deep structure in a person's personality, *but there is a price for not having them* in the individual. She even goes so far as to say that "There is no person whose life does not need to unfold in a coherent symbolic system" (Douglas 1996: 53). Group, in particular, seems strongly related to a well-defined personal identity, though in g/G cultures, grid becomes a substitute for group, and members define themselves on the basis of their hierarchical roles within the culture. We see this in many middle-class United States communities, for example, where one's career is placed over practically everything else. In g/g cultures, however, roles, groups, rules, formality, and all forms of control are rejected (or at least perpetually challenged), leaving personal identity vaguely defined by choice of clothing, hobbies, interests, and so on.

The Problem of Identity Formation

While this situation of g/g allows for much greater personal freedom and autonomy, it is not without consequences for the individual, as Douglas argues:

> Alas for the child from the personal home who longs for non-verbal forms of relationship but has only been equipped with words and a contempt for ritual forms. By rejecting ritualised speech he rejects his own faculty for pushing back the boundary between inside and outside so as to incorporate in himself a patterned social world. At the same time he thwarts his faculty for receiving immediate, condensed messages given obliquely along non-verbal channels.
> (Douglas 1996: 56)

Douglas thus argues that the cost of such rejection of grid and group, for personal identity, is rather high. As we will see in the next section, a number of other anthropologists, psychoanalysts, and sociologists have noted this function of ritual as well. For now, we note that Douglas quotes psychoanalyst Melanie Klein (Spillius, 1988), who referred often to the unsatisfied longing for non-verbal understanding and connection which may reflect the most primordial nourishing relationship between mother and infant. Recall that Klein began scholarly discourse on the concept of projective identification—this type of unspoken connection represents the healing and emotionally relieving component of this projective identification, not the pathological kind. Such a connection, argues Douglas, is impossible in ritually rejecting environments with low group and (to a lesser extent) low grid. Douglas elaborates that those who continually champion non-ritualized intimacy in social relations unknowingly undermine their own longing for wordless bonds between members, since it is only ritual which can express this non-verbal bond (Douglas 1996: 54). Later she explains that this is due to the fact that "Formality signifies social distance, well-defined, public, insulated roles. Informality is appropriate to role confusion, familiarity, intimacy" (Douglas 1996: 79).

Many other depth psychological approaches discuss the unconscious bonds between individuals and their surroundings and corroborate this assessment—especially the difficulty with role confusion in psychological development. Erik Erikson (1963), for example, identifies one of the major developmental milestones as "identity vs. role confusion," which according to Erikson happens between the ages of 12 and 18. It is probably not a coincidence that so many coming-of-age rites occur at these ages, which we will discuss in Chapter 10. Such rituals provide exactly the sort of well-defined role and group structure that psychologists suggest is needed for strong identity formation. With the loss of grid and group, however, such formal ritualism is rejected in favor of anti-ritual sentiment, which offers the allure of equality, freedom, and autonomy, as well as relief from what are felt to be oppressive social structures. But it leaves the sense of identity wanting. Thus Douglas makes several very psychological arguments that grid and group, and the ritualism that accompanies them, provide a kind of nourishment to the universal need for identity, role, belonging, and interconnection such social structures provide.

The Problem of Suffering

A person's view of why they are suffering—encountered so often in various guises by medical providers—is also affected by grid and group. Since we have learned that narrative, explanation, and meaning are so relevant to physiology and psychological health, it is worthwhile to examine the cultural dimension here. As shown in the above table, high grid correlates with well-defined explanations for suffering in terms of violations of formal rules of behavior. In such systems, suffering can be alleviated via rituals that aim to rectify the transgression and restore the original order. High group, however, correlates with suffering being explained as caused by evil outside forces. Such suffering can be alleviated ritually by placating, exorcizing, or purifying these forces—or expulsion from the group in the case of "witchcraft"-style accusations common in G/g cultures. In g/G settings, however, there is no ritual way to reinforce group solidarity and its concomitant state of purity, and suffering is simply a result of stupidity and is shamed. There is no system in place to rectify it apart from desperate efforts to avoid such judgment through a renewal of role positioning in the grid. Shame over suffering becomes a common consequence. As is the case with identity formation, here grid can substitute somewhat for lack of group. In g/g settings, however, suffering is seen as something that must be endured, with only a utopian dream of a glorious future without suffering offered as a cure. There is no evil in the g/g setting, as there is no group and hence no "outside" (where evil always dwells), nor is there grid and hence no ladder upon which to strive to avoid suffering and no roles or formal rules that can be transgressed or rectified. Thus in g/g settings there is no explanatory framework with which to conceptualize suffering from this perspective. We will encounter this theme again when we discuss death rituals in Chapter 11. This state of affairs leaves the sufferer with no real ability to take advantage of the tools provided for by narrative, meaning, and even synchronicity, since very little that happens in the physical world has any real social (and hence, emotional) meaning, which is perhaps why, in g/g settings, the spiritual world becomes valued far more greatly than the material world, which is rejected it its entirety.

Grid and Group in Psychotherapy

Most *psychological* explanations for suffering fall under these categories as well; in cognitive therapy, suffering is explained as a result of irrational thinking, which is reminiscent of g/G explanations. In many kinds of dynamic therapy explanations are offered that are variants of the "lack of sufficient love" ("you suffered an empathic failure," "you were traumatized," and so on)-type explanations found in g/g settings. With insufficient grid and group, however, ritual solutions to these ailments are those of psychotherapy and medication management—highly individualized and deficient in role, group, identity, and connection, but strong in personal freedom, autonomy, and individualism. That ritual is now used in psychotherapy, as we saw in Chapter 5, suggests, however, that addressing deficits of role, group, identity, and connection with ritual can be significantly healing.

It is evident that the gain of anti-ritualism—freedom from obligations, rigid structures, and stifling of expression—comes with a cost. The cost of anti-ritualism, anti-grid, and anti-group is greater alienation, suffering, and inability to access the symbolic, non-verbal, and cohering forces that operate in ritual. Thus, in g/g and g/G settings, members must be taught how to ritualize.

Douglas also emphasizes the importance and non-dismissible function of symbolic, non-verbal communication offered through ritualized behavior (Douglas 1996: 40). Thus we see that higher degrees of grid and group can provide a sense of belonging, a clear sense of identity and role, and an explanation for suffering with a clear method for rectifying or at least improving suffering. Within such a structure, individuals are relatively immune to the rootlessness, anomie, confused identity, and poorly narrativized suffering that are encountered by those in settings with low grid and group. What is gained by rejecting such structure, however, is freedom, individuality, and a release from perhaps stultifying and repressive constraints. We are reminded here of the tedium effect of excessive doctrinality—a mode more likely in a setting of high grid and/or group. In such a setting, members may feel a pull toward the vivid emotionality and liberating confusion of imagistic modes of ritual expression. The burst of undifferentiated life that emerges from the imagistic mode can either renew a doctrinal system or shatter it to pieces, only to later petrify into a new structure over enough time. Thus we have seen again that there is a strong, complex relationship between social structure and individual psychology, and in particular there appear to be a number of costs and benefits to various amounts of social structure and anti-structure—the subject of Victor Turner's work, discussed below.

Ritualism and "Sincerity": An Important Observation

Before we discuss Turner, however, one more observation about the balance of ritual and anti-ritual attitudes can be made. An important development in ritual study that builds on Rappaport's model is that of professor of religion Adam Seligman, anthropologist Robert Weller, historian Michael Puett, and psychoanalyst and psychiatrist Bennett Simon in their *Ritual and Its Consequences: An Essay on the Limits of Sincerity* (2008). In this work, Seligman *et al.* observe that the study of ritual itself has been influenced by post-Protestant, post-Enlightenment assumptions that need to be understood. In their analysis, they define this particular worldview—our Western worldview—as extremely individualistic and hyper-focused on internal, deeper subjective meaning, and label it the "sincerity" mode. They view ritual as not merely a religious activity but a crucial way of framing activity that offers its own ability to foster human realization and fulfillment. In this view, ritual fosters a continued shaping of a continually degrading world through ritual construction of an "as-if" world. Contrasting this, the sincerity mode focuses on attaining these goals by eschewing all forms of ritualization in favor of seeking "what *really* is"—i.e. with a never-ending quest for the truly true and the really real. It seeks not the world-constructing action of ritual, but a plunge into the depths for the "truly authentic" in each of us. One illustrative example is the difference between traditional Catholicism, with its entrenched ritual modes of action in many spheres of life that aim at a continual renewal of the world, and the impetus behind the Protestant Reformation, with its emphasis on individualism, deep contemplation of salvation, and an intensely personal relation to deity.

The sincerity mode is not unique to post-Protestantism, however. It can be found throughout history and across cultures, for example in Hasidic Judaism, Zen Buddhism, Chinese Mohism, Renaissance French literature, expressivist art, and even atonal or punk rock music. When in the sincerity mode, old ritual forms are continually challenged and considered tired and worn out or "inauthentic" and meaningless (or "too mainstream"), and participants focus energy on scrambling them up, discarding them, or even consciously negating them in their quest for even more truly authentic expression.

Seligman *et al.* view ritual along this spectrum, arguing that both aspects of framing experience—the ritualistic and the sincere—are needed for human balance, but that in modern first-world nations we are far too weighted in the sincerity mode, and lack the resources ritual provides. This is because if the sincerity mode runs without the balance of ritual, it tends to absolutize thought and boundaries, either by eliminating them altogether in visions of universal love and "equality," or by apotheosizing them into unassailable categories (Seligman *et al.* 2008: 13) in *reaction* to the lack of boundaries—the situation seen in many fundamentalisms. Ritual, on the other hand, "plays" with boundaries, both by defining them (but not too strongly), then by transcending them. Through numerous examples, Seligman *et al.* show that for ritual-rich societies, the world is in need of continual repair. Left on its own, the world is seen as drifting toward entropy at every step. Performing the ritual acts to realign the world to the symbolic ideals contained in the rituals themselves—but only for a while. In these societies and subcultures, boundaries are clearly defined through the ritual, but they are slightly permeable, and the imagination plays a large part of the "serious play" of ritually constructed worlds. Because of this effect, and unlike the sincerity mode, ritualistic societies do not depend on a coherent belief system (much to the consternation of post-Protestant, post-Enlightenment anthropologists). Sincerity mode interaction, however, practically demands rigid adherence to a coherent belief system in order to provide any sort of lasting structure because of its persistent distrust of boundary and ritual form (one is reminded of the continued pressure of "politically correct" belief in this regard).

The problems with unbalanced sincerity modes of action, therefore, is similar to what we have seen in g/g settings, only Seligman *et al.* provide us with a deeper understanding of them: if the matrix of social order is ruled by sincere feeling rather than ritual action, the sincerity mode will forever seek ways to prove itself even more truly sincere, but by nature it will always fall short. For example, the sincerity mode would assert that all we must do is sincerely feel more love toward each other to improve harsh relations. When posed with this challenge, of course, no amount of evidence can ever prove one is "truly sincere"—this Rappaport has shown, because the specters of deception and alternative hang over all communications without the help of ritual. Thus the social ambiguity of the anti-ritualistic environment will continue unabated, leading to more role confusion and ambivalence. Ritual modes, however, allow participants to act *as if* they loved one another, which can—through various non-discursive, and even unconscious mechanisms discussed throughout—actually create a more peaceful surrounding, irrespective of what everyone's "true, inner feelings" (whatever that is supposed to mean) actually are. In the sincerity mode, however, the only tool available is the discursive search for hidden meanings and disguised motives, which is bottomless. This fundamental limitation of non-ritual culture is what Seligman *et al.* argue are the "limits of sincerity," and this aligns well with the limitations we have seen of low group and to a lesser degree low grid societies. Finally, they observe that Western society, due to various historical *momenta*, has reached an unprecedented level of imbalance between modes in favor of sincerity.

The way ritual plays with, defines, and then paradoxically transcends *boundaries*, however, is an important tool ritual has that the sincerity mode *does not have access to*. Seligman *et al.* explain:

> playfulness dies when social boundaries are denied. Individuals become private, atomized selves, each identical in its core characteristics and everyone merges into a great mass. This is roughly the contemporary image of a market society . . . Today, it is often this atomized individual who imagines that there is only one possible world—a world *as is* instead of one of the multiple *as if* worlds that ritual allows.
>
> (Seligman *et al.* 2008: 98)

The Sincerity Model and Modern Psychotherapy

If all this talk about the dark side of the sincerity mode is worrisome, that is a good thing: Seligman *et al.* have, I feel, firmly identified one of the blindsides of much Western therapeutic practice—ritual impoverishment. Though the Western world is too varied to make it possible to say that the sincerity mode dominates all spheres of it, I think it is fair to say that this mode is very commonly encountered, especially in mental health settings. This is because in settings of high ritualism, mental health issues are often handled via internal mechanisms. The modern obsession with sincerity can be found in the endless talk shows which valorize the inner wellspring of feeling, or with teens' endless concern with the truth of their "inner feelings" of love, their "true self," and so on. Unbalanced sincerity is also concerned with the quest for utopian paradise—this is another way that the sincerity mode also matches well with Douglas's low group (and to a lesser degree, low grid) designation. But now we know *why*: ritualized cultures do not seek for the perfect society or future that lies "beyond" the material world, but work with the world by constantly (re-)correcting it. The ritual mode does not concern itself with the quest for the one, inner truth, but socially creates many *as-if* truths that correct the world through continued ritual *action*.

Today, the sincerity mode dominates most psychotherapy approaches. A sincerity-based psychotherapy, however, must endlessly plumb the depths in search of the deeper, truer truth forever, leaving therapist and patient forever in doubt about whether or not they have achieved the "most true" expression; that this describes most forms of psychotherapy is downright eerie. Thus it may be that a healthy dose of ritualization, rather than the endless search for the "true self" may be a more effective tonic for the suffering member of a sincerity (sub)culture.

Ultimately these modes can be detected through their method of praxis: ritualized action, for example, tends to be performative, repetitive, non-verbal, social, and conservative in nature, whereas sincerity-based action is biased toward the unique, the verbal, the idiosyncratic, the private, and the perpetually reformative. These patterns can be found not only in religious expression but in political movements, art, music, and narrative styles, and for our purposes, psychotherapy.

We should be careful, however, not to demonize the sincerity mode too much—it is necessary, though it needs the balance of ritual to be complete. What the sincerity mode provides is the energy and emotion of a sense of inner truth that goes "beyond" the ritual as-if world, viewing it as a "reflection" of the truly real divine world. It invigorates ritual forms, and it provides the strong emotional "pull" of ritual for those who participate in them. It keeps ritual forms from becoming stale, rote, or empty, as the practitioner seeks the "real truth" behind the forms. It is only when it attacks *all* ritual forms relentlessly and eschews them as a matter of course, leading participants to try to function without the balancing effect of ritual, that we see the above problems manifest. In small doses, the sincerity mode can transform outmoded ritual forms into reinvigorated, powerful new ones. In excess, however, it leads to atomization, inner disquiet, and social chaos. When *combined* with ritual, it produces an experience of tremendous beauty. Examples of this combination can be found in Victor Turner's classic discussion of *communitas.*

Victor Turner and the "*Communitas*" of Ritual

Anthropologist Victor Turner argues in his *Dramas, Fields, and Metaphors* (1974) that rituals share a narrative quality that carries over into large-scale social dramas. Turner developed the concept of "*communitas*"—a social and psychological state that is found in many cultures, and he here expands upon van Gennep's "liminality"—a state in the periphery of everyday life. Often a sacred condition (or near-sacred), it is characterized by a number of qualities in which various "anti-structure" components coordinate. Subjects in a state of *communitas* are socially in a state that is non-hierarchical, egalitarian, and non-rational (though, Turner adds, not *ir*rational).

Turner begins by defining structure and anti-structure/*communitas*. Structure he generalizes to a mode of thinking that holds people apart, creates differences, defines social roles and categories (Turner 1974: 47); we see here the parallels between Turner's definition and Douglas's more precise definitions of high grid/group. *Communitas*, on the other hand, is characterized by lack of structure in relationships, interconnection, and emphasis on spontaneity and freedom, a lack of gender and other kinds of social differentiation. It shares these characteristics, then, with low grid and group, and with the sincerity mode. Turner differentiates *communitas* from the social state of liminality, however. He psychologizes *communitas* as "a sphere or domain of action or thought rather than a social modality" (1974: 52). *Communitas* is engendered by ritual humiliation, stripping of structural insignia, ritual leveling, and so forth, that emphasize humility, equality, and general lack of grid and group (he also shows how some cultures can actually use the ritual mode to create an environment of sincerity). In a similar observation to previous scholars we have reviewed thus far, Turner notes that millenarian and revivalistic movements crop up often when societies are in transition between large-scale structural changes. Such movements seem to non-verbally symbolize and embody the liminal state of the whole society. Pilgrimage, monastic asceticism, millennial cults, and controlled, elaborate rituals all utilize the imagery of *communitas*. Thus Turner is taking a primarily social construct, liminality, and correlating it with his essentially psychological mental state of *communitas*. Ritual is an important part of how this is done.

Turner makes several observations about the anti-structural elements found in *communitas*: "An important component of the liminal situation is, as we saw earlier, an enhanced stress on nature at the expense of culture" (Turner 1974: 252). Here natural symbolism is predominant, that of wild vegetation, beasts, birds, and so forth, dominating the dress, imagery, and art of the *communitas* state. He continues, concerning the rite-of-passage nature of such states: "One dies *into* nature to be reborn *from* it" (Turner 1974: 253).

Communitas, argues Turner, appears as a balancing effect on excessive structure, which despite its benefits can be straining over the long term:

> Since communitas has a strong affectual component, it appeals more directly to men; but since structure is the arena in which they pursue their material interests, communitas perhaps even more importantly than sex tends to get repressed into the unconscious, there to become either a source of individual pathological symptoms or to be released in violent cultural forms in periods of social crisis. People can go crazy because of communitas-repression; sometimes people become obsessively structural as a defense mechanism against their urgent need of communitas.
>
> (Turner 1974: 266)

Note here how Turner is already combining his sociological observations with depth psychology-like statements about repression and primitive emotions. These observations also help us to see the strong emotional component and natural tendency that exists to overturn grid and group structure—hence such a state is not merely an absence of structure but a positive force in its own right within the human condition, according to Turner, that must be repressed by structure. Recall also the balancing act observed by cognitive scientists between the doctrinal (structure) and imagistic (anti-structure/*communitas*) modes, and the observations of Douglas in terms of grid and group (structure) or lack thereof (*communitas*) and the observations of Seligman *et al.* in terms of ritual (structure) and sincerity (anti-structure). Like low grid and group cultures, *communitas* is often equated with themes of universal love according to Turner.

But like the others, Turner recognizes the largely rejuvenating but ultimately unsustainable state of *communitas*. For Turner, the liminality of *communitas* cannot survive long without structure—often new structure—to organize and sustain it. Hence Turner provides one reason why the sincerity mode is in a perpetual state of reform. "Vision becomes sect, then church, then in some cases dominant political system or a prop for one—until communitas resurges once more against it from the liminal spaces and instants every structure is forced by its nature to provide" (Turner 1974: 293). This process is simply a part of human nature: "man is both a structural and anti-structural entity, who *grows* through anti-structure and *conserves* through structure" (Turner 1974: 298). This sentiment finds strength in the biological and cognitive branches discussed so far, particularly in our discussion of decentering.

Regarding the role of *communitas* in various cultures, Turner remarks that in the simplest societies, *communitas* is hedged around by significant constraints, taboos, ideas of purity, and so on, and surrounded by potent emotional symbols. As societies become more complex, this tendency is lessened and *communitas* is given a wider currency and longer reign (Turner 1974: 203).

Communitas can be seen in traditional rites of passage, in millennial movements, in monasteries, in counterculture movements, and on countless informal occasions. Turner also observes that the myths used to describe the liminal state of *communitas* are set in a "place that is not a place, and a time that is not a time" to emphasize the psychological/experiential differences between structure and anti-structure (Turner 1974: 239). Moreover, consistent with its association with anti-structure (and, I argue, with low grid), *communitas* is associated with poverty and low rank. Liminality draws upon poverty for its symbols. The myths and images of *communitas* also blend the genders—not surprisingly, since gender is often used in the service of structure to varying degrees.

Turner states that *communitas* emerges spontaneously in times of crisis or transition, to either revitalize the old structure or to replace it with a new one, citing as examples the various reform movements within the Catholic Church over history, the Protestant Reformation and the many evangelical "revivals" within Christianity, Islamic Sufism and Sanusi movements, and the many Hindu movements which originated in attempts at dissolving the rigid caste structure, including Buddhism, Jainism, Lingayatism, and Sikhism (Turner 1974: 250). Thus we can see that *communitas* corresponds to situations of low grid and group, typically associated with rejection of structure and "rejuvenation" of old systems, along with expressions of universal love and utopian millennial visions. *Communitas* is also associated with transitory periods within states in high grid–group environments, though in those cases such states are highly contained by limited access, secret societies, and so on. From the vantage point of sincerity, we can see that the sincerity mode can provide an important counterbalance to ritualization despite its limitations.

Turner's definition of *communitas* as a psychological state corresponds to several theoretical models already discussed; in particular *communitas* appears to be associated with anti-structure, with spontaneous sincerity and anti-ritualism in search of "inner, absolute truth," with the breakdown of grid and group, with the imagistic mode of ritual, with liminality, and with large-scale cultural transitions or renewals. Like the cognitive scientists who argue that doctrinal modes are continually challenged, overthrown, or renewed by imagistic modes, Turner notes that *communitas*, however expressed, often can become structured over time, in which case anti-structure becomes structure. The imagery of *communitas* is that of non-differentiation; similarities among members are emphasized (like military recruits all given the same haircut and uniform, as well as low rank), normal constraints on behavior are overturned or ignored, emotional urges are unbound, sexual and other taboos are lifted, universal love (the antithesis of high group) is emphasized, and imagery is millennial, apocalyptic, and/or utopian.

Example: Imagery of Communitas in Clinical Practice

I had a patient, Mr. Green (name and other details changed to protect confidentiality) who was functioning well up until his mid-thirties, whereupon he began to have recurrent dreams of walking through a neighborhood, right through houses, unnoticed, until finally stopping in a central area where a huge garden grew. The vegetation became so wild and overgrown that he was buried in vegetables and fruits. This began his descent into a nearly intractable depression, followed by severe but rare manias. In this dream imagery, one can see the (distorted and exaggerated) imagery of *communitas*, anti-structure, and liminality: recall that the imagery of liminality and *communitas* is often that of unchecked Nature—in these dreams dramatically and concretely embodied by vegetation overgrowing the literal "structures" of the nice, orderly neighborhood. Also note the invisibility of the dreamer to those inhabiting the buildings—neither a part nor not a part, the dreamer is in the liminal state. Note also the marriage of the abstract, the concrete, the intellectual, and the visceral in this dream symbolism, so often paralleled in ritual and mythic symbolism due to the ability of such symbolism to communicate non-verbal messages (even to oneself). Interestingly, subsequent symptoms led to a permanent state of liminality in the dreamer, who lost his job and finances and was forced to live at home for decades. Structure broke down, and the alienation and meaninglessness associated with lack of group (endemic in our culture) was amplified by his inability to accept the usual response to this state—sentiments of universal love, acceptance, and utopian future: such sentiments utterly failed to account for his suffering, which shows the weakness of the liminal, g/g setting. Unfortunately, this patient left my care before I was able to attempt re-ritualization as a type of therapy for him.

To recap, *communitas*, low grid and group, the imagistic mode, the quest for sincere inner expression and individual spontaneous changes in consciousness correlate with anti-structure, imagery of Nature and non-differentiation, blurred gender, liminality, future promise, and ill-defined universal connectivity. High grid and group, ritualism, the doctrinal mode, and tight constraints on consciousness correlate with structure, imagery of control, tightly defined and constrained Nature, clearly defined states of role and identity, and well-defined images of boundary and connection to the eternal and timeless rather than to the future. Therapists who know where their patients are on these spectra will be better equipped to use the ritual of psychotherapy to heal their patients.

Catherine Bell: Ritualized Behavior

We have spent a great deal of time discussing ritual in the abstract. But what do rituals look like more specifically? What are the main characteristics of rituals? In her wide-ranging and nuanced survey of ritual and what she terms "ritualized" behavior, anthropologist Catherine Bell addresses these questions (Bell 2009: 136–137). Like others, Bell states that ritual activity feels created by the divine powers, *and* due to its particulars significantly *creates* those same feelings through its various biological, emotional, and cognitive mechanisms. Ritual and the divine are thus neither created nor bestowed but somehow *both*. Bell also argues that ritual fosters heightened interconnectedness, allowing each participant to become a part of a larger organic whole—i.e. it allows them to participate in something greater. Briefly, Bell summarizes the main features of ritual as:

- Formalism—communications and behaviors have a more restricted, conventionalized, restrained, abstract, generalized, impersonal, and less idiosyncratic nature. Formal oratory tends to be louder, and have stereotyped tonal structure, limited vocabulary, and a more rigid order and style. This type of communication appears to promote social cohesion: it often reinforces the status quo, but also forces communication along non-verbal channels, which are more difficult to disguise, thereby subtly reinforcing the social relationships involved. The greater the social distance between participants, the greater the formality of their interchanges will tend to be, and the potentially more potent the communication will be (Bell 2009: 137).
- Traditionalism—traditionalism uses ancient garb, repetition of older customs, and archaic language, and promotes a sense of continuity with the past, giving a ritual an authentic, legitimate, and satisfying feel. Modern examples include the use of academic robes in academia, and wigs in the British legal system. Traditionalism of action connects human activity with the ancient past, harmonizing the participants with the very order of the cosmos, blurring the boundary between self, world, and time. Significantly, appeals to "immemorial tradition" are often invented when a rite is created, giving the impression that all that is needed is the illusion of tradition to achieve the effect. "We have always done this" may frustrate anthropologists inquiring as to the meaning of a ritual, but in the mind of the practitioner, it is *entirely the point*, and it is its own explanation.
- Invariance—ranging from the procedures of Zen meditation to the routines of Alcoholics Anonymous (an expression of group), to what I have observed in the ritualistic way in which students and residents report information to attending physicians (an expression of grid), invariance of form emphasizes discipline and conscious control of the body and mind. It emphasizes conscious effort over chaotic nature, and reinforces structure via careful choreography and memorized oration (Bell 2009: 152).
- Sacral symbolism—religious or other sacred, dense symbols are often reinforced by rituals and subsequently utilized by rituals, creating a positive

feedback effect. Ritual caretaking of the American flag, for example, creates a sacredness and non-verbal symbolism to the flag which therefore calls for ritual handling. Sacred symbols or holy sites are often sacralized (and therefore will demand further sacred handling) through the use of boundaries, staged progression, accompanying narratives, appeals to the "four corners," and the tripartite division of the cosmos into Earth, the heavens, and the underworld, thereby making the ritual an expression that (temporarily) orders the whole universe.

- Performance—the deliberate, self-conscious, public, symbolic actions involved in ritual communicate and create a sense of sacredness on multiple sensory levels, and actively participating in a ritual pulls one into the theme and purpose of the ritual through bodily action. The framing of a performance as understood by all as a "performance" sets the communication aside as special and important. It creates a complete and condensed model of the world and emphasizes holism (Bell 2009: 160). Thus the performances of ritual dramas, shamanic otherworld journeys, public "media events" and social protests reduce the chaos of the real world to an ordered and coherent system of symbols, rendering it meaningful and validated through more visceral and non-verbal channels of communication (Bell 2009: 139).

Like the cognitive scientists and Mary Douglas, Bell places heightened emphasis on how cultures and ritual systems change with time. Bell observes that large influxes of cultural exchange can disrupt a stable cultural system: "If the exposure to plurality—that is, to other value systems and alternative forms of social organization—is intense and sustained or occurs at times of internal social chaos, it can begin to undermine the coherent sense of a unifying order that underlies a traditional society" (Bell 2009: 200). Subsequent breakdowns of individual ideas *and* ritual reinforcers lead to the rapid breakdown of a system, usually punctuated by an outburst of millennial cults and/or protest movements which carry with them strong indicators of liminality, low grid/group (with the usual concomitant "rejecting-the-old-order" rhetoric), a rubric of sincerity over ritualism, and imagistic modes and *communitas*; these are imaged via Nature symbolism (fleeing to the wilderness, leaders who are unshaven or disdain hygiene), vivid visionary literature that is both apocalyptic and utopian (or at least cyclical), talk of universal brotherhood and universal love, and so forth. Recognizing when patients are in the midst of such (sub)cultural upheavals can help frame their own inner turmoil and chaos by clearly identifying the cultural origins of it.

Integrating the Psychology and Anthropology of Ritual

We have discussed how biological, cognitive, and psychodynamic factors contribute to ritual, and we have reviewed a number of anthropological theories of ritual that illuminate the phenomenon of ritual immensely. We have also seen where the anthropological formulation can be improved via the data of the other disciplines, and vice versa. Each perspective looks at ritual from a particular point of view, and none of these perspectives are mutually exclusive in any obvious way.

What we have seen so far in the theories of van Gennep, Rappaport, Douglas, Turner, Bell, and others are a number of similar lines of thought that, when combined with the observations of the cognitive scientists, lead to a number of common themes. When it comes to ritual it appears that there are two different styles of expression which can be seen in various guises in many settings. Using Turner's terminology to label them, we see that these modes of ritual expression are associated with:

Anti-structure	*Structure*
Low grid and group	High grid and group
Imagery of freedom from obligation	Reinforces obligations between group members
Emphasizes the spirit	Emphasizes the material
Emotional and rejuvenating	Pragmatic and instrumental in execution
Utopian visions of future release of suffering	Practical explanations for suffering and solutions
Connection with paradisiacal future	Connection with the past and the eternal
Imagery of freedom from oppressive structure	Provides role, identity, and context
Communitas—all is one	Integral parts—each a separate part of the whole
Rubric of sincerity: the quest for "what is"	Ritualized "as-if" (re)construction of a world in need of continued realignment
Boundaries are non-existent	Boundaries are clear but permeable

Rituals tend to emerge and/or be sustained by the social and psychological factors that contribute to these two "attractor positions," and lead to either a continually changing ritual environment within a culture, where various anti-structural splinter groups and millennial movements break off from an established structural system, or sometimes to a more stable dynamic system wherein anti-structure is allowed a constrained expression within the structural system at specific intervals. This interplay appears to be associated with forces that work within individual minds and in between minds within a culture to serve various somewhat opposing but sometimes overlapping needs:

Here we can see the various poles of interacting "forces" that operate to help us understand what rituals are doing (or *not* doing) in a particular context. Not only are they responding to the biological, psychological, and social situations of a person with the above qualities, but they help to create what they are aiming at (or don't create, via their absence) through various biological, psychological, and social mechanisms. The above comparison should not be taken as an absolute categorization, however. There are times in any religious system when ritual expression will be framed around a decrease in structure at one point while later ordered around an increase. Van Gennep has provided numerous examples, in that

Expressions of anti-structure	*Rituals of structure*
Dissolves forms felt to be obsolete	Create order from chaos
Refreshing emotional involvement/vivid	Pragmatically organizing and instrumental
Frees from excessive over-involvement/ obligation	Provides identity through involvement with group
Frees from oppressive hierarchies	Provides clearly defined roles
Provides vision of freedom from suffering	Provides explanation for suffering and remedies
Connects with utopian future	Connects with divine past, dream time, Eternal
Fertilizing death	Rebirth, recreation
Imagery of Nature overwhelming culture	Imagery of culture taming Nature
Idiosyncratic, spontaneous expressions associated with sincerity	Traditional, proscribed, rigid

the liminal transitional state will be given by rituals that reflect/create the essentially anti-structural state that participants will be a part of temporarily. What is common to both types of expression, however, is *participation*. In both cases the practitioners of a ritual are participating in something outside themselves, and this appears to be one of the primary functions of rituals, both created by and helping to contribute to what rituals do. Thus it will help to finish the chapter on the subject of participation.

Participation

Anthropologist Susan Greenwood (2009) bases her approach to ritual on a modern revisioning of the work of philosopher-anthropologist Lucien Lévy-Bruhl (1985) and of anthropologists Stanley Tambiah (1991) and Bradd Shore (1998). Greenwood argues, similarly to the biogenetic structuralists, neuroscientists, depth psychologists, and cognitive scientists we studied earlier, that the "as-if," imaginary worlds of rituals often involve a different "type" of thinking that is symbolic, holistic, and ambiguous rather than literal, sequential, particular, and so forth. Greenwood stresses that this ritualistic or "magical" thinking is a natural kind of thinking available to all humans but especially important in ritual. Thus, for Greenwood, ritual accesses a type of consciousness that involves not analytical, linear thinking but "analogical" thinking—thinking that emphasizes connections and associations between ideas and things rather than differences and distinctions. This kind of thinking differs in its treatment of time also, in that events and objects are connected not through cause/effect chains in time or space but through similarity and association independent of time or place.

According to Greenwood, the magical or "mystical" mental process involves "participation" in something outside of oneself. Unlike analytical thinking, magical thinking involves viewing the self and other as aspects of a coherent whole, rather than as separate objects. Self and fellow co-ritualist, self and magical object, self and god are seen not as fully distinct from one another but blended in a symbolic, mystical, or magical manner. This participation is characterized by a de-emphasis on specifics of time and place, is often highly metaphorical, is holistic, and is dominated by emotional, non-discursive concepts. Rather than equate the analytical and the magical types of thinking to unsustainable classifications of "primitive" vs. "civilized" thinking, Greenwood emphasizes that Tambiah and Lévy-Bruhl argue both kinds of thinking are present in people of all cultures to varying degrees.

Greenwood explains the difference between causality and participation as styles of thought. For causal thinking, self and world are rigidly separated, as are all individuals and objects. Space and time are precisely distanced and events and objects can be continually atomized into systems of interacting parts acting in the space and time field. Participation, however, blurs self and environment, emphasizes holism of language, objects, and people. Space and time blur and objects interact with one another based on their emotional, holistic impression in an intersubjective field of self and other. Importantly, Greenwood prioritizes neither and rejects a rigid dualism between these two types of thought: "Participation and causality do not form a dualism, but rather, intertwine in any one person's mind; these aspects of thinking are not diametrically opposed; rather, they intertwine in the wider process of consciousness . . . In actual practice, we all probably use both types of thinking intermittently" (2009: 42).

Updating Sir James Frazer's (1921) classic classification of magical thinking, discussed earlier, Greenwood classifies magical thinking into *homeopathic* and *contagious* magic. Homeopathic magic is founded on the idea that "like produces like" and connects ideas by virtue of their apparent *similarity*. Contagious magic is founded on the principle that objects that are in contact with one another stay in contact forever—something akin to the more recent idea of "quantum entanglement" (Manousakis 2006). Evidence of the adherence to homeopathic magic principles has been found in rituals from ancient India, Babylon, Egypt, Greece, and Rome, as well as in rituals described in the Americas. Ideas of contagious magic have widespread cross-cultural distribution also, examples of which exist in the numerous rituals dealing with the power of menstrual blood, or as can be seen in the reverence for holy relics throughout ancient Europe. The connection of ideas via similarity or contact is augmented in magical thinking through the use of what Greenwood calls "persuasive analogy", in which the value or meaning is transferred through sympathy by way of ritual language, narrative, or imagery. Greenwood also emphasizes the cultural aspect of ritual and magic (2009: 100). Here we see agreement between Greenwood's examination of participatory thinking and the cognitive scientist's exploration of it.

Jung actually presaged this division of thinking types with his own formulation of the "two kinds of thinking," perhaps due to his relationship with Lévi-Bruhl, and he discusses this classification in his work *Symbols of Transformation*:

> We have, therefore, two kinds of thinking: directed thinking, and dreaming or fantasy-thinking. The former operates with speech elements for the purpose

> of communication, and is difficult and exhausting; the latter is effortless, working as it were spontaneously, with the contents ready at hand, and guided by unconscious motives.
>
> (Jung 1954: para. 20)

Biogenetic structuralists also corroborate Greenwood's classification system, stating that ritually altered consciousness is a near universal (Bourguignon 1972), and may work by down-modulating the dominant, analytical workings of the left hemisphere in favor of the non-linear, imagistic, holistic, and emotional modality of the non-dominant right hemisphere (Laughlin *et al.* 1990; see also Goodwyn 2012). These effects are brought on via the rhythm, repetition, entheogen use, pain, vivid emotionality, and so on, of ritual performance. This right-dominant mode of thought may furthermore flow into a more co-dominant mode of thought in the context of a performed ritual through the stylized and meaning-imbued movements involved. Thus, abstract ideas of the sacred are enforced upon the physicality of the nervous system and body. The state in which both hemispheres share dominance rather than alternate may also correlate with ritually altered consciousness and experiences of holy union (d'Aquili and Laughlin 1979).

Evans-Pritchard (1937) provided an example of how analytical and participatory modes of thinking complement, rather than oppose one another. When Evans-Pritchard was working with the tribe he studied, the Zande, there was a tragic granary collapse that killed two people who were sitting under the granary. When asked why they thought this happened, Zande informants explained to Evans-Pritchard that though they knew that termites had damaged the granary supports, for them this explanation was necessary but insufficient. It only explained the mechanical cause of the collapse, not *why* the granary collapsed at just the right time to kill the two victims. It therefore did not reveal the *meaning* of the event. Thus, to answer this, the Azande people explained the event in terms of witchcraft—that is, in terms of intentionality and participatory or "magical" thinking. Evil witches had intended the collapse and therefore participated in the deaths of their victims. Thus we have a good example of a (commonly encountered) magical explanation used to relate unusual events to belief systems, and to use those same systems to influence further events with the same mysterious forces. It is a method, not of explanation, but of *interpretation* that is best suited to magical thinking: "Zande belief in witchcraft in no way contradicts empirical knowledge of cause and effect . . . [they] are not mutually exclusive. On the contrary, they supplement one another, one accounting for what the other does not account for" (Evans-Pritchard 2009: 116–117).

Evans-Pritchard continues that this dualism of thought is not unique to traditional societies but is pervasive in all cultures to varying degrees (Evans-Pritchard 2009: 118). This type of participatory mental processing is therefore universally available, but variably utilized from one culture to another. Greenwood argues that participatory thinking or magical consciousness has suffered from too little study thus far. This is probably right. In any case, what all the branches appear to be saying with respect to the mentality of ritual is that ritual evokes a different type of thinking, behavior, and language from mundane forms of behavior, and this is seen to varying degrees in both anti-structural and structural ritual expression (though participatory thinking may be more prominent in anti-structural ritual modes).

As Geertz puts it: "in a ritual, the world as lived and the world as imagined, fused under the agency of a single set of symbolic forms, turn out to be the same world" (1973: 112). This ritually created story connects the divine to the human in the same way it connects the highest ideals with the most powerful human emotions. In fact, it appears that ritual and emotion do not cause one another but interact to co-create each other in a densely interactive manner (Metcalf and Huntington 1991: 4).

We have reviewed a huge amount of literature on ritual thus far, and made a number of connections along the biological, psychological, cognitive, and anthropological branches. We have, however, necessarily had to stay in the abstract in the discussion, speaking in themes, large over-arching patterns, and concepts. The question is: do these abstract patterns hold when we look at specific rituals? We will see that they do, and that we can understand the developing "big picture" on what rituals do, by examining specific rituals in greater detail. In Part III we will do just that, and we will explore how we can use the principles learned so far to shape psychotherapy using the knowledge of ritual studies. We will then take a comprehensive look at this open question in Part IV.

Part III

Applications

In the next section of this book, we will look at examples of rituals across many cultures and across many centuries. This will give us data to compare to the theoretical model of the previous two sections, in order to put together a dynamic interdisciplinary theory of ritual to apply to mental health settings. In Chapter 7, we will look at magical inscriptions in Northern Europe as evidence of ancient folk magic ritual. This particular example is chosen because magical inscriptions are examples of quasi-oral "folk" magic that we nevertheless have historical access to that we would not otherwise were it purely oral in nature. This situation gives us an opportunity to observe folk practices (however imperfectly) across several centuries, giving us an idea of longitudinal stability, and hence psychological resonance as well as common patterns. The same sort of analysis could easily be done in any region known for magical inscriptions, but I am more familiar with Northern Europe and so I will confine this inquiry to that region, and even then defer more often than not to the experts in history, archeology, and mythology. In any case, the inquiry will open up thought on a number of ritual details only hinted at by the general theories given previously, allowing us to put them in a real historical context and possibly use these principles in a therapeutic setting. In subsequent chapters we will expand from this paradigm of purely historical analysis to look at various *kinds* of rituals: healing, manipulative, transitional, and rituals involving death, all of which have examples from the history of runic inscriptions as well as in-depth historical analysis and modern ethnography. Thus we will be looking at even more specific rituals not only from a historical but from a cross-cultural perspective, to inspect what all these rituals might be doing and explore how such themes might be usable in mental health treatment in our otherwise ritually impoverished society.

Chapter 7

Magic Inscriptions and Other Creations

As has been noted by religious scholars since Frazer, rituals often employ the concept of "similarity," where two objects or ideas are considered to have an essential link because of similarly appearing features, such as the mandrake and the man. This "similarity," says Sørensen, is felt to show the shared essence of the two things. This allows one to manipulate one object via a different object because they are felt to have a "similar essence." This concept is manipulated ritually by emphasizing sameness and de-emphasizing difference. We will see how this is accomplished shortly (Sørensen 2007a: 58–59). *Origin as essence*, for example, where the origin of an object is equated with the essence of that object, is a commonly used concept. The sort of universal symbolic thought discussed here involves conceptual mapping, or

> structuring more abstract and less coherent domains by reference to experientially salient and highly structured domains . . . [it] is the result of quite ordinary cognitive procedures whose products are deeply entrenched in the conceptual system of all cultures.
>
> (Sørensen 2007a: 132)

As we can see, an important ritual principle is related to the ascription of "essence." That is, symbolic associations that are based on perceptual similarity—iconic and indexical signs in the above terminology—will lead to the ascription of a *common essence* to them. Holy/magical objects will be seen as the outward manifestations of the inner, blended "essence." This intuition will facilitate the transfer of properties between manipulated elements. The care with which people treat photographs is a good example of this kind of magical thinking; that is, in many societies a photograph is felt to share the same essence as the person that photograph is of. Lest we smugly reassure ourselves that those of us in modern industrialized nations are above such "superstitions," I suggest taking a photo of someone you love dearly and trying to grind it under your foot or set it on fire. If you can do it, you should notice that even the most hardened, anti-ritual skeptic will feel reluctance that is likely to override the more "rational" belief that destroying the photo in such a manner will not harm the person photographed. This effect is evidence of the emotional intuition that motivates this principle of ritual effectiveness—the intuition that similar appearing things share a common essence. Anthropologist Susan Greenwood argues convincingly by reviewing a number of empirical studies that this sort of thinking is just as prevalent in Western societies as it is in so-called primitive ones: "we in the West think as magically as they do . . . Magic is a universal aspect of human consciousness; it is inherent in the mind" (2009: 4).

Runic Inscriptions: Ancient Folk Magic Rituals

Ritual probably predates all linguistic activity, and it simultaneously serves multiple functions. It should be no surprise that rituals are absolute universals and share numerous characteristics even when developed independently by unrelated cultures separated by great distances in time and/or space. In northern Europe, magic inscriptions using runes were so resonant that they survived cultural transmission for over thirteen centuries. Here we will see numerous patterns that we have discussed in previous chapters, including potential biological, psychological, and cultural effects related to "rune magic." Runes are useful to look at because they are simultaneously "folk" magic and written *by the practitioners themselves*—a rare combination, since folk practices are rarely written down. This allows us to look more at the ritual thinking not so much of learned elite specialists, which is what one gets when one studies the written traditions of many ancient cultures, but of how the everyday folk constructed their world in ritual terms.

Since such traditions were mostly passed down orally, they were more shaped by psychological resonance through every transmission. Therefore they were more likely to be influenced by universal cognitive structures. The present analysis gives us the opportunity to see *how* these structures interacted with prevailing cultural ideas. In addition to the fact that rune magic was passed down orally, and hence subject to greater constraints of cognition, emotion, memory, and so on, they are also, however, written on various items of wood, metal, or stone. Thus the study of rune magic informs our overall approach. On top of this there are written works about runes scattered across wide areas that can give us cross-cultural evidence to explore and augment this data, and even the later medieval and modern antiquarian interest in rune magic has a dynamic interdisciplinary framework to it. Thus a potentially obscure and esoteric field of study can actually tell us quite a bit about universal ritual structures and give us clues to effective ritualization in therapy.

Runes: Magical Symbols of Northern Europe

Magical alphabets are known to all cultures that use writing, and the Germanic tribes of Northern Europe are no exception. In order to assess the psychological resonance of rune magic, as well as to understand any biological and cultural components to this particular kind of ritual magic, we must understand the long history of the use of these symbols. Several theories exist concerning the origin of the runes; the most popular currently is that they are derived, in part, from a north Italic script that quickly became adapted for use by the Germanic tribes of the area.

The word "rune" means "secret, mystery" and runes fulfill their ritual function, in part, because they emphasize the iconic and the indexical rather than the semantic aspect of a symbol:

> In most important aspects, the linguistic signs written on amulets and talismans have lost their symbolic reference. This is replaced with indexical references based on the conception of a direct connection between a given sign and its referent, in which the sign is seen as "originating" from, or having "power" over its referent.
>
> (Sørensen 2007a: 72)

Dating somewhere around the first century CE, the Germanic tribes of Northern Europe developed a system of symbols known as the "Elder Futhark," a collection of twenty-four letter forms, called runestaves or simply staves, after their staff-like appearance. Each stave has a name, like "Gift" or "Ice," and so on, and these names appear to date back to the earliest common Germanic times in which the runic script developed. This is attested to by the fact that as the rune name changed, so too did the phonetic value of the rune over time, suggesting that the names of the runes were relatively resistant to change even when the language itself was changing over the centuries. By 200 CE, Elder Futhark runes were already spread fairly widely across Europe (Page 1987: 25). This rapid spread and subsequent persistence is our first evidence of the psychological resonance of these particular symbols, from which we can infer that they may correspond with universal or near universal collective elements of the minds of those using or thinking about runes.

The names of the runes date back possibly to their invention (MacLeod and Mees 2006: 8), and persisted remarkably well through the many centuries of their use, again suggesting resonance. This perhaps innocuous practice, particularly in the *choice* of names given to the runes, I will argue has had profound consequences for their later usage, especially with respect to their ease of use in magical systems. This is particularly in light of the various cognitive and anthropological theories regarding the special use of symbolic language and thought in rituals worldwide. We know about the rune names from later documents, including the Old English, Norwegian, and Icelandic rune poems, composed around the eighth, thirteenth, and fifteenth centuries respectively but likely representing much older traditions. This is because, despite their differences in age and region of origin, they are remarkably similar in theme and structure, which suggests all three came from a common older tradition. In Table 7.1 I provide a quick reference view of the runes of the Elder Futhark.

The Use of Symbols: Magic and Mundane, Ancient and Modern, Indexical and Semantic

Over the centuries since the beginning of their developed use in the first centuries CE, runes have been used both as magical scripts and as a prosaic system of writing. It is interesting to note that the use of runes for magical purposes appears to

Table 7.1 The Elder Futhark. The Elder Futhark was used until approximately 700 CE (which means 500–700 years of cultural transmission already), whereupon linguistic changes leading into the Viking age also caused changes in the runes. Briefly, where the Anglo-Saxons expanded the rune row to include four or more new staves, the Scandinavians compressed the Elder Futhark into the so-called Younger Futhark, which only had sixteen staves. Both, however, were used in magical inscriptions as well as more mundane inscriptions.

Rune	*Reconstructed Proto-Germanic name*	*Name/meaning*	*Transliteration*
1. ᚠ	Fehu	"wealth, cattle"	**f**
2. ᚢ	Uruz	"aurochs, water/slag"	**u**
3. ᚦ	Thurisaz	"the god Thor, giant"	**þ**
4. ᚨ	Ansuz	"a chief god, Odin"	**a**
5. ᚱ	Raiðo	"ride, journey"	**r**
6. ᚲ	kaunan	"burning ulcer, torch"	**k**
7. ᚷ	Gebo	"gift"	**g**
8. ᚹ	Wunjo	"joy"	**w**
9. ᚺ	Hagalaz	"hail"	**h**
10. ᚾ	Naudiz	"need"	**n**
11. ᛁ	Isaz	"ice"	**i**
12. ᛃ	Jera	"year, good harvest"	**j**
13. ᛇ	Eihwaz	"Yew-tree"	**æ**
14. ᛈ	Pertho	unclear? "lot box, pear tree"	**p**
15. ᛉ	Algiz	unclear? "elk"	**z**
16. ᛊ	Sowilo	"sun"	**s**
17. ᛏ	Tiwaz	"the god Tiwaz/Týr"	**t**
18. ᛒ	Berkana	"birch"	**b**
19. ᛖ	Ehwaz	"horse"	**e**
20. ᛗ	Mannaz	"man"	**m**
21. ᛚ	Laguz	"lake, leek"	**l**
22. ᛜ	Ingwaz	"the god Ingwaz/Freyr"	**ŋ**
23. ᛞ	Dagaz	"day"	**d**
24. ᛟ	Oþila	"inheritance, estate"	**o**

depend on the relative commonality of their use. Recall that Sørensen (2007a) and many others have noted that nearly all magico-religious systems use a separate type of language for ritual that is set apart from everyday language. The use of runes appears to be no exception. I base this assertion on the following evidence. The time during which runes have been used for magical purposes corresponds to their relative lack of use as mundane script denoting simple messages, legal documents, or other non-magical use. Two principles appear to apply that contributed to their use as magico-religious symbols versus mundane script. First, it is during the early development of the system that we see runes used most commonly as magical scripts. Then, with time it appears this usage of runes waned, though never completely died, where we see a gradual shift in their use from magical symbols to a more mundane use as prosaic linguistic signs. During this period runes were still used in magic rituals, but it appears that the runes themselves had lost their primary magical significance and become used to convey magic *words*; hence the magic seems to have shifted from the runes themselves to the words they represented.

A few centuries after our earliest records of runes as used for magical purposes, the runes slowly began to be used more and more commonly for prosaic linguistic signs, and magical use as symbols became less common. With still further passage of time, however, a massive influx of continental influences on the primarily Germanic cultures which used runes caused their use to decline in favor of Latin scripts. The last use of runes in a magical context of which I am aware comprises the Bergen finds of Norway, which date no later than 1450 CE, representing approximately thirteen centuries of time in which runes were used as magical symbols (to varying degrees). During this massive span of time the runes were also used for mundane communication to varying degrees throughout the Pan-Germanic world, which includes Scandinavia, Germany, Anglo-Saxon England, and the Viking settled areas of Europe.

Once their use as linguistic signs died out, however, and they became subject to antiquarian curiosity in the Middle Ages, it was not long until the runes were once again thought of primarily as magical symbols, an idea so infectious (and hence, resonant) that most modern runic scholars are continually having to remind readers that the runes were used for prosaic writing. In any case, in the nineteenth and twentieth centuries, various "revivalist" orders such as the Rosicrucians came to use (sometimes modified) runes as magical symbols, mostly disregarding the ways in which they were used by ancient practitioners and adopting the runes for use in their own newer magical systems. Then, in the mid-twentieth century, riding the wave of neo-pagan religions that began in the 1950s, new magical systems were invented that incorporated Elder Futhark runes (and occasionally Anglo-Saxon runes) into their own magical theories (for example, in Ralph Blum's popular *The Book of Runes*, 2008) that had little to do with ancient practice, but were perhaps popular because of the antiquity of the runes, uncommon usage in the general population, and the ever fascinating idea that foreign and/or ancient mysterious scribbles have potent magical power—an idea we have already encountered in discussing the European use of Egyptian hieroglyphics. Generally, as in other places, Germanic sources ascribe great power to foreign magicians, including Celts and Saami peoples, and Anglo-Saxon sources cite Greek, Irish, Hebrew, and Latin. Therefore, in general, cultures tend to project their magical fantasies on to their foreign neighbors, as observed by Storms: "a number of charm formulas evidently owe their effect to the mystification of a foreign tongue" (1948: 1). This is likely due to the awe and mystery inspired by foreign peoples and alien customs, which can be seen today in New Age movements in which modern Americans turn to Hindu, Buddhist, or Taoist traditions due to their apparent efficacy.

Runes: Dynamic Interdisciplinary Perspectives

According to some runic scholars, the runes may have been spoken aloud *during* their carving to "enhance" their magical power (Flowers 2010). If this is correct, then we have a ritual act that includes carving, intoning a highly indexical sign, and subsequently inscribing onto a physical object the rune in question. Biologically the ritual process of rune inscription will have the potential to evoke placebo effects on performance, whether it be healing, success in battle, and so on, through the effect of the image, the narrative behind the inscription (mythic or otherwise), and the beliefs of the practitioner, and could conceivably affect brain, immune, cardiovascular, respiratory, gastrointestinal, or skin physiology.

From the cognitive branch, we would expect any narratives associated with this ritual to be resonant narratives that therefore stimulate deeply universal systems. The equation of force with effort may also be a part of the process of inscribing a ritual object, in that larger numbers of runes likely correspond to a perception of greater power in the ritual. Conceptual blending is prominent in the idea that whatever the rune may be a sign for now blends with the object upon which it is inscribed—an example of contagion magic, and the object will therefore be seen as partaking of the "essence" of the rune. From a linguistic perspective, it is significant that the runes appear to have an occult meaning outside of their semantic meaning, which is to be expected since, in ritual, the indexical and non-verbal aspects of language use as a ritual act is always emphasized over the literal and semantic use of language. Furthermore we should expect to see nonsense words, scrambled words, or encoded words, since these obscure semantic meaning in favor of occult, indexical meaning. From the psychodynamic perspective, projection is prominent in such symbol-making activity, in that items treated in this manner will likely take on strong psychological significance and therefore become linked to a person's emotions, much in the way one might treasure an otherwise worthless necklace because it was one's deceased mother's favorite. The object becomes a representation of a part of its owner, but also the personality of the inscriber as well. These intuitions are so powerful they can no more be eradicated than can the automatic way we think of the sun "rising" and "setting" instead of the earth rotating.

As for the ancient magicians, unfortunately we know very little of the rune inscribers beyond their names. If the runic object, say a weapon, was successfully used in battle, the ritual itself would be more likely to foster a sense of meaningful coincidence and therefore feed into the belief effect discussed from the biological angle, thereby reinforcing the ritual structure. A weapon might also be pro-dissociative in a functional sense, aiding the warrior in summoning up a functional battle rage. Culturally, we know that engaging in the act of having a runic object made is a clear communication to self and culture that one is preparing for war; ambiguities and alternative are eliminated by this physical act. It signifies to the practitioner a clear, undeniable signal of intent and purpose.

So does all this analysis hold when we examine specific artifacts? We will discuss whether any of the above properties apply to runic objects uncovered by runic scholars and archaeologists.

Magic Words: alu, salu, auja, wiju, laþu, leub, laukaR, gagaga, hagala, sœri

Recall that Tambiah (1968, 1985, 1991) argues that ritual is often based on a highly creative use of the metaphorical properties of language, connecting Frazer's law of similarity to the law of metaphorical relations, and the law of contagion as the metonymical connection. We saw further elaboration of this idea in the work of Sørensen. Ritual language, argues Tambiah, exploits the properties of language to achieve its effects. Ritual furthermore is performative (Bell 2009: 51) and a creative (and not merely descriptive) act. The very performance of the ritual and the inscribing of the runes, therefore, becomes a sacred act that imbues the inscribed object with multi-level significance.

Words often give form substance and substance form, and so most rituals have material objects which are "imbued" with symbolic verbal meaning through the ritual act, and rituals often have the quality of a creation myth, in which abstract form is given substance and raw chaotic substance is given form. Objects in ritual are given a narrative, reiterated and reaffirmed through ritual (Rappaport 1999: 166–167). Thus there is a "near universal attribution of magical or creative power to words and to certain acts informed by words" (Rappaport 1999: 49).

Rappaport observes that ritual speech is stereotyped and stylized, often archaic, repeated with precise enunciation, and that this contributes to the clarifying role of ritual by its avoidance of gradation, qualification, nuance, and endless alternative. Through its archaic nature it assimilates participants in a timeless past or ageless category of being. We do not know what or how the original rune-masters may have verbalized while performing their inscribing; however we do know that runes were referred to as "god-descended" or "glorious," which further suggests magical power in the runes themselves outside of what the runes are being used to write (Page 1987: 30).

There are relatively large numbers of brooch/amulet finds called bracteates, all inscribed with Elder Futhark runes and dating to around roughly 500 CE. A portion of these have well-known magic words on them, including **alu**, **auja**, **laþu**,

laukaR (I follow convention and represent staves in bold type), their known variants **al, lkaR, lauR, lþu**, and some rhyming groups such as **salusalu** or **luwatuwa**. These are interpreted as charms of some kind, and some of these have the familiar formula where the rune-master names himself, which reinforces or "increases" the magic of the charm. An example of this is on a fifth-century Danish amulet: **hariuhahaitika:farauisa:gibuauja**, which Page translates as "I am called Hariuha: the one wise to danger: I give good luck." The ancient concept of "luck" (a Germanic concept discussed in great depth by Grønbech 1912) meant more than simply good fortune, but personal power and vitality. Here are some of the known charm words found on a variety of runic finds:

Alu: "divine power"
Auja: "luck"
Wiju: "consecrate"
Laþu: "invocation"
Laukaz: "leek"
Gagaga: "roar"
Hagala: "hail"
Sœri: "invocation"
Tuwa: "offering"
Maga: "power, strength"
Salu: "invocation"
Ehwaz: "horse"

Laþu, *alu*, and *laukaz* were particularly common favorite charm words during the Elder Futhark period. As mentioned, charm words appear in abbreviated form, for example, **lþu** for *laþu*, or **l** for *laukaz*, or **hag** or **h** for *hagala* (MacLeod and Mees 2006: 88). Other inscriptions reverse or scramble the runes of these charm words, such as the Migration Age amulet from Allesø, Denmark that reads **lauz [swastika] owa zlut:eaþl**, *Lau(ka)z* [swastika] *owa z(a)lut e(u)aþl.* This inscription appears to have the words *laukaz*, *tawōz* (a variant of *tuwa*), *alu*, and *laþu*, cleverly intertwined and scrambled according to McLeod and Mees by comparing it to other similar inscriptions (MacLeod and Mees 2006: 91). We can guess at why the staves were scrambled. Hiding, encoding, or otherwise obscuring runes is in fact observed on numerous runic objects, and this fact likely serves the indexical purposes discussed earlier. Moreover, such effects not only preserve a "secret" meaning for the rune writer, but also serve to de-emphasize the semantic meaning of the staves, in favor of a more indexical and symbolic meaning more amenable to magical thinking and ritual.

Since magic often uses archaic, poetic, obscure, or somehow "separate" language for its use, the runes provide a great deal of evidence gathered across several centuries of the principles we have discussed so far in action. As noted previously, mythological concepts are often used in rituals but used idiosyncratically, to achieve various goals. This theme appears cross-culturally and persists across history. For example, a fifteenth-century Swedish work, *Comfort of the Soul*, states that prayers in Latin are "more effective" than those in the vernacular; thus this idea has been recognized before, and Christianization did nothing to change this effect. In fact, MacLeod and Mees observe (2006: 210), "Christian terms, names, and titles rapidly acquired a mystical taint and were frequently employed in runic magic." In all these cases, the literal, semantic meanings of the words are set aside in ritual in exchange for their more iconic and indexical (and hence essentially non-semantic) meanings. Other tricks used by ancient rune-masters to shift meaning from semantic to indexical/iconic include interweaving runes, repeating them in sacred repetitions of 3, 8, or 9, using rhythm, alliteration, and prosody, and other techniques like writing the runes in obscure codes.

Similia Similibus: Participating in the Resonant Divine

One very common technique of ritual incantation that incorporates mythology—resonant narratives—is the *similia similibus* or "just as . . . so too . . ." pattern. Here the inscription describes a well-known myth, using it as a kind of template of the situation for which the spell is designed, followed by a description of the effect the spell is intending to bring about. A famous example of this is the *Second Mersberg charm*, a charm which survived into recent times in a variety of forms in Scandinavia, England, Scotland, and Germany. The ninth-century High German version reads:

> Phol and Wodan rode to the wood; then Balder's foal sprained its foot. Then Sinthgunt sang over it and Sunna her sister, then Frija sang over it and Volla her sister, then Wodan sang over it, as he well knew how, as for this bone-sprain, so for blood-sprain, so for limb-sprain, bone to bone, blood to blood, limb to limb, as if they be glued together.
>
> (Trans. MacLeod and Mees 2006: 154)

Later versions of this charm exist with the heathen gods replaced with Christ, Mary, and the apostles, but without replacing the essential "bone to bone, joint to joint" structure. MacLeod and Mees point out that the Atharva-Veda, 1,500 years older than the Merseberg charm, has a similar sounding text in it, though it is uncertain whether this is an independent invention or a survival of an ancient Indo-European charm. Either way, it represents an excellent example of psychological resonance. The key feature here seems to be the *structure* of the charm rather than the particular story or deities involved, so long as they are well-remembered deities in the living faith of the magician and recipient.

In any case, the charm appears to be recalling an ancient story in which some action or another took place in its archetypal form—recalling the origin = essence concept so common to magical or participatory thinking—and this story is applied to the current situation in the magician's and recipient's mind. This "just as . . . so too . . ." structure can be found in numerous examples, pagan and Christian, throughout the medieval world.

Talking Form: Personification

Many runic inscriptions have a style of "so-and-so inscribed me . . ." as if the object itself were talking about the rune-master; this personification may be a useful instance of using the universal concept of intentionality as a magical technique (Greenwood and Goodwyn 2016). This practice personifies the object, which may promote projection of self into the object psychodynamically, and cognitively frames the object as having mentality, intent, and so forth, which makes it amenable to being reasoned with or persuaded to do one's will.

For example, a fifth- or sixth-century pendant from Zealand, Denmark reads *Hariūha haitika, Farawīsa. Gibu auja* [tree symbol], "Hariuha I am called, Danger-wise. I give *auja*," which contains the name + name amplification, plus the giving of *auja* loosely translated as "luck." Here the object is speaking as if it were the rune-master, or the object is made alive through the act of the inscription.

This practice spanned centuries, as shown by a twelfth-century bronze amulet from Högstena, Sweden, which has inscribed in Younger Futhark runes *Gal anda viðr, gangla viðr, rīðanda viðr, viðr rinnanda, viðr sitianda, viðr sign(and)a, viðr f(a)randa, viðr fliuganda. S[kal] alt fyrna (?) ok um døyia.* The rhyming and heavily alliterating verse translates as "I incant against the spirit, against the walking (spirit), against the riding one, against the running one, against the sitting one, against the signing one, against the traveling one, against the flying one. It shall completely wither (?) and die." This amulet was found in a grave and appears to be necromantic magic to prevent the body from becoming a revenant. Alternately, it protected its owner from harmful entities, personified as spirits doing various vague, image-schematic activities such as "riding," "traveling," and so on, causing them to shrivel and die. Recall that finding the exact "true meaning" of the ritual is a sincerity-related drive. Ritualism, on the other hand, involves creating as-if worlds where boundaries and effects are created; furthermore the non-discursive aspects of ritual will always confound discursive analyses, so any attempts to elucidate the "true meaning" of a ritual must be viewed as only part of the full understanding of it. This is why I do not try too hard to determine the meaning so much as observe the *action* of the rituals discussed throughout this volume.

The personification of the object, then, is another resonant practice in runic inscription that survived centuries of cultural transmission. The placing of a name on an item is a psychological act of significance that is not likely always registered completely consciously. Names are picked out quickly and easily, and likely represent an extension of the owner, or are viewed as containing the "essence" of the owner. Names thus quickly invoke participatory thinking with regard to the name and its owner. Inscribing one's name on an object encourages projection and semantic blending of object and owner—two potent participatory ideas. So regardless of the "intent" of the owner or inscriber (the names of which are often *both* on runic items), the mere act as a general psychological principle will be significant and likely contribute to any magical effect even if this is not intended—much scholarly debate centers around whether or not such and such an inscription was "intended" as magical; in principle such intent is important and psychologically relevant, but it is not everything, as naming could have an effect in any case, because it is a symbolic expression. The inscribing of a name on an item, then, while easily dismissed as "mere graffiti," is not so easily dismissed at the psychological level.

Several finds, usually brooches from the Elder Futhark period onward, consist of a name, followed by a word like "comfort," "protection," "joy," "blessing," perhaps signifying an amulet which confers a magical influence on its named wearer. We can see now a variety of dynamic interdisciplinary participatory processes that may go into this deceptively simple procedure. Weapons often carry names, either of the owner or the weapon (a boundary that is psychologically blurry anyway due to projection), and reflect the common mythological image of a god or hero like Odin, Thor, Sigurd, or Beowulf wielding named weapons. Weapons with names like Howler, Router, Thither-Rider, and so forth have been unearthed, and sometimes the runes are accompanied by complicated non-runic magical symbols. In many cases it is clear that the inscription is of the owner's name, followed by a series of magical symbols.

Many finds have the name of the object inscribed as a precursor. For example, a hart's horn will start out with "hart's horn" as the first part of an inscription, such as the eleventh-century Younger Futhark inscription found in Dublin. Another find at a woman's burial site in Gårdlösa, Skåne (Sweden) contains a brooch upon which is inscribed **ekunwod(iR)**, "I, UnwodiR, (cut these runes)," emphasizing the rune-master rather than the owner or maker of the brooch—an interesting priority. From the previous chapters, we can speculate that the act of inscribing the rune-master's name on an item imparts to that item a part of his "essence," by contagion.

Summary: Magical Inscriptions

Reviewing ritual study, from the biological branch we have little to go by, since none of the participants of these inscriptions is alive today; however, we can speculate that the rhythmic aspects of the inscriptions, coupled with the likely charismatic personality of the inscriber, could invoke placebo responses in the recipients of these ritual objects. This is because we already know that image, narrative, belief, touch, eye-gaze, and psychological complexes can evoke placebo responses, and there is evidence of narrative and image (both described and depicted iconically) in the foregoing, and strong belief was likely common if not universal in ancient culture, much as it is today.

From the cognitive branch we see that the mythic narratives often used in runic inscriptions contain clear stories with many of the features proposed to account for their psychological resonance: clear-lined stories that are easy to visualize, minimally counter-intuitive, extreme (with gods, and so on), containing rhythmic elements, simple plots, atemporality (the "long ago" of mythic time), and interconnection—the "as above, so below" element connects divine with material in no uncertain terms. Conceptual blending allows the magician to put his or her own essence into the object through inscribing their name, and repetition of specific runes shows evidence of the equation between effort and "magical force." Furthermore the essence of the rune is incorporated with the object through the ritualized act of inscribing. Naming the object personifies the object and imparts intentionality and personality to it, further blending categories between "I–it" and "I–thou" and opening up greater possibilities for projection. This is further confirmed by the common practice of having runes "speak," meaning the inscription is written as if the object were speaking for itself. Furthermore, the non-semantic use of runes via the techniques of nonsense words, foreign words, scrambling words, framing words, palindromes, or using single runes to signify words or concepts associated with the name of the rune all de-emphasize the linguistic sign in favor of the mysterious indexical sign.

From the psychodynamic side, all of these techniques likely put the recipient into a more participatory cognitive frame, allowing him/her to projectively identify with the object. The use of narrative in particular has more effects beyond the resonant, as we have seen, in that it aligns the disparate parts of the psyche with each other and has a cohering ability. The tendency of many rituals to put practitioners in a state of mind that expects meaningful coincidence enhances the likelihood of subjectively feeling synchronicity and all the effects that ensue from that. The "as above, so below" aspect of magical inscription not only connects object with owner and rune-master, but also connects the owner with the divine realm—and hence the collective element—providing a clear, resonant explanation for the power of the item and justifying its existence with commonly known stories about the gods through the equation of origin and essence.

Which leads us to the cultural branch, whereupon the recipient of such an object reinforces his or her place, belonging, and role within a culture, merely based on the common language, shared myths, and (however passing) familiarity with runes as a valid magical practice. The various encryption and verse forms used in charms and runes set them apart as ritual utterances. We do not know if there was any tripartite structure of ritual akin to van Gennep's formulation in the case of rune inscription, but participating in a ritual in which one receives a blessing from a rune-master is clearly an unambiguous communication to self and group of one's acceptance of the canon that goes with it, reinforcing all the other branches. Such rituals make the abstract, ineffable, and intangible expressions of the collective element into concrete physical objects with weight, volume, and physicality. Finally, the formalism, archaism, invariance, and sacral elements of rune inscriptions can all be seen in the above examples, and we may speculate that there was a performative aspect to inscribing such objects as well, as evidenced by the practice of calling magic "galdr" or specifically *sung* incantations:

> the evidence from medieval literary sources indicates that much Germanic magic was expressed, as in classical tradition, by stylized, or actually sung language . . . the Old Norse term *galdr* "incantation, magical charm", the

> Scandinavian equivalent of Anglo-Saxon *gealdor* . . . clearly describes the type of magic that was expressed in runic inscriptions.
>
> (MacLeod and Mees 2006: 10; see also Flowers 2010)

Thus we find it plausible that runic inscriptions had significant biological, cognitive, psychodynamic, and cultural effects, and this is because we see evidence of the usual mechanisms that these various fields have put forward with respect to what rituals do—evoking a participatory frame of mind through image, rhythm, performance, psychological resonance, universal and intuitively easy ideas, conceptual blending, indexical use of signs, projection and projective identification, narrative, synchronicity, the tendency of the mind to dissociate, decenter, and reconstruct, the clear, unambiguous communicative nature of ritual, and the tendency of ritual to connect the sublime and ideal with the physical and visceral. These all prime the practitioners to adopt a strongly participatory mode of thought that has dynamic interdisciplinary effects.

Clinical Applications

There are a number of ways we can incorporate what we have learned about magical inscriptions into modern medical practice. As we will see, we already do it unconsciously, and we repeat many of the above ancient patterns. I would like to make what we are doing conscious. Furthermore by making such practices more clear, new ideas suggest themselves, since though we repeat many patterns, there are things the ancients may be able to teach us about maximizing placebo/ritual responses in clinical care.

The closest thing modern medical practice has to a full-blown magically inscribed object is the humble prescription. I invite the reader to think about this in the ritual framework we have been developing. The patient must go through the effort of arranging his/her schedule to journey to the clinic on a predetermined day and time, which allows for a great deal of mental building up of the narrative leading to the encounter. There they must endure various barriers including a parking space, waiting room staff, and they have tasks to perform such as filling out forms, and so on. Then, from a hidden, inaccessible place (only to be reached by those who know the code to enter the door), the healthcare provider arrives and they travel to a secluded place that is "set apart" (i.e. "sacred")—the doctor's office. This is a rite of separation in miniature, as is the liminal phase (sitting in the office), followed by reincorporation (returning to the waiting room).

The physician discusses the patient's problems and symptoms, listens closely (theoretically) and then provides a story for your suffering. "You have clinical depression," "Your bipolar disorder is getting worse," "You're stressed about X," and so forth. This contextualizes the patient's suffering in a magical language set apart from everyday language (medical jargon) and offers hope. In an ancient/traditional setting, such explanations might be "You have angered the ancestors," or "The spirits of the land need an offering," and so on. The physician then writes down a prescription, again in a special language, often with cryptic symbols. This prescription comes from a limited access area, on special paper, with a printed label representing the clinic and its logo. On the script itself is the physician's name and signature, and hence she has projected her "essence" into the piece of paper—recalling the psychological glamour that accompanies names. Now the patient has a concrete, tangible, physical object that represents the entire process in a physical object. Alternately, the physician uses mysterious machines to transmit information about the patient into a giant invisible brain-like database of information (the electronic health record/internet) using her socially (and ritually) granted superior access.

The patient then leaves the office through the various channels and, having returned to everyday life, collects the physical/tangible medication from a pharmacy that is part of the huge cultural medical complex. It also will carry with it the associations of any popular advertisements, with all their colorful easy-to-remember diagrams and cartoons, to create a non-verbal "story" of their illness in abstract form. Pharmaceutical advertisements tell pictorial stories of patients traveling from illness to wellness as a result (naturally) of their pill. Colorful and memorable as these may be, they notably *lack* any sacred/divine meaning. The reasons for this I will explore in the chapter on healing rituals. In any case, the lack of sacred meaning to the illness may reduce ritual efficacy and is the first example of our ritual impoverishment.

Anyway, this tangible projection of the physician—the pill—is then *ingested into the body of the patient.* All the symbolic, emotional, mental, projected, metonymic meaning that has been invested into that pill is now being absorbed into the patient's very body substance! Anthropologists Thompson *et al.* claim that the pill is a significant ritual object, arguing that the pill is a metonym for the physician and biomedical technology in general (Thompson *et al.* 2009: 127, n.16). Thus, ritually impoverished though we are, all of this amounts (still) to a powerful experience.

Nevertheless, modern practice lacks some of the processes discussed in this chapter when it comes to ritual objects. We do not use rhythmic songs or incantations. We do not draw upon a collection of commonly shared and culturally agreed-upon "magical" symbols, or a mythic *similia similibus* of some kind to relate the ritual object to some ancient mythic narrative, such as Christ on the cross, a story about Buddha, or a god or ancestor in a creative act. We do not typically use visual depictions of "increased power" as ancient rune-masters did via repeatedly inscribed runes or other methods. Furthermore, unless the patient is a neo-pagan who subscribes to beliefs in the magical efficacy of symbols (although Christians sometimes feel such feelings about crosses and bibles/verses), no such non-verbal indexical signs are typically used on ritual objects given to patients by providers.

We do not personify the medication used (as many ancients did with herbal remedies or ritual objects), though in my practice I have noticed that some patients do this on their own (though in some cases it is hard to tell if this is merely a poetic flourish or if they genuinely feel spirits "in" things like medicines). Modern treatment may also be suboptimal via the lack of decentering in the context of the use of ritual objects. Neither the patient nor the practitioner utilizes any altered state of consciousness in typical practice, thus we may miss out on the potential advantages (but also dangers) of this process. Finally, throughout typical medical treatment there is a notable lack of sensory pageantry in general, which may be very weakening overall to memorability—recall that vivid memorability is a critical feature of ritual in general and contributes greatly to its efficacy.

It may seem that it would be difficult to use some of these techniques without appearing bizarre or hokey to the patient. However, it can be done—never underestimate the human tendency to think ritually. It emerges spontaneously when you let it in the consulting room. For example, on several occasions I have worked with patients on focusing their attention on a particular concept such as "health," "stability," "I will be fine," and so on, in the manner of mindfulness or focused breathing. This takes little time and can be done in quick med-check settings. To assist in this process, I will write on a prescription pad the concept we are working on as a ritual object for meditative practice, or simply instruct the patient to put it on the refrigerator (or some area encountered frequently). If necessary, I frame it with "this may seem silly, but it can really help to remind you." As a script is a relatively low-pageantry object (as is the whole therapeutic process in general), we know we must compensate for that with high-frequency practice. Something as seemingly innocuous as a handout about anxiety or depression can also function as a ritual object—be sure to write something on it symbolically meaningful to help your patient think ritually about the handout. Ideally you would do something to the handout to emphasize its non-verbal, indexical status as a ritual symbol of improved health. Briefly holding the handout together (a non-verbal act of connection) and having a brief, intense discussion about the theme you are trying to foster (trust, hope, calm, stability, and so on) can "imbue" the handout in this manner.

Having patients draw can also provide you with raw materials for symbol creation. There is some evidence that drawing mandalas can lead to alleviation of post-traumatic stress symptoms (Henderson *et al.* 2007)—in this case, subjects were instructed to draw a "symbol of yourself"—the only instructions being to make a circle and not use any words. Note how both of these instructions bias expression toward the non-verbal and the indexical, and away from the semantic and the literal. That such symbolic expression helped reduce trauma symptoms suggests that any symbolic themes from such work could be used on ritual objects as well, perhaps carried much as a talisman or bracteate might be; it is not identical, but it contains similar ideas.

A final case is illustrative: Ms. D presented with severe depression and incessant nightmares following an abortion she was ambivalent about. She dreamt continuously about watching helpless animals die that she was tasked to care for. In therapy, we discussed how her symptoms followed the abortion and were clearly about her guilt and loss, and a sense that her child was angry with her. She had mentioned in passing thinking about getting a tattoo to "commemorate" the child, and I invited her to think about the tattoo on a much deeper, more symbolic and emotional level. As we discussed this I invited her to imagine the child in the next world (she had the commonly encountered vague, unaffiliated spirituality of many Americans) and try to imagine her now. We discussed how birds are often symbols of the soul in many cultures (*similia similibus*), and that perhaps we should think of her tattoo as connecting her to her lost child, while at the same time allowing the child to "move on" to the next world. We will revisit these grief-related themes later. For the time being let us note that through this treatment, the tattoo became a "magical inscription" and the addition of it created a physical, rigid boundary, resulting in a clear, undeniable mark (much like what happens in rites of passage worldwide) of the process she went through that was permanently inscribed on her body. The bird represented the child as well as a great deal more that is inexpressible. The results surprised me: her symptoms, and in particular her nightmares, completely remitted once the tattoo was complete.

Art and symbolic drawing have the power to transform *if* you utilize the ritual mindset which emphasizes the indexical, conceptual blending between abstract, holy ideas and concrete, physical objects, one that incorporates resonant narrative and belief, a *similia similibus*, projective identification, and (perhaps above all) cultural reinforcement whenever possible, remembering that in ritually impoverished environments this will be the most difficult to utilize.

Chapter 8

Healing Rituals

He cures most successfully in whom the people have the most confidence.
– Galen

In ancient Greece, at the temple of Asklepios, a god of physicians and healing (Meir 1968), there was a ritual for healing that had several interesting features. First the patient was isolated for a time, then she/he was engaged in relaxation exercises. Then patients were expected to make a sacrifice, attend to their dreams, and pay a substantial fee. Afterwards, the physician would interpret the patient's dreams and offer a variety of remedies to cure their condition. Kradin (2008) suggests that the psychological effect of this practice made the patient receptive to mental imagery and unconscious processes, and we see here the plausibility of that assertion given a much wider database from which to draw. Anthropologists Thompson *et al.* have this to say about similar rituals:

> social performance is not merely representative of social life; it has the power to be constitutive of physical and social wellbeing by mobilizing the support and resources that set healing in motion and see it through to completion. While these types of healing rituals . . . exist across cultures, what is significant is that they are local, creative and adaptive responses to the need for healing, on an individual and social level.
>
> (Thompson *et al.* 2009: 133)

In this chapter we will look at healing rituals from a variety of sources and use that data to compare it with our dynamic interdisciplinary applications. Healing has many definitions and dimensions, and many cultures do not make a distinction between healing the mind and healing the body. As we saw in Chapter 3, rituals can affect our physiology in a variety of ways. But what ritual characteristics are most effective at invoking physiological or neurological change? Placebo researchers have determined that the beliefs of the patient and physician, the setting, the images of the ritual, and the objects used in the ritual are all factors.

Patient Beliefs

A large number of studies show that the beliefs and expectations a patient has going into treatment can actually affect the outcome of the treatment. Flaten *et al.* (1999) showed that you can change the effect of a medication by changing the expectation of the subjects, even if the expectation is the opposite of the drug's supposed effect. This has been demonstrated in muscle relaxants (Flaten *et al.* 1999), asthma medications, and stimulants (Flaten *et al.* 1998; Luparello *et al.* 1970; Lyerly *et al.* 1964). The effects of placebo caffeine on motor performance differed based on the recipient's beliefs about the treatment (Kirsch 1999: 173). In one study on Parkinson's disease patients, the patient's perception of which group they were assigned to was the strongest predictor of outcome—the actual treatment did not matter. This result applied not only to the perceived quality of life, but also to actual motor functioning (McRae *et al.* 2004).

Koshi and Short (2007) emphasize that placebo responses likely have to do with expectancy of cure, the symbolic meaning of the treatment experience, and the context. Expectancy alone can actually override a drug's effects (Kirsch 1985), and according to Benedetti (2009), placebo effects are stronger when doctors are friendly and reassuring, as this appears to enhance positive expectation. Benedetti also reports that what a patient expects will happen strongly affects their placebo response, and not merely in subjective reports, but also in terms of objective measurement of physiological functioning. He proposes that positive expectations could potentially lead to cognitive (conscious and unconscious) readjustment of behavior, decrease self-defeating thoughts, affect memory and motivation, and alter the meaning of the experience as a whole (Benedetti 2009: 40).

Conversely, lack of trust can have detrimental effects. Distrust of medical personnel and therapies increase the nocebo effect—or negative placebo—as do high-intensity visual cues (Benedetti 2009: 83–84), and in one study (Krell *et al.* 2004), 90 percent of subjects who reported that an antidepressant would be "very effective" responded to treatment, whereas only 33.3 percent of subjects who thought the treatment would be "somewhat effective" responded.

Generally, adolescents and children show stronger placebo effects than adults (Benedetti 2009: 231), presumably because they tend to be more trusting in such situations. It has been observed that enthusiastic, definitive statements from doctors are nearly twice as likely to be effective as the same treatment from a doctor who is skeptical of the outcome (Benson and McCallie 1979). In a large study (Shapiro and Shapiro 1997), it was found that subjects who deferred choice of treatment to their doctors reported greater improvement. Also, those who liked their doctor reported greater placebo effects. Misinformation about whether or not a treatment was a bronchoconstrictor or bronchodilator reduced the effectiveness of the treatment by up to 49 percent (Luparello *et al.* 1968).

Dramatically, it has been observed that placebo injected painkillers are approximately equivalent to hidden injections of 6–8 mg of morphine (Colloca and Benedetti 2005) in terms of pain relief. Put another way, these researchers found that it took 6–8 mg less of morphine to alleviate pain when it was injected in full view of the patient and with their knowledge of being treated, as compared to being given morphine via hidden injection intravenously (IV). As Moerman put it: "What patients know . . . and what things mean, is what accounts for the effectiveness of much of medical treatment" (2002: 46).

Doctor Beliefs

But what the patient believes is going to happen is not the only important factor when it comes to outcome. Thomas (1994), for example, found that the odds of a positive therapeutic outcome were improved when patients saw their doctor as optimistic, experienced, and competent, and that doctor skepticism reduced therapeutic benefits. Even the so-called "gold standard" double-blind placebo controlled clinical trial has its problems, as shown by a study by Pollo *et al.* (2001). In this study, patients recovering from surgery could request IV pain medication and were divided into three groups. The first group was told nothing about the infusion. The second group was told they would either receive a powerful analgesic or placebo (mimicking the "gold standard" conditions of a clinical trial), and the third group was told they were receiving a powerful painkiller. All groups received placebo IV painkiller, but could request buprenorphine for additional pain management. The third group requested the least buprenorphine, followed by group two, and then group one, showing that placebo effects in settings mimicking real practice are stronger than those reported in so-called "gold standard" clinical trials. I have worked with researchers doing drug trials who have actually *used* this phenomenon in an effort to *reduce* placebo effects; the purpose was to maximize the difference between the placebo group and the active medication group. In other words, they consciously made skeptical or vague statements about expected outcome to patients in order to deliberately reduce placebo responses to treatment. The ethics of this practice remains dubious in my opinion, and furthermore muddy the waters when it comes to real clinical practice, since it does not duplicate real clinical conditions and doctor–patient interactions.

In another study, Gracely *et al.* (1985) divided *doctors* into two groups—in the first group the doctors knew they had a high probability of giving a powerful painkiller, and the second group knew they had a low probability. Patients in the first group who actually were given placebo showed a stronger placebo response than patients in the second group who got placebo. The doctors did not tell their patients anything about the possibility of treatment, yet somehow the patients picked up on the fact that they were less likely to get relief, possibly from unconscious cues from the doctors who were told they might be giving placebo. In any case, Moerman argues that:

> What is important is that doctors—healers of any sort or type—are *convinced* that their techniques are powerful and effective, and that there is undeniable evidence of this effectiveness. In some places, such proof comes from gods

> or spirits, in some places from personal experience, and in other places from the assertions of science.
>
> (Moerman 2002: 43)

Thus the beliefs of both the patient and the healer play into the effectiveness of an otherwise biochemically non-specific healing ritual.

Ritual Setting, Objects, and Images

Other visuo-sensory cues go into such responses and include the setting in which one is treated, the shape and color of the objects used, and the images discussed or used in a treatment. IV administration of placebo medication, for example, is more effective than intramuscular (IM) administration, which is more effective than tablets (Wall 1993), and pain pills that are reported to be more expensive are more effective than those reported to be "discounted" (Waber *et al.* 2008). Other variables that appear to influence placebo efficacy are the credibility of the therapist, therapeutic setting, treatment, administrative ritual, and the practitioner's reputation (Wickramasekera 1985).

Neuroimaging studies have shown that placebo treatment is associated with changes in brain physiology in patients with Parkinson's disease, depression, and pain, and the response depended on the illness:

> This suggests that the placebo effect goes where it is most needed, or serves a protective or adaptive function based on the environmental context in which the subjects find themselves . . . to some extent in clinical trials, it is remarkable that, based on the evidence to date, the neurochemical placebo effect appears to mirror the pharmacological effect which it is designed to mimic . . . This indicates a crucial role for the context, particularly the expectations generated by the environment, in the manifestation of placebo responses, whether it is a clinical trial or an experiment designed to study the placebo effect itself.
>
> (Lidstone and Stoessl 2007: 182–183)

Here we see that the setting and context of a ritual play into the expectations held by the practitioners. As we discussed earlier, so-called "sham" procedures and devices have shown stronger effects than placebo tablets (Kaptckuk *et al.* 2006), which is another instance of context and setting specifically affecting outcome. One study (Ammirati *et al.* 2001) showed that a sham pacemaker device was greatly superior to placebo anti-arrythmia medication. In one study of Ménière's disease, Thomsen *et al.* (1981) showed that sham implantation of ear tubes showed up to 70 percent improvement in symptoms, and this effect was still present nine years later (Bretlau *et al.* 1989; Welling and Nagaraja 2000). Other examples of successful "sham" surgery are procedures for heart disease, knee surgery, deep brain stimulation, and fetal cell transplantation for Parkinson's disease (Benedetti

2009: 244). These procedures are the closest we come in the West to large-scale healing rituals with multiple participants. Other examples of such multi-part, multi-player rituals will be given later on.

The Psychology of Healing Rituals

Though the belief of participants is clearly an important factor in how healing rituals do what they do, Sørensen correctly points out that "The question of 'belief' is extremely complex both linguistically and philosophically . . . Perhaps it is not a question of belief in the first place, but a combination of suspension of disbelief effected by the ritualized context and of basic mental representations evoked by the ritual actions performed" (Sørensen 2007a: 185). An example of the distinction is the observation that patients who strictly adhere to treatment recommendations respond more robustly than those who do not, regardless of whether or not they are taking placebo or "active" treatment (Horwitz and Horwitz 1993). Thus belief may mean "commitment" to treatment. The important point is that when it comes to rituals, if we think of a belief as a prediction, ritual beliefs are a special kind of prediction. They are *predictions which can affect their own outcome.* Whether such self-fulfilling predictions can be fairly described as "beliefs" I shall leave as an open question for philosophers.

As mentioned, imagery is likely a significant part of ritual that communicates with participants on a deeply emotional, non-verbal level. Price and Fields (1999: 126), for example, argue that desire for relief and expectation of relief occur as imagery. We already know that imagery can affect physiology; one dramatic example is the observation that sensory imagery related to food was shown in various studies to induce insulin secretion (Benedetti 2009: 165); it appears imagery triggers unconscious physiological/emotional responses *in addition to* conscious thinking responses.

Psychological symbols use images and Brody (2000) argues that the placebo effect is a change in the mind–body unit that results from the symbolic meaning which a subject attributes to a significant event or object. Symbols induce expectations of a meaningful outcome along non-verbal channels and are a part of context, as mentioned. Context is the therapeutic environment, and Mayberg *et al.* have shown that altering the therapeutic environment can significantly contribute to clinical improvement in depression (Mayberg *et al.* 2002).

The Anthropology of Healing Rituals

Even in supposedly "advanced" and "rational" (whatever that is supposed to mean) Western society, cultural variables have been shown to affect healing rituals significantly. For example, the placebo response to depression treatments has increased in recent decades (Khin *et al.* 2011), by roughly 7 percent per decade between 1980 and 2000 (Walsh *et al.* 2002), and the mass media has been shown to increase negative reactions and side effects in patients via verbal suggestion

(Oftedal *et al.* 2007). Thus healing rituals have a significant cultural component to them and these are a significant part of what rituals do.

Cross-culturally, anthropologists classify healing rituals as rites of affliction. Rites of affliction "seek to mitigate the influence of spirits thought to be afflicting human beings with misfortune" (Bell 2009: 115). Many cultures identify maleficent spirits as the cause of various human afflictions. Among the Ndembu, it is the spirits of the dead. The ancient Anglo-Saxons viewed the ylfe (elves) as the cause of many types of afflictions, along with demons. According to Bell, rituals of affliction

> heal, exorcise, protect, and purify. The type of ritual and ritual expert used will depend completely on the way in which a culture interprets the problematic state of affairs. One culture might diagnose some illness or bad luck as the result of an incomplete process of creation at the beginning of the world or as possession by spirits and prescribe a formal exorcism. Another culture might diagnose it as the ravages of sin and prescribe confession and rigorous penance, while a more secular society might diagnose the problem as a repressed childhood trauma and advocate three to six years of expensive ritual visits to the couch of a psychoanalyst . . . the dynamics of the ritual attempt to redress the development of anomalies or imbalances. Across the board, this takes the form of purging the body and mind of all impurities, which are nothing other than forces that have intruded upon the body–mind holism [and] may involve the intercession of powerful beings to rectify intrusions and imbalances that go beyond the body of a single person.
>
> (Bell 2009: 115)

Going beyond the body of a single person, as Bell puts it, could mean for us the collective element of the psyche. Importantly, rites of affliction deal not only with the mechanical causes of an illness, which is what Western medicine has traditionally been more concerned with, but with that element of illness that is more often of greater concern to the patient: the meaning of the illness. Cause and meaning are not identical, a fact that modern medicine lets slip by in its search for mechanistic causes for everything. But mechanistic causes do not address the more important question of *why* I am getting sick, now, or why one child becomes ill while another does not (Bell 2009: 116).

Such factors include ideas that diseases are caused by imbalances in social relationships, among the living, the dead, and/or the gods/spirits. In most systems, health or disease are conceptualized as part of a larger realm of order that sees no division between self and community, mind and body, material and spiritual. Hence, most systems utilize some kind of system that advantages *participation*. Moreover, many rites of affliction contain a great deal more sensory pageantry and rich symbolism than the modern mechanistic model of illness (along with the mechanistic solutions we prescribe) encountered in Western medicine.

Contrasting Ritual Modes

In the last chapter we reviewed the ritual elements of Western healing practice. Let us now contrast these with a traditional Korean healing ritual described by Bell. First, the client is questioned by the (usually female) shaman, who occasionally goes into a trance (utilizing decentering techniques), until eventually identifying the spiritual cause of the affliction of her client. Commonly it is an angered spirit or ancestor. After this a long ritual is performed, lasting from dawn to dusk, consisting of a series of three-part séances with a fixed pantheon of gods. During the séances, the god will possess the shaman and explain the illness to the client and how to heal it. Sometimes this involves driving out an evil spirit, and a straw doll with the client's clothing will be burned. For now, note the intensely collective nature of these rituals and the intense sensory pageantry involved. In such a case, psychological projection and projective identification would be intensified, as would memory and all the other biological and cultural effects discussed so far.

The question of whether or not such rituals are effective would benefit from rigorous empirical study, but for now efficacy is not really in question, as Bell observes that ritual responses have "proven quite capable of effecting psychotherapeutic cures" (Bell 2009: 117). This is due to the fact that typically elaborate rituals such as the Korean example above involve a powerful emotional catharsis for the afflicted, involving confrontations with fears and social tensions, but also involve the afflicted's entire family in addition to ancestors, gods, and spirits. This results in a broad-based group/family therapy which reaffirms important roles for individual grudges, griefs, and fears which are allowed to vent during the ritual (Bell 2009: 117).

Such rituals, ranging cross-culturally, link powerful outside forces to the individual as opposed to within the individual (like Jung's archetypes). Trance and possession rituals also typically involve elements of rebellion against social constraints, and "they may even institutionalize methods of inverting, reversing, or undermining other dimensions of the religious and social order" (Bell 2009: 119). Thus we see the symbols of grid and group temporarily break down to afford a brief interlude of *communitas* and liminality, during which the patient is broken down in order that they may be reformed again in a stronger, more expanded manner, much like what neuroscientist Patrick McNamara observed in his studies involving decentering of the Self.

In rites of affliction, furthermore, purification is particularly important, and usually generated through fire or water (which recalls the cosmological cycles of fire and water destruction observed in numerous myths of creation and renewal—this is a *similia similibus*). Such rites "present an argument, to use Geertz's terms, for a cosmos of ordered and interdependent components" (Bell 2009: 120). Thus rites of affliction often have imagery of creation and destruction, which goes along with the comments regarding liminality.

Historical Examples: Europe

The principles and themes found in various healing rituals persist across many generations, demonstrating resonance in their patterns. For example, an eighth-century runic inscription on a skull fragment, found at Ribe, Denmark reads *Ulfr auk Oðinn auk Hotyr hialp Buri es viðr þæima: værki auk dværgynni. Bur.* This translates as "Ulf and Odin and High-Tyr is help for Bur against these: pain and dwarf-stroke. Bur (carved)." MacLeod and Mees (2006) observe that Bur is the father of Odin and his brothers, who in Germanic myths created the world and are another example of a *divine triad*, which is very common in ancient European material, particularly in regard to Odin, who is mentioned in the triads Odin–Vili–Ve (the Prose Edda), Odin–Hœnir–Loki (the Poetic Edda), Woden–Logaþore–Wikiþonar in the sixth-century Nordendorf brooch, Odin–Thor–Fricco (Adam of Bremen's description of the three heathen statues at the famous temple at Uppsala, Sweden), and so on. Odin is an expert healing magician and creator god, which always suggests bringing order from chaos (Sproul 1979). Note also that the ubiquitous "origin = essence" idea gives primacy to the creator god as "essence" of the created world, since he is the origin of it. Furthermore, MacLeod and Mees (2006) observe that the first name, Ulf, means "wolf," an animal closely associated with Odin and Tyr. High-Tyr may also refer to Odin himself. Recall also that Tyr is the name of the **t** rune in the rune poems. Interestingly the name Bur has the **u** rune carved twice, perhaps for emphasis. The name of the **u** rune is perhaps also being used symbolically to indicate "strength" since its name is the aurochs, wild ox.

This rune inscription therefore contains numerous elements discussed so far, including the use of meter in the original language (which may have been chanted during carving), psychologically resonant images of myth and creation, *similia similibus*, conceptual blending, the origin = essence idea, the non-semantic use of the **u** rune to "strengthen" the name Bur, which may be a pseudonym for the carver, adopting a divine persona as father of Odin (which indicates a possibly dissociated state), and the concept of projection of the carver's real or imagined persona into the fragment. The use of a skull to inscribe such runes on should not be overlooked either, as the skull was likely thought of as containing a magical essence of some kind depending on the person to whom it belonged. The closely related Celtic tribes of Northern Europe in particular revered the head as seat of the soul (Monaghan 2006: 241–242), and Odin is described (Hollander 2006) as keeping the preserved head of an all-wise giant with whom he converses to gain wisdom. Narrative is a strong element here also, as the runes are telling a short story of how the gods helped Bur overcome pain and "dwarf stroke"—an ancient label for numerous ailments.

That was thirteen centuries ago in the eighth century. But across the centuries, the basic themes and structures persist, though the details may change. In the tenth century an Anglo-Saxon book of remedies for various ailments known as *Leechbook III* describes a remedy for an "old headache"—that is, a headache that is persistent. Ancient Anglo-Saxons felt that such headaches likely had a magical cause and so required a magical/ritual solution (Pollington 2008: 381; Storms 1948: 39). The *Leechbook III* states:

> Against an old headache. Take pennyroyal, boil in oil or in butter, rub the temples with it and above the eyes, moving on to them from the head. Though his mind be turned, he is hale.
>
> (Storms 1948: 39)

Later, it reads:

> For a very old headache . . . find little stones in the stomachs of a swallow's fledglings and hold them so that they do not touch earth nor water nor other stones, sew three of them together in whatever you want, put them on the man to whom they are needful, better will soon be for him.

Historian Godfrid Storms analyzes the first passage, noting that the Old English name of pennyroyal is *dweorgedwostle*, a compound containing the word *dweorh*, which means "dwarf"—a spirit which dwells in stones, hills, and mountains, akin to the various nature spirits found in cultures worldwide. Simply the name of the plant, therefore, is enough to make a connection to the mythical imagery, as much symbolism and collective cultural meaning goes into a name. Furthermore, Storms notes that the rubbing appears to contain a magical tripartite symbolism of rubbing the temples, forehead, and crown. Finally, the verb "turned," *oncyrran*, sometimes means "perverted by magic" and so the final phrase is an expression of will—a magical speech act that creates its aim.

The Canterbury Charm, a runic manuscript inserted into the margin of an Anglo-Saxon manuscript dated to the eleventh century, translates as "Gyril wound-causer, go now! You are found. May Thor bless you, lord of ogres! Gyril wound-causer. Against blood-vessel pus." Here an infection is personified into a named agent, and follows a pattern observed by MacLeod and Mees (2006: 120), which is the "you are found" phrase, a naming formalism, in which the illness is named and personified (much like the exorcism of demons in later Christian rituals and the naming of mental illnesses today), followed by a banishment, invoking the god Thor, who was renowned for his enmity with trolls, giants, and other malicious beings, and praised for his skill at smashing them with his mighty hammer.

Other beliefs common to ancient healing include the cross-culturally encountered idea that illness is caused by evil spirits in blood, which rituals can eliminate by causing an incision and collecting the bad blood, then throwing it across a road, river, or other clearly defined boundary (Storms 1948: 60). Spittle is also used in many cures as an indexical symbol of the magician's essence and power, such as when the magician spits into a holy salve in order to make it more effective, or spits on the painful part of the body in order to heal it. This is not unlike the symbolic effect of prescribing a pill in modern medicine. In the case of spitting, the spittle becomes a symbol of the "power" of the magician "flowing" onto the patient, like a mother kissing the cut of a child. Breath is also a recurrent symbol of the magician's essence or spirit (note the etymological relation between *inspiration* and *spirit*). Breath carries the "power" from the person into the ritual target. Do not underestimate the importance of the effect of the symbols on the magician as well as the recipient, in the case of unknown concoctions. Honey is often used—gold color, sweet taste, use in making mead, the holy drink, source of poetry, myth, and so on. Water is always used in some modified form, probably to distinguish it from prosaic water.

The fat of animals is used because of the symbolic qualities of the animal—as the part represents the whole, and both are seen to contain the same "essence." Furthermore the idea of contagion connects the part with the whole also. Marrow and milk are used in the same way; human milk is especially powerful. Ale, beer, and wine are also very often used, usually with modifications to add distinctness (Storms 1948: 69). Wax, honey, whey, and sweat are used to make salves or potions, and the vessel used is typically chosen for its symbolic qualities (Storms 1948: 72), being brass, earthenware, copper, "new," sacred, and so on. Running water has a special quality, argues Storms (1948: 74), because it is clear, fresh, murmuring as if alive, active and "quickening," and culturally speaking is normally full of elves (i.e. animate spirits), whereas the stagnant pool is dead, dark, and oppressive (like Grendel's mere in *Beowulf*). Herbs are often pounded into dust and mixed with butter/fat to make a salve, as if to imbue it with the "essence" of the herb.

Herb magic is usually based on the behavior and growing habits of the herb—nightshade grows in dark, moist places and so must be "stronger" than the dangerous things that dwell in dark, moist places, like evil elves or dwarfs. This is fascinating because it means the placebo effect evolved to work with our subjective impressions of things in a very complex manner. Importantly, Storms notes that: "magical practices and formulas are hardly ever directed against visible, tangible dangers, such as bears and other wild animals, but always against invisible, shadowy menaces, such as . . . malice, ungratefulness and the unknown danger of charms pronounced by an enemy" (Storms 1948: 136). Thus we see *these effects are directed at specifically mental and non-physical phenomena*. These observations have been corroborated by many others discussed in this volume. In any case, we can understand this process as making visual and tangible that which is invisible and intangible: ideas, feelings, emotions, pains, and concepts.

The idea that pains and illnesses are caused by the bolts or shots from evil or malicious spirits is very widespread (Storms 1948: 142) and hence resonant by definition. Many ailments are called *elfstone*, *elf-flint*, *elf-arrow*, *elf-bolt*, and so forth in Germanic tongues. This is a good example of the externalizing and objectifying bias in action that we have discussed already: an internal disorder or sensation is seen as an external object, agency, or mentality flinging physical objects at the victim of the disorder. A charm against such "elf shot," *Wiþ Færstice* (Storms 1948: 140), describes a sudden twinge or rheumatic pain in pictures of "mighty women" riding forth and hurling spears at the victim, to which the magician responds with a return volley and several chants of *Ut spere, gif here inne sy!*—"Out little spear, if you are in here!" The charm then speaks of mysterious smiths making war spears helping the recipient whether he has been shot in the blood, bone, limb, or flesh, whether it be shot of the "Aesir, or the shot of elves, or the shot of hags, I will help you now" and instructions on how to treat the magic knife by dipping it in a butter salve of feverfew and red nettle that grows through the wall of a house—chosen for its penetrating and rugged character, i.e. the subjective impression it gives the observer. Storms notes that in this charm the magician states that he firmly knows of the source of this illness by describing how the mighty women came charging over the hill-burial mound, which thereby puts him on the level of clearly understanding the illness. He utilizes the equation of origin with essence to know the essence of the illness. He tells a story that he has heard the harmful spirits and seen them, and counter-attacks. As Kradin recommends, he has "psychologized" and "symbolized" the patient's somatic discomfort, which he has seen lead to relief from (especially psychosomatic) illnesses. Consider, in light of these intertwining aspects, how effective such a charm might be if it did *not* contain the elements we have been discussing—without the narrative, the vivid imagery, the metonymically charged items, the definitive statements, and so forth: it is unlikely it would be nearly as effective at generating placebo-based physiological change and healing.

In a variety of medieval European charms, such as found in the manuscript known as AM434a (Waggoner 2011), the *Leechbook*, and other sources (MacLeod and Mees 2006), several patterns can be found:

1. Writing a word repeatedly or progressively lengthening or shortening it to effect a cure. In some cases, each day comes with a word reduced by one letter, the idea that the thing to be eliminated shares sympathy with the concept being affected magically. Note the way such a ritual creates a "light at the end of the tunnel" by setting a specific timeline on the cure via the word reduction method. The patient can see the word diminishing, which may correlate somehow with non-linear mind–body effects to nudge the immune system in a particular direction.
2. Magic words are stripped of semantic meaning and used for prosodic qualities, such as in the charm listed in AM434a to protect against "troll-riding": "res, fres, pres, tres, gres, I expel from me ogres and ogresses, trolls and evil beings, I ask the sweetest lady Saint Mary that I may save both my own life and others', in the name of the Father and Son" (Waggoner 2011: 1).
3. The location of a written charm is significant. Placing charms under the pillow, for example, is used to treat sleeplessness.
4. As in many cross-cultural examples, myths are used to narrativize the illness. In the case of medieval European rituals, one may see, for example, the story of Shadrach, Mesach, and Abednego (who survived a furnace in the name of God), to combat skin inflammations and against burn injuries (parallels exist on runic objects; MacLeod and Mees 2006). Also the myth of crucifixion is used to staunch blood flow: "Just as you, my Lord, stanched blood

from your own wounds at the ninth hour on Good Friday, may your blood be stanched, n., whether bleeding from hostility or a nosebleed, and all blood be stanched from wherever it runs, in the name of the Father and the Son and the Holy Spirit" (Waggoner 2011: 2). The crucifixion is an image often found in blood-stanching charms in medieval manuscripts and folklore; the story of Jesus stopping the Jordan River is also common in such charms.

5. Heavily symbolized objects are important elements (Waggoner 2011: 78). For seizures, for instance, the AM434a recommends taking the "red stone found in a swallow's belly, and let him always carry it" (Waggoner 2011: 9). This "swallow stone" remedy dates back to the first-century Greek herbalist Dioscorides, and variations of it were being prescribed into the seventeenth century in Europe (Eadie 2004: 698). Thus we have sixteen centuries of this clearly resonant idea (echoed in the *Leechbook* discussed earlier). Stones found in birds would be difficult to acquire, following the effort = power idea discussed by cognitive theorists of ritual. Another example is that of uterine vellum, which is made from the skin of unborn animals or still-born animals. Uterine vellum has a long history of magical use (Kålund 1907) and contains obvious highly indexical symbols of birth, new life, and creation.

As we can see, the ancients really knew their symbolic objects and techniques! By comparison we are impoverished in Western medical practice—we use very few of these "technologies."

Spirits and Personification in Healing Rituals

As mentioned earlier, many healing rituals involve personified nature spirits, and clinically I occasionally come across patients personifying their medications or blaming their illnesses on "the Devil." I do not argue with such statements—I *use* them.

Ancient European rites of affliction are illustrative. In Anglo-Saxon belief, elves (Anglo-Saxon *ælfe*) were supernatural beings of intermediate status between civilization and the monstrous creatures of the outworld (such as giants), who were often associated with land features such as open fields, groves, hills, and valleys, as opposed to the more unambiguously hostile trolls and giants, who occupied watery areas or depressions (Hall 2007). Elves were described as mysterious, beautiful, often androgynous, capable of powerful magic, sometimes malicious, sometimes benign, and paralleled the Old Irish Sídhe folk and other "fairy beings" discussed in Welsh, Latin, French, and Scottish sources (Hall 2007: 68). Such nature spirits have parallels all over the world (Üther 2004). The highly resonant nature of such beliefs will be evident as we continue.

Some afflictions were believed to be caused by elves—these ailments required additional magical methods beyond the usual demon banishing performed by holy folk. Afflictions attributed to elves included possession, sudden sharp aches and pains, sudden fevers, epilepsy, skin eruptions, hallucinations, and nightmares, often in response to some transgression of the sufferer. They could also, however, grant altered states of consciousness that benefited the receiver. The elves (Hall 2007: 130) appear to have been thought of as experts at mind altering, seductive, and manipulating magic also practiced by folk magicians (Old Norse *seiðr*, Old English *síden*), and folk magicians skilled in such arts were sometimes said to have elf ancestry, another example of the origin = essence idea. Historian Alaric Hall explains:

> The new evidence . . . contextualized with thinking in medical anthropology, which has established clearly the power of ritual, particularly in manipulating social forces with a bearing on an individual's health . . . and of placebo and nocebo effects . . . are gradually being absorbed into thinking on medieval charms. Less often noted is the capacity of psychological disorders to produce somatic illness: some societies, indeed, systematically conceive in somatic terms what Western clinical medicine would define as psychological disorders. The focus of our Anglo-Saxon medical texts on somatic diagnoses may disguise the treatment of psychological problems, for which the psychological treatments of charm, ritual and other manipulations of belief-systems were liable to be key elements in healing.
>
> (Hall 2007: 108–109)

I would certainly agree, given the wide evidence base discussed here as well as clinical experience. Hall explains, for example, that the charm *Wið Færstice*, analyzed by Storms earlier, "renarrates the sufferer's experience in martial and heroic terms. If recited only to victims of the illness, the charm had the potential to help them renegotiate their self-perception, but if intended for public performance, it could extend that renegotiation to the whole community" (Hall 2007: 112). From a psychodynamic perspective, having the community participate in such rituals likely intensified any mass-projective identification effect. Culturally, the collective element would be intensified as well.

As mentioned, elf beliefs were very resilient and hence resonant, as they survived efforts at eradication by the imported Christian belief system that had no place for them in its cosmology: in the strict dualism of good–evil associated with Christian cosmology, elves were in the gray area. Rather than the elimination of elf-beliefs, however, the elves survived Christianization and numerous other social changes and lasted for centuries, despite their being impossible to fit neatly into Christian categories of spirit-beings (Hall 2007: 153, 174). Anglo-Saxon clerics well versed in Christian cosmology were nevertheless careful to ensure elf-caused illness was dealt with by more than the usual devil banishment, as they were not seen as equivalent beings, despite the attempts of some to demonize elves (Hall 2007: 174). Elves were often seen as ancestors to cunning folk, and therefore sources of supernatural power that was not simply demonic or angelic.

Psychocultural Effects

Recall that narrative is a key element (along with participation) to healing in all disciplines studied. From a cultural perspective, rites of affliction change narrative and allow participants to experience a (temporarily) expanded mental state in which the ritual can transform a person's mental narrative, and hence self-structure (Greenwood 2009: 125; see also McNamara 2009).

Interestingly, Hall shows how the depictions of male and female elf-beings changed over the centuries, correlating with changing gender roles in society. In the oldest period, such beings were often effeminate men or warlike women—inversions of the usual gender roles assigned to men and women in that society. Such inversions suggest the powerful but dangerous *liminal* elements of ritual action. In the Anglo-Saxon world, warlike women and effeminate men were not non-existent, only rare, but still able to function in society. In this society and in most European Iron Age societies, gender transgression (in ritual settings) could be empowering and had an important supernatural role. This is likely due to the usual reason for deliberately inverting the usual social structure—it provides the wild, untamed natural force of *anti-structure*. Such images are uncanny and dangerous, but powerful. As before, we saw how some societies were often able to balance structure and anti-structure in a dynamic equilibrium. It is likely ancient Germanic/Celtic societies did this in part through the cultural valuation of inverted gender norms—within strict boundaries, of course. As time progressed, however, war-fierceness and effeminate behavior became more and more tied to physical gender rather than simply personality traits exhibited by either sex (Clover 1993); this was linked to a gradual erosion of female social power (the causes of which are likely complex but possibly related to the ideologies imported via Christianity) that correlated with a shift in how elves were viewed as almost entirely female:

> Christianisation introduced concepts of sin, and associations of sin with sexual behaviour, which had not previously existed in Anglo-Saxon culture and would both have encouraged the idea of female seductiveness as a spiritual threat to men, and the idea that male sexuality needed to be constrained . . . Their appearance may also relate to the gradual curtailment of women's power and independence.
>
> (Hall 2007: 166)

In the increasingly male-dominated world of formal power, *women* came to represent anti-structure. Elf-beliefs, then, appeared to reflect social norms of the day. But there is likely more to elf-beliefs than that; unlike monstrous trolls and giants who threatened society as a whole, elves, fairies, and so on, were only dangerous to those who transgressed *social, internal* norms, rather than the external threats from Nature and rival tribes. Thus such beliefs served to strengthen the social norms as well in a complex interaction of culture and beliefs. I am belaboring this point to remind us of the powerful effect culture can have on specific models of illness.

Healing Rituals: Cross-Cultural Themes

We have dived into the historical record to look at themes that survive centuries in terms of healing rituals. Now let us look cross-culturally. Religious scholar Mircea Eliade (1954: 82) argues that one of the most important mythological and narrative elements of the healing ritual is cosmogony, citing examples among ancient tribes of India, the Bhils, the Santals, and the Baigas. Eliade also shows how in many places the cosmogonic myth is recited at birth, marriage, and death rituals. The cosmogony is "the creative act *par excellence*" (Eliade 1954: 83). Also related to healing rituals is the use of quaternary circle symbolism, such as American Indian sand paintings and Indo-Tibetan mandalas, which Eliade connects with cosmogony. From psychodynamic theory, it is interesting that Jung (1954) identifies such images with what he called the Self archetype. The Self archetype, often imaged as a circle with quaternary symmetry of some kind, is postulated by Jung to be a fundamental organizing center of the mind that encourages healing (see Goodwyn 2012: 153–162). Such quaternary circles have been found in all corners of the world, giving the image near universal status as a recurrent theme in symbolism and suggesting strong psychological resonance.

Among Navajos and Polynesians, and in the ancient Near East, Europe, and many other places, Eliade identifies the importance of *narrative* as a ritually effective element found in the other branches of our model. He remarks that remedies only become effective if their origin (and hence essence) is declared known, and made contemporary with the moment of their discovery. For Eliade and so many others, the healer must recite the history of the disease or the demon who caused it, along with the story of the good spirit that conquers the demon (Eliade 1954: 84).

This effect of narrative and belief on healing symbolism was empirically studied in one paper examining "flower essence" therapy, a healing method developed originally by Edward Bach (1987) in which thirty-eight "essences" are purchased by the client and self-selected based on supposed links between psychological symptoms and the "spiritual nature" of the flower essence. Biochemically, all essences are an identical mixture of brandy and water. But the psychospiritual meaning of each essence is presented by Bach in his writings, and this discussion therefore likely influences the outcome for those who read his discussion of the flower essences. In a study of the efficacy of the rituals associated with this therapy used to treat various ailments, Hyland and Whalley (2008) showed that *taking the spiritual interpretation of the remedy seriously* was able to predict outcome *independent* of expectancy: "Thus the effect of expectancy is not *only* mediated directly—there are also effects that appear to derive from the behavior of engaging in the ritual . . . doing the ritual rather than believing the ritual may be the important factor for long-term placebo effects" (Hyland and Whalley 2008: 411–412). This is startling support for our model of ritual efficacy, as we can see the effect of image, essence, narrative, and performance in action to evoke placebo changes in physiology *even independently of* "belief" or expectation.

In many American Indian cultures, Hultkrantz reports that "the agent of diseases is a supernatural factor, and among the most widespread causes given for disease we may note enchantment, transgression of a taboo, intrusion of foreign objects or beings, and soul loss" (Hultkrantz 1979: 88). Being afflicted with a harmful enchantment is a very widespread attribution of illness, as we saw earlier. The enchantment is often, but not always, linked with the second two, the transgression of taboo (sin, sometimes of ancestors rather than the patient) and intrusion of a foreign object or being. In the case of taboo, confession is required. In the case of intrusion, the magician must identify the source of the invading entity (whether it be malicious spirit or evil magician/witch) and extract it. The healer then sets out to extract the entity through sucking, pulling, blowing, massaging, and so on, whereupon the object is displayed to all to see, either as a literally extracted object (in which case the shaman is obviously using sleight of hand), or by transferring the "essence" of the malicious invader to the displayed object.

In the case of soul loss, the ill person is deemed to have separated from his body through choice or compulsion, and must be retrieved. The soul is seen as having wandered off or been abducted into Nature or into various spirit worlds, both fraught with hazards. The healer then sends his own soul or that of his guardian spirit to retrieve the patient's soul. The healer must brave various hazards of these harsh realms, including treacherous environs, battles with monstrous enemies, and the malevolent dead. This feat often requires the healer to go into an altered state of consciousness; however, there is evidence that in some cultures the healer merely enacts the soul retrieval journey without any descent into an ecstatic state—so called demonstrative or imitative shamanism (Hultkrantz 1979: 91–95), which shows how the ritualization process can sometimes overtake genuine psychological experiences, and with similar effect. This change often coincides with a change in overall social structure from hunting society (genuine ecstatic state) to agrarian (rites and imitative skills). We will return to these cultural variations later.

Countless examples exist of the themes and concepts developed in this chapter in areas unrelated to ancient Europe. Just a few examples illustrate: water, as discussed above, is commonly used to symbolize rejuvenation and renewal (provided the water is clear and flowing rather than stagnant and dark). This idea can be found throughout the world of American Indian folk remedies, as explained by Hultkrantz (1979: 62). Another example is that of the confession of sins to a religious expert in order to alleviate the suffering caused by the sins—this practice is also found in the Americas. In fact, early Catholic missionaries were so shocked at the similarity of such practices among the Mayans that they thought the aspostle Thomas must have somehow preached to them (Hultkrantz 1979: 233). Barring this possibility, it is more likely that the practice of sin confession is a highly resonant practice due to its appeal to commonalities in our human mental architecture across cultures and throughout history.

Clinical Applications

In this chapter we have explored numerous cross-cultural examples of healing rites. A number of themes emerge from this survey, and we can summarize a dynamic interdisciplinary ritual approach to healing therapy using what I call the "7 Ps":

1. Psychological resonance. Using an indexical story, object, or image that has strongly recurrent features and connecting it to the patient via *similia similibus*.
2. Pageantry. Vivid sensory engagement along multiple channels to enhance memory retention of the ritual (for low frequency rituals especially).
3. Performativity. Manipulating objects in a conceptually blended manner using the body, including the non-semantic, prosodic use of language that is sacral, invariant, traditional, and formal.
4. Personification. Personifying the illness and/or the remedies involved in order to engage the universal cognitive structures that engage intentionality and *meaning* (Bruner 1998).
5. Participation. Using decentering and other methods on this list to participate with the environment/others/objects/and so on, in order to *become part of something larger than oneself.*
6. Purification. Manipulation of objects and spirits to symbolically "clean" the self and renew it, and/or rid the self of the ailment, here symbolized as an external object or entity.
7. Projection. Projective identification of ideas and healing elements, especially of other humans engaged in the ritual. Here we can see how firm beliefs of cure can transfer from doctor to patient and influence healing also.

In modern Western therapy, some of the 7P themes are detectable, but often in a muted or diluted manner:

1. Psychological resonance is barely taken advantage of or recognized, with Jungian therapy a rare exception, using mythic narratives and *similia similibus*, and even then it can be challenging due to the low ritualism and the often-encountered lack of commitment to any particular myth. In these cases atheists and agnostics must be given some rationale for taking myths seriously in order to use this technique.
2. Pageantry is minimal, making what happens in therapy rituals difficult to remember due to the properties of memory. It winds up being high frequency to compensate for that—but this is wrong-headed. Psychotherapy, being a healing ritual, should be a high pageantry/low frequency event that transitions a person from sick to liminal to well, permanently. Afterwards, maintenance of healing can be maintained with low pageantry/high frequency rituals of "purification" or rejuvenation.

3. Performativity is hardly used. We frequently do not give patients anything in particular to *do* to address their mental issues. Instead we encourage continued cogitation and abstraction. This is a legacy of the sincerity mode discussed in Chapter 6. Mainstream Western medicine is largely anti-ritual (and either denies or does not recognize when it is being minimally ritualistic), and hence it is the endless search for the "truly true" self at ever deeper levels of sincere meaning, with none of the playful reinforcing and transcending of boundaries seen in ritualistic cultures. Furthermore, in a society that worships the "new" and "improved" it is hard to find sacral, traditional, formal, and invariant forms to use—they often must be invented and/or borrowed (but never fear: borrowing has a long history!).
4. Personification rarely occurs (or we ignore it as superstitious hokum in religious patients or pathologize it as psychosis when it may not be true psychosis), which leaves us unable to truly address mental problems on their own terms—those of intent and *meaning*—and instead we focus on cold, mechanistic explanations of illness in terms of neurotransmitters and brain circuits. Intentionality is a property of the mental realm; mechanistic explanations therefore are unlikely to take advantage of the full arsenal of universal cognitive architecture we have that is designed to navigate the integrative subtleties of personification. Clinically, I do not debate the reality of demons or harmful spirits with patients. That is a blind alley that will eliminate discussion with me and destroy the therapeutic bond—moreover, pursuing that question tends to be serving the therapist's need for scientific "certainty" rather than understanding the patient's experience. Neither do I ignore such experiences, which is even more commonly done in Western practice. Rather, I ask what can we *do* to appease/banish/placate them? (Naturally I adjust their medication as well—just in case). I find it often fruitful to ask: what does this spirit want? What can be done to come to terms with this desire? Assume it is real (after all, psychologically, *it is*), and then ask how to deal with it. To do so is to invite the playful as-if nature of boundary/structure formation of ritualism.
5. Participation is so fundamental it is hard to avoid even in the most staunchly anti-ritual environments. Nevertheless, the most ego-restructuring kind of participation typically is enhanced by some kind of decentering, which is rarely found in mainstream Western healing methods. Again, some off-beat modes of therapy use this technique with hypnosis, entheogens, active imagination, and so on. But generally it is little-used. The practice of guided imagery is a close cousin.
6. Purification. The idea of purification is fundamental to healing rites, and has limited coinage in typical Western therapeutic settings. The practice of mindfulness meditative practice may be the closest thing to a full-blown ritual purification that we have. I believe this is an untapped resource, since purification is often of the low pageantry/high frequency variety that could potentially augment any sort of therapy. The concept of a spiritual cleansing is

universal and highly resonant, and likely would benefit from objects, physical enactment, and so forth.

7. Projection. In Western medicine, the default ritual use of projection/projective identification is in one-on-one therapy settings. Patient and doctor beliefs still have their effects in this case, but the often-encountered scientific skepticism which is so necessary in empirical research can actually hinder treatment if it is not made conscious and attended to. Furthermore, while in one-on-one treatment this can be very helpful (especially in low pageantry/high frequency rituals), I believe more might be possible, at least ritually, in a group setting, particularly if it involves a patient's close and trusted attachments. Support groups such as Alcoholics Anonymous have a baseline level of ritualism that fosters group projection, but it is nothing like some of the traditional rituals we have discussed so far. This is due to our modern post-Enlightenment, post-Protestant setting of extreme sincerity mode, low group, and overall anti-ritualism. I suggest that therapists should try to coordinate ritual techniques with a patient's spiritual counselors, if there are any, to help bring others in to participate in the patient's healing. If there are none, *we* become the spiritual advisors, for better or worse. Bringing loved ones, however, into the ritual process is the default setting in traditional cultures, and it is an untapped resource for many patients today.

A good example of the difference between Western and traditional approaches to depression can be found in psychologist Andrew Solomon's popular writings on depression (e.g. Solomon 2015). Andrew Solomon, himself having suffered from depression, once volunteered for a traditional Senegal remedy for what they called depression, which they explained as being covered in harmful spirits that were jealous of his sexual partners. In order to be cured, Solomon went through a day-long ritual that involved the entire community. Placed in the center of the activity, he was first covered in millet seeds which were then collected. Then he had to hold a ram close to him and he was covered in blankets as music played. He became very hot, then the blankets were pulled off and the ram (and other animals) were sacrificed and he was covered in their blood. After this he was wrapped in ram intestines and instructed to move (with great difficulty) to a pre-designated place with holes dug into the ground. There he had to take pieces of the ram and put them in the holes and say "spirits leave me alone, and know I will never forget you." Given a piece of paper where the millet was gathered, he had to give the millet to a beggar who had good hearing and no deformities and that would finish the affliction. To end, the women spat water all over him, rinsing the blood away. Afterwards, everyone danced, the ram was cooked, and, as he describes it, he felt extraordinarily "up," and even though he did not believe in the principles, he found the experience exhilarating. As we saw earlier in the study on flower essence therapy, performance can bring about change even in the absence of belief—imagine how much stronger this effect is than the relatively diluted flower essence therapy treatment.

Solomon continues to recount his encounter with Rwandans who had experienced Western mental health methods, who told him:

> We had a lot of trouble with Western mental health workers who came here immediately after the genocide and we had to ask some of them to leave. They came and their practice did not involve being outside in the sun . . . where you begin to feel better. There was no music or drumming to get your blood flowing again . . . There was no sense that everyone had taken the day off so that the entire community could come together to try to lift you up and bring you back to joy . . . There was no acknowledgement of the depression as something invasive and external that could actually be cast out again. Instead they would take people one at a time into these dingy little rooms and have them sit around for an hour or so and talk about bad things that had happened to them . . . We had to get them to leave the country.
>
> (Solomon 2008)

This anecdote provides a good picture of the difference between ritualistic and sincerity-based modes of thought and action.

Identity and Explanations of Suffering

We have seen some clinical examples of incorporating ritual (to varying degrees) already in the case of the tattoo, Orlandini's (2009) ritual, and the use of ritual objects. We have also seen that many times the above 7P techniques are missing due to the nature of our low group (and often low grid) cultural settings that overemphasize the sincerity mode. Recall that while this situation is not unique to modernity, ritual scholars argue that it has never been so extreme. As such, our typically runaway sincerity, low group, anti-ritual environment comes with a particular set of challenges for its members I see constantly in clinical work: the lack of group identity and the problem of suffering.

In settings of low group and, to a lesser degree, low grid, obligations and expectations are ambiguous, hazy, undefined or non-existent. Hence individuals in such settings typically have no idea where they stand or even who they are as members of a group because we define ourselves in large part through our obligations to others and not *only* by listening to the "inner voice of our deeper self." But the sincerity-mode response to this dysphoria of identity is more soul-searching and navel-gazing, which cannot ever satisfy because it can never be enough. The intense desire for belonging, universal in the utterly social animal *Homo sapiens*, then, is never sated.

The second problem involves explanations for suffering. In g/G settings (commonly seen in middle-class settings of excessive careerism and corporate climbing), suffering is due to simply being a failure and/or stupid. The anxiety this provokes is therefore severe, and the prescription is more striving, more competing, and more isolation from loved ones in the relentless search for greater status;

career choice becomes the group identity. It is a poor substitute. Similarly, in g/g settings, suffering is simply due to a lack of enough love. More love, more sincerely felt, and more universal acceptance are seen as the answer to suffering and everything else. Family therapists, of course, will tell us that this is just wrong-headed—it is structure, boundaries, and the resolution of ambiguities that are needed—"more love" simply doesn't cut it (Seligman *et al.* 2008).

I continually encounter these problems in modern clinical practice. Every day I hear some variation of "I don't know who I am," "I don't feel like I belong," "I'm the black sheep" (the latter one is a full-blown cliché). Without group identity—obligation and attachment to others—we feel worthless, life feels meaningless, empty, and terrifying. Modern life, with its media-saturated consumer culture, however, often encourages us to imagine we are alone in a faceless mass, with nothing to distinguish ourselves from it or to identify with one another except whatever we can cook up with our fantasies. Children begin to really feel this in middle school, which is probably why intense cliques start forming at that age. I speculate that this identity confusion is derived from a lack of group, runaway sincerity, and low ritualism. This situation encourages extreme individualism and a valorization of independence from any and all constraints to one's freedom. The problem is that such freedom from others is a double-edged sword. After all, if nobody needs me for anything, I may be joyously free of all constraints, but I'm also bitterly alone. The commonly expressed empty sentiment "I support you in whatever you want in life" is often code for "I don't really care what you do because none of it affects me, so do whatever you want." A truly connected person cares very deeply because their fates are intertwined with yours! Western psychology, however, often labels such situations "enmeshment" and seeks to help by separating people from each other even more, to encourage them to begin their sincerity-driven quest for Authentic Self-Actualization.

Couple this problem with the problem of suffering—either it's your fault because you're a failure or stupid, or you're just a victim of not enough love. I hear variants of these beliefs every day in clinical practice, too. I think both of these problems are culturally influenced contributors to much of the mental illness that I encounter every day. The solution suggested by the study of ritual is to counterbalance these forces with the appropriate amount of ritualism—and this is because the above problems are well addressed by the ambiguity-resolving, playful boundary forming-and-transcending, non-verbal and ineffable expressing power of ritual.

Creative use of the 7Ps of healing rituals may therefore help overcome some of these problems. Resonant narratives and *similia similibus* are a reason to discuss world myths and the psychological reasons to take them seriously with agnostic patients, whereas learning the myths of devout patients and co-creating ways to participate in such narratives can introduce this theme into therapy. The extremely resonant story of the passion, crucifixion, death, and rebirth of Jesus, for example, could be used in such a manner with devout Christian patients—remember the goal here is *participation*, or allowing the patient to see that their own transformation from illness to wellness has "gone before" in such archetypal narratives (they do not have to engage in *imitatio Christi*, but the instant popularity of Thomas à Kempis's work on the subject says something about the resonance of the idea). As we have seen, many ancient healers saw the potency of the *similia similibus* and incorporated it into their healing encounters, and such practices survived for *centuries*. No modern psychotherapeutic technique has that kind of track record—hence I take notice at such resonance.

Helping patients find their identity is often facilitated greatly with the pageantry of cultural/ethnic and local community objects and creations, including food, music, crafts, stories, and clothing, that are derived from a particular group identity that a patient is drawn toward. Sometimes it can simply be the patient's own ancestry or local community. Perhaps your patient has Native American ancestry she has previously ignored. Perhaps he comes from an Italian family but has never considered it part of his identity. Perhaps they have yet to explore local community gatherings. Other times it is a mysterious connection or attraction that is difficult to quantify. Use what works; so long as you both can co-create a narrative explanation, it will typically suffice. Let them explore such cultural expressions/crafts/art/lore, but make explicit what you are doing with it—building group identity and belonging.

It is the desire for belonging that is, I think, a large part of the cause for what Freud called the "repetition compulsion"—a classic example is the woman whose father abused her growing up finds a man later in life who continues to abuse her. She is not seeking punishment. Rather, she is simply duped into thinking these are the people to whom she belongs; it is testament to the power of this desire that one would endure so much pain to avoid feeling like one did not belong.

There are likely many ways to foster a sense of community/ethnic/group/cultural belonging—this is but one. The drive to do this is universal, but without raw cultural material it is awkward and incomplete. Observe how modern middle-school children clumsily try to create group identity from scratch by creating cliques that consist of (again) clothing, music tastes, and hobbies—what is lacking, however, is *resonance*, since they nearly always draw from faddish pop culture that will be forgotten tomorrow. Hence it never lasts or satisfies as a symbolic representation of group identity. Moreover, in our hyper-individualist culture, such group ties rarely consist of real-world obligations; hence they know deep down that it is a charade. For our purposes, when faced with a patient troubled by poorly defined group identity, the end goal is to help them find something *outside themselves* that they can participate in; this is accomplished by helping them find a tradition of some kind that has stood the test of time (i.e. is resonant) and encouraging them to express it in ritual terms. This can be in the form of various heritage, religious, ideological, or community associations—those that involve real-world obligations will be the most powerful in identity building. Ideally ones to which a patient's family belongs will be potentially easier for the patient due to familiarity—though sometimes the patient's family is chaotic and toxic, so that is not an option.

In any case, a word of caution is in order here: the desire for belonging can be incredibly strong. Any force of such strength should never be treated lightly. Rather than needing to be encouraged to find something outside themselves, some patients will need you to put on the brakes for them and avoid extremism—as Seligman *et al.* (2008) point out, in the modern setting of runaway sincerity, extreme fundamentalisms such as millennial cults, extreme ideological crusades, or hate groups are often found as crude, primitive substitutes for true group identity. Those with poor identity are drawn to such groups because they feed their longing, however clumsily. But all of these share one thing in common: a lack of psychological resonance. They never stand the test of time—as cognitive anthropologists show, such groups quickly splinter apart into even more extreme groups or they implode. Thus, the building of identity should be a rapprochement. It should be a slow, solid building of group/cultural identity, consisting not of navel-gazing or airy analysis, but of concrete, physical, sensual expressions of symbolic participation in something larger than oneself. This might be an ethnic/ancestral identity, a religion, a non-extremist social group with a long history, local community organizations (difficult in our environment of constant mobility), or perhaps most of all: one's own family traditions, to the extent that is possible. It might be engagement with music, festivals, games, arts, or crafts that have a cultural or community significance to the patient. Since our patients come from such a huge variety of backgrounds (the United States alone having immense diversity), flexibility and creativity will be required. Also, when balanced by family, community, religion, and/or heritage, career is a fine choice to augment one's developing identity. It is extremes of any stripe we wish to avoid. The important thing to remember is that identity is defined by *context*. It is practically impossible to create identity out of nothing despite the widespread modern fantasy of self-invention. Rather, it is created by a set of important relations and attachments to others—this is the legacy of our nature as a social species.

The second benefit of building group and grid is that it fosters an explanatory framework for suffering. This may result from the way ritualism naturally draws us away from sincerity-based thinking that constantly seeks the One Authentic Truth and builds room for the playful "as-if" worlds. Doing this frees the patient to construct narratives of their illness that allow for suffering to be explained in culturally meaningful terms, such as the ancestors, the will of God(s), the Great Mystery—all *collective* constructions/recognitions. Here, too, is where the personification of ritualism plays a part: spirits, dead ancestors, and gods have will and intent—these are expressions of meaning. God, of course, has will and intent. Various "spirits" do also. If illness and suffering can be framed in terms of intent, they can be addressed in meaningful terms. The way ritual fosters the experience of meaningful coincidence likely contributes here as well, again, drawing patients out of the extreme solipsism of runaway sincerity and allowing the very events in their life to be concrete expressions of something much larger than them, whether it is the ongoing battle between Good and Evil, the hinted needs and will of the ancestors or spirits/angels/elves, God's great plan, or what have you. Again, however, caution is needed: this is powerful stuff, and patients often come to therapy with *negatively* framed explanatory systems: God is punishing me, God hates me, nothing goes my way, the Devil is going to kill me, and so on. As you help your patients build group identity, real obligations follow, and a collective identity begins to develop. When this happens, the shared fate of the group becomes primary, and personal setbacks become secondary. Through "as-if" worlds, the ritual system creates and then reinforces a narrative that is inherently inclusive, even of suffering, and past traumas can become integrated into a larger narrative. Such pain is much easier to bear if it is for some kind of purpose—even if that purpose is merely to use it to help others. This is why nearly *any* meaning—even a negative one—is preferable to meaninglessness, as several placebo researchers have concluded.

In this chapter we have merely scratched the surface in terms of how ritual themes can be used to build identity and aid in many other ways. In the next two chapters we will build on the 7P framework to add additional detail and elaborations to help transition our patients from sick to well and to help them deal with grieving and loss—a universal aspect of human life.

Chapter 9

Transitional Rituals

Man truly does not live by bread alone; he is "turned on by legend, literature, and art, and his life is made glowingly meaningful by these and similar modalities of culture.

– Victor Turner (1974: 165)

In Chapter 6, we saw how Arnold van Gennep looked at rituals as rites of passage; rituals for van Gennep allowed members of a culture to transition from one clearly defined role to another by dramatically symbolizing in high-pageantry image and performance. Recall that ritual participants first separate from the old role, then endure a period of time in a neither/nor place of "liminality," and then finally reincorporate into the new role. In many rituals, this tripartite structure is prominent, but in rituals of transition the pattern is particularly clear. Overall, as Bell puts it, "life-cycle rituals seem to proclaim that the biological order is less determinative than the social" (Bell 2009: 94). We will see how this plays out in this chapter.

Passage into Adulthood

In the rituals that signify passage into adulthood, initial separation rites accompany physical maturation and serve to separate the child from the mother, and often include burning of old bedding, changing living quarters, seclusion—often in the wilderness—whereupon the youth is rigorously separated from the opposite sex. These separations serve to highlight the distinctiveness of the initiate by dramatically removing him from his old context. Often at this time the initiate is considered among the dead. During the transitional period, initiates are untouchable, dangerous, sacred, and imbued with the gods and the dead, outside social norms and rules, but separated from mainstream society through various taboos. At this point he is in a transitional state where he is forced to endure various physical and mental tortures, often imbibes intoxicating substances, is painted—usually white, black, or red—and is taught tribal lore and various mysteries, whereupon he is resurrected and marked somehow in a way consistent with the other adult members of the society through various rites of incorporation. These rites of incorporation into the world of sexual activity and adult responsibilities are often permanent and involve cutting off a finger, bashing out a tooth, cutting an earlobe, piercing, hair cutting, or scarification among other things. On this subject van Gennep says the target organs of these mutilations are always chosen "because they project [and because] of their histological constitution, [they can] undergo all sorts of treatment without harming an individual's life or activity" (1960: 73). These markings serve to identify members within a group via an outward, undeniable physical sign. Often during this time new members feign learning how to walk and eat, as if they were infants, which highlights the overall birth/death symbolism.

Van Gennep emphasizes that during the liminal phases of these rites, the great mysteries are revealed to the initiates, and often demonic spirits that roam the wilderness and make terrifying noises are shown for their true selves: adults in masks using bullroarers, and so on. This unveiling is often a very dramatic aspect of such rituals. Sometimes these initiation rites contain a double initiation: separation from birth environment, transitional period, incorporation into the sacred environment, transitional period, separation from sacred environment, transitional period, then reintegration with tribal environment. "But as a result of this passage through the sacred world," van Gennep adds, "the initiate retains a special magico-religious quality" (1960: 82). Such rituals likely have a dramatic effect on the biology, psychology, and cultural constitution of the participants.

Van Gennep's analysis holds true for rituals in groups as widespread as Australian Aborigines, Native American tribes, Pacific Islanders, and even ancient ritual texts such as those of Egypt and India, or the Elusinian mysteries. The structure can be seen in various priestly and knightly orders throughout history, through various "shamanic" initiations, and the structure holds also for the ancient rites of Orpheus, Dionysus, Mithras, Attis, Adonis, and so forth as analyzed by the myth-ritual school of James Frazer (1921) and others.

In her analysis of the Cretan Wiradthuri initiation ritual, in comparison with initiation rituals found in Africa, America, Australia, and the Pacific Islands, religious scholar Jane Harrison says "When a boy is initiated . . . he belongs to something bigger, more potent, more lasting, than his own individual existence: he is part of the stream of the totemic life, one with the generations before and yet to come" (1998: 73–74).

Even relatively new rituals such as Wiccan Witch initiations of the mid-twentieth century (Haining 1972: 51–56) involve bathing, removal of clothing (stripping of prior social status and demonstration of liminality), a concern over boundary—in this case the magic circle, a recreation of the cosmos in the four directions, a chant of words chosen for rhythmic and prosodic quality rather than semantic value, and the use of archaisms such as "thee" and "thou" in the ritual dialogue between priestess and initiate. As part of liminality, sexual rules are negated not only by nudity but by the use of ritually sexualized behavior such as kissing of feet, knees, sexual organs, breasts, and lips in a prescribed manner, and imagery of neither/nor, such as stating the initiate is neither bound nor free—an emphasis on humility (negating social rank structure). Also part of this ritual are concerns of purification—so common in rituals worldwide—accomplished in this case by striking the initiate 3, 7, 9, and 21 times (for a total of 40, like Jesus—I wonder if they noticed that). At this point the secrets of the order are revealed to the initiate, followed by more kissing and anointing, and bestowal of various material objects necessary to their future craft, which completes the incorporation.

A Dynamic Interdisciplinary Analysis of Transition Rituals

In initiation rituals, biogenetic structuralists observe not only that vivid imagery is universal, but that such imagery is often alternated with conceptual material, shifting back and forth between the abstract concepts of a cosmology and the vivid imagery of it (Laughlin 1990: 30). The example given is that of Tibetan Vajrayana initiation, which alternates between ritual performance and text reading; another example is Western education in the physical sciences, in which lectures and ritualized laboratory procedures (not really *ritual* per se, but containing ritualistic elements) form the corpus of education of a scientific profession.

Turner observes that the liminal phase of transitional rituals in particular appears to be dense with imagery of anti-structure:

> In rituals, especially in the seclusion rites of initiations into manhood, womanhood, or into tribal associations and secret societies, there may be episodes of real or symbolic cannibalism . . . here there are regularities and repetitions indeed, yet they are not those of law and custom but of unconscious cravings which stand opposed to the norms on which social bonding secularly depends.
>
> (Turner 1974: 257)

This opinion is echoed by anthropologists Metcalf and Huntington, who observe the prominent *nature over culture* theme common in such states, where symbols are drawn from the biology of sex and fertility. Ritual actions channel toward strong affect and often taboo affect, which sacralizes such feelings and gives them a positive value (Metcalf and Huntington 1991: 38). Turner comments that "Perhaps Freud and Jung, in their different ways, have much to contribute to the understanding of these nonlogical, nonrational (but not irrational) aspects of liminal situations" (Turner 1974: 257).

Psychologists Otto Rank and Carl Jung have both used the model of van Gennep's initiation rite to analyze the structure of many myths as well as the process of human individuation—development over a lifetime. "These theories support the idea that rites of passage not only effect transitions in the social sphere but also concomitantly in the psychological sphere" (Bell 2009: 102).

The rites of transition involve prolonged, highly ritualized periods in which participants are likely affected in a number of ways. Rappaport argues that:

> The alterations of consciousness of which ritual is capable . . . are in the service of the integration of those multiple levels of mind of which one extreme

> is called consciousness and the other the unconscious, an integration which may be, for the novice or learner in a rite of passage, a novel synthesis, a new and deeper understanding of the world.
>
> (Rappaport 1999: 388)

In particular, the rhythmic drumming, chanting, fasting, ordeals, vivid imagery, colors, and so forth are very prominent in these rituals and seem particularly targeted toward certain decentered states of consciousness. Biogenetic structuralists argue that the holistic, connective right brain is activated in such rituals and likely puts participants into a receptive state. Given the extent to which even so humble a "ritual" as going to the doctor can elicit powerful physiological placebo responses, one can only speculate as to the physiological changes occurring during these extended, much more pageantry-heavy rituals.

Participants, especially when in the liminal state corresponding to the imagistic mode, are saturated with images and ideas that resonate powerfully with the universal cognitive structures and functions of the mind, and this likely allows such ideas to sink down to an unconscious level. It certainly makes them *memorable*, and memory is a critical element to the building of new ego structure. Indexical signs dominate, opening up the pathway for non-verbal and visuo-spatial processing that presumably has greater access to universal emotional structures.

Psychodynamically it is plausible that projective identification is utilized to a high degree in incorporating the images and ideas of the collective element. As many psychoanalysts have noted (not just Rank or Jung), initiations have a strong narrative flow to them, and narrative (again) saturates the entire enterprise, as the initiate flows through a timeless story of growth from child to adult, and all the heroic sacrifices, terrors, joys, pains, and ecstasies that may entail. The rituals themselves encourage the detection of meaningful coincidence/synchronicity, as well as decentering (before and during the liminal phase) and reassociation (reincorporation phase).

As we saw in Chapter 5, among the Charrua of Uruguay, for example, young initiates seeking a guardian spirit will go to a lonely hill with a stone mound on it and then torture themselves with various fasting and self-mutilations until they see the spirit. This practice is also found in North American tribes (Hultkrantz 1979: 71), and variations and elaborations of the guardian spirit-as-alter-ego idea can be found in places ranging from Tierra del Fuego to the Algonquin tribes of the northeastern United States—this widespread distribution demonstrates the resonance of the practice and belief in guardian spirits. It is not unique to the Americas, either, as we have evidence of guardian spirit beliefs among the medieval Vikings. In general, the guardian spirit is communicated with via vision and/or dream (see also Goodwyn 2012: 61–87), and is typically most closely linked with hunter-gatherers; cultivators often relegate such ideas to specialists such as shamans or priests, or do not have the idea at all (Hultkrantz 1979: 74), and other ritual practices take the place of such elements in initiations. We will discuss the mechanisms of such cultural variations in Chapter 12.

Religious scholar Åke Hultkrantz discusses the obviously decentering aspect of Native American initiation rituals, which normally include intense visionary experiences (Hultkrantz 1979: 75–79) either spontaneous or solicited. Spontaneous visions include vivid dreams, whereas solicited visions include those induced by various aesthetic rituals such as fasting or deprivation, mutilation, seclusion, or other hardship, and also by various entheogens such as peyote, tobacco, or marijuana. The vision usually includes a spirit who gives divine gifts including songs, various taboos, supernatural skills, divinatory revelations, or communications to the ritualist. These rituals are in many tribes combined with coming-of-age rituals. One example is the Mandan Indian ritual of the *okeepa* where the young initiate is suspended from the roof of a ceremonial lodge by needles stuck through his chest. From other needles piercing his legs drag buffalo skulls. From this painful dazed state, it is believed, come the most profound visions. Whether the guardian spirit is the recipient of outright worship is debated by religious scholars, but examples exist among some peoples of giving food offerings to their spirits, and of devotees tattooing themselves to resemble their spirit, assuming a spirit name, decorating their clothes with the fur, feathers, claws, and so on, of their spirit (if animal), and so forth. Here we see concrete evidence of identity building in action—the initiates are building their identity through ritual participation in something outside himself using resonant mythic narratives as well as spontaneous decentered visions. In these cases the integration of conscious and unconscious forces is one of the central aims of the ritual. Still others are to create an unforgettable experience that will transform the self of the initiate, allowing—indeed forcing—them to let go of their old childish ego and transition into an adult ego.

The above practice can be compared to the Nordic practice of "mound sitting" or "going under a cloak," described in a variety of Icelandic sagas, or the ancient Irish practice of *imbas forosnai* in which a person seeking visionary help or advice from the elves, dwarves, ancestors, or gods will come to inspire the mound-sitter. This practice, too, heightens the capacity for meaningful coincidence and likely encourages altered states of consciousness.

In any case, the transitional ritual serves many cultural functions as well as the above: grid and group structure (or lack thereof) is reinforced by going through these rituals, as they clearly define roles and hierarchies of participants through multiple lines of communication, and in a manner that thwarts deception and alternative, and they continually connect the abstract ideals of the collective psyche with the physical, visceral, and material of the here and now. They almost always contain elements of controlled *communitas*, particularly in their liminal phases, and these highly emotional and imagistic phases likely etch themselves onto the psyche of the participants in such a way as to reinforce the ritual structure and narrative. Through all branches, again, we have the element of participation as an overarching theme.

By contrast, societies which eschew ritualism for a permanent rubric of sincerity (that is, cultures with low grid/group not balanced by ritualism) do not take advantage of these ritual effects, leaving members with the potential for perpetually ill-defined roles, identity and role confusion, a continual and nearly limitless but ultimately circular discursive exchange and negotiation of roles that is disembodied from the physiological and emotional levels of the mind. It leaves members on a perpetual search for one's "true self" in the face of bewildering and limitless individualism, which blurs everyone into a huge mass of atomized individuals disconnected from all distinction (Seligman *et al.* 2008). This situation ironically encourages still more desperate quests for distinction and "authenticity," which as discussed can never be satisfied without the tools ritual provide. As we discussed in the previous chapter, we are then left with a society of people who are constantly trying to figure out who they "really" are—a state common in the Western world. As ritual and culturally derived answers to the question "who am I?" are continually attacked as oppressive and in need of reform, we are left with the only answer the mode of sincerity can provide: "I am whoever I want to be!"—that is, arbitrary self-invention. This, of course, is no answer, but simply an opening of even more questions.

Rituals provide the longed-for answer to the question, however, by creating roles, obligations, relations, boundaries, and ideal forms. They are felt as satisfying answers because they derive from the collective element, rather than arbitrary self-inventions; by definition, they draw from outside the self. Anti-ritual self-inventions are not satisfying because they are *disconnected* from the collective element—that is, disconnected from the surrounding culture and disconnected from our universal human nature. Through its biological, psychological, and cultural effects, the ritual connects the bare, ever-malleable ego with not only the divine, but the bloody, the messy, the muscular. It does this through non-discursive, metaphoric, and imagistic methods of a powerfully emotional imagination that can never be pinned down to a "one, true self." It provides roles and boundaries that are nevertheless permeable and non-arbitrary with which to build one's sense of self and identity through its *relation* to those boundaries and collectively derived definitions. After all, the first step to defining the self is to delimit its boundary. The effects of ritual flow through our cultural relations to our very cognitive structures all the way to our bodily functioning, and transition us from role to role as human life requires.

Clinical Applications

Transition rituals are important for helping people move from one important role to a different important role. Without these transitions, individuals are left in an ambiguous state. Even in our largely anti-ritual culture, there are still some ritualized attempts at transition, but as usual comparatively they are muted, watered-down, or overly intellectualized and focused on consumerist values. I will explore two major transition problems that manifest often in clinical work: the transition to adulthood and the transition from singlehood to couplehood.

Adulthood Transitions

Suspicions that Western cultures do not have adequate rituals of transition to adulthood have been entertained since at least as early as van Gennep's work and they have continued since. It is a subject of continued interest. Rappaport (1999), for example, observes that since physical maturation varies so widely from one person to the next, it is far too vague and ambiguous a guide for individuals to know whether to behave as children or adults, and furthermore for others to behave toward them. Things such as undertaking more rigorous work, engaging in sexual activity, valuing greater self-discipline and self-reliance, seeking a long-term mate, having children, seeking separate living quarters, and so on are all common activities that have a clear child/adult differentiation. Adulthood rites bring clarity, precision, and certainty to what is an otherwise messy, ambiguous process. When not tyrannically imposed, such structures can be comforting, helping one to know one's role and place among important contacts. Moreover, those undergoing a transitional ritual, whatever their inner feelings about it may be, cannot deny having undergone it, and the physical markings and vivid memories will be continual reminders of their new role—it will be a continual communication to others and themselves of their new role. When supported by a community of some kind, others will respond in turn (projective identification), and will reinforce the role.

In the absence of such rituals, however, one will continually encounter people in an ambiguous and role-confused state, who have a poor sense of their place, how they are to behave, and how they are to respond to others—a situation I find in clinical work regularly. The social structure transition rituals provide help to the ego structure, and in its absence it is much weaker and subject to the continual chaos around it created by ambiguous roles. Let us also not forget that rituals can filter down into our very physiology and affect our biological state—it is possible, then, that rituals quicken physiological and mental maturation in subtle ways not yet explored by empirical work. We will leave that for future research to determine.

Though school graduations, turning 18, and the awarding of a driver's license are vaguely ritualized in America, they suffer from a lack of most of the features discussed in this volume with respect to adulthood rites. There is no real separation to highlight the former state. There is no liminal phase, decentering, imagistic anti-structure, or pageantry. There is no reincorporation phase, and there is no permanent marking. They typically lack resonant narratives or *similia similibus*, non-instrumental performativity, personification, or purification, except in diluted forms. Thus they are not as convincing to the participants and others as they could be, and do not resolve inner ambiguity or uncertainty. There is an exception to this: the military. The military rites of transition are significant, and the military continues to utilize many of the technologies of ritual, probably because, as for hunter-gatherers, there is a constant survival-oriented pressure to use what works. The US military, for instance, continues to use heroic narratives about the

Founding Fathers or great war heroes, and uses sensory pageantry with meticulous attention to uniforms, ceremony, and proper form and technique. Ritualized language is used, and no doubt projective identification and participation are encouraged through the decentering effects of rhythmic marching in unison, or "drill," along with ascetic physical routines.

Clinically, the lack of ritualism is difficult to address because social roles require social settings to recognize, ritualize, and reinforce them, and we only have a therapist and a patient in a private room, and a rubric that encourages all changes to be viewed as "self-inventions"—a legacy of the sincerity mode, no doubt. Without the patient being able to participate in something outside her private thoughts, identity building and role transitions can be extremely difficult. One avenue that can help is dream exploration. This is because the human instinct to ritualize emerges spontaneously in dreams quite often (but typically in fragmented, "raw," and/or idiosyncratic ways), and when a person senses on whatever level that they need to transition into a new social role, mature, or develop into a new ego structure, they will often dream of "initiation" ceremonies complete with purification with water, going through thresholds, separation states surrounded by nature symbols, and so on. Recognizing the ritual, emotional, and deeply universal symbolism of such dreams, and the implications thereof, with a patient can help them to co-create rituals with you to physically enact these transitions. Treating dreams as "messages from the unconscious" is in many cases the modern equivalent of saying they are messages from the ancestors/gods/spirits/God. This can have a powerful effect of allowing the patient to realize there is more to phenomenal experience than their own self-generated fantasies. Furthermore, many dreams are crafted largely from collective elements and so, in a sense, patients using dreams are accessing something outside their own ego.

Using mythic narratives and pageantry, as well as interacting with various dream characters, mythological characters, ancestors, or what have you used in the narrative *as if* they were present will deepen the experience and allow it to "sink in" to the physiological level through the meaning-constructing effect of intentionality. A tripartite structure using decentering can be useful—but as ever, use caution with decentering techniques such as active imagination or light trance/hypnosis. These suggestions are unlikely to provide an experience that is as powerful as a full-blown cultural ritual where a whole community is present to provide projections and add to participation, but it will give the therapist an additional tool for use in treatment.

Relationship Transitions

The transition from a single person interested in pursuing their own self-interest to a "serious" couple capable of producing a stable environment in which to raise children is a major transition. In most cultures, there are a number of extensive rituals that assist in this transition. These follow the tripartite structure, where the couple is ritually separated, then isolated for a time, then incorporated in the marriage ceremony. Mock battles, seclusions in the wilderness, changing clothes, hair cutting, consecrating one's toys/jewelry to a deity, changing food habits, taboos, giving away possessions, washing, destroying old objects, changing one's name, and many more rites accompany the separation phase of marriage rituals. Communal feasts, exchanging clothes or valuables, tying the couple together, using objects belonging to one another, drinking each other's blood, consuming from the same dish, washing each other, entering the new house, and of course sexual intercourse (regardless of whether it is the couple's first or not) are among the rites of incorporation reviewed by van Gennep (1960: 131–132).

With funerals and military rites, marriage rituals are among the last rituals we have left in our society to contain any significant amount of the features described by ritual experts. And yet, comparatively, we are still impoverished. Marriage ceremonies in our culture of course exist, and they do utilize pageantry. But that pageantry seems more driven by consumerism rather than sacred meaning or a tradition outside the couple's idiosyncratic fantasies. Moreover, the whole array of relationship rules and dating conventions in the lead-up to marriage that we once had no longer exist. In the past, for example, courtship had a typically extensive set of expectations and conventions. These gradually died out, starting in urban areas and filtering into the rural areas (we will review similar changes when we talk about funerary rites in the next chapter). Mock abductions separating the groom from the bride, for example, were practiced in Appalachia as recently as the middle twentieth century—though tellingly it was regarded as "backward" even then. Conventions such as bachelor parties no longer have ritual elements and differ little from every other revel, which disconnects them from the whole purpose of reinforcing the phenomenal experience of the marriage ritual.

The state of modern "courtship" (now an archaic term) can be summed up in a satirical cartoon I saw once, depicting a couple in a bed, staring at each other. One says to the other: "So does this mean we're dating now?" Clinically, I observe how relationship status is constantly ambiguous, ill-defined, and a source of perpetual anxiety. As in rites of adulthood transition, when it comes to couplehood, we are ritually impoverished comparatively, and the fact that divorce rates are roughly double now what they were in the 1940s may not be a coincidence. This question deserves much greater empirical scrutiny, but anecdotally, I encounter confused people in extremely ambiguous relationships constantly in clinical work. This confusion creates anxiety that contributes to chronic mistrust, relationship chaos, and endless drama, because it does not feel stable or grounded in anything except the couple's imagination.

In any case, the problem I'm highlighting here is that the breakdown of ritualism has led to tremendous ambiguity, confusion, and anxiety in relationships, simply because the structures that guided people along the path from "me"-oriented singles to "us"-oriented couples have mostly evaporated in the setting of runaway sincerity. It should be evident by this point what may help: creating distinctions using physically concrete and memorable events and using the "7Ps." Co-creating a tripartite structure of some kind, in coordination with a couple's family or other traditions, will facilitate the emotional, psychological, and even physical changes that the ritual is to foster. Co-creating these kinds of structures and connecting them to a tradition outside the couple themselves may help considerably in the transition from singlehood to couplehood.

As a final note, all of the above could be said about the rituals that transition childless adults into parents—as usual, in our society very little beyond the odd baby shower is done to ritually transition people into the most important role of all. Cross-culturally, our rituals of parenthood are very lightweight and dilute. Is it any surprise, then, that clinically we encounter so many parents with boundary confusions when it comes to their own children?

Therapy is not only a healing ritual; it is also a transition ritual. This is why beginnings, middles, and ends—i.e. initiation and termination, need to be emphasized to whatever degree they can if we are to take advantage of the various ritual effects on memory and self we have been discussing. The 7Ps can be used here also, to guide the patient from illness to wellness in a non-ambiguous, concrete, and socially clear manner using non-verbal, enacted ritual tools in addition to more conventional methods. The ways in which this can be done are nearly limitless—I encourage clinicians to work with patients using these principles to create their own unique ritual expressions.

Therapy termination is a large part of this—it is fraught with difficulties due to the intense (often unconscious) bonds that form in psychotherapy, wherein both therapist and patient sometimes avoid the pending separation, and therefore do not deal with it properly. But without a clear, strong termination, the patient is robbed of an important ritual moment: the moment of "graduation" from therapy, during which time the patient can be said to have completed an officially sanctioned therapy. For this reason, an inadequate termination may erase any benefit the patient may have gotten out of therapy. This moment is enacted dramatically and with great pageantry in cultures worldwide—take the example of when the women of the village spat water all over psychologist Andrew Solomon to wash away the blood. It is unlikely he will ever forget that moment, and it is in that manner (among others) that the multi-channel effects of termination can be maximized.

The process of termination, however, can be difficult because it involves saying goodbye. And as many therapists know, saying goodbye can be very challenging, particularly for mental health patients. This leads us to the ritual way in which the ultimate goodbye is navigated: rituals involving death. In a sense, termination is like the death of the therapist for our patients. Thus, as we continue to look at how ritual study can inspire psychotherapy, death rituals provide an important guide to not only managing termination, but managing complicated grief—a very common goodbye that challenges any psychotherapy.

Chapter 10

Death Rituals

Death rituals are also transition rituals. At first glance, they serve a number of interconnected functions, and like all rituals studied so far, death rituals appear specifically designed to strengthen the connections of participants, not only with each other, but with the deceased whom they have just lost. Catherine Bell explores how this works:

> A Korean widow grieving over the death of her spouse and frightened about how to manage alone in the world invites a ritual that demonstrates the continuation of relations after death, the subordination of her loss to an enduring value system, and a catharsis of her anger that enables her to reassume control of her life.
>
> (Bell 2009: 136)

Death rituals do indeed appear to serve these purposes, and as we progress, we will see that they do even more. Funerals, according to van Gennep, are perhaps the most dramatic rituals of all. Like other rituals, funerals have a similar structure with the separation of the corpse from the world of the living, followed by a dangerous liminal transitional state in which mourning is observed, recognized, and often subject to rigid structures, followed by an incorporation phase which often involves second burial and involves the dead person being finally incorporated into the land of the dead. During the transitional period, the dead are subject to wakes, night-long vigils by close surviving relatives, who themselves share the dead person's transitional state and subject to numerous taboos and proscriptions. The corpse is given food and treated as if still alive, as death is normally thought of as a process rather than an abrupt change of status. During this time also it is commonly held cross-culturally that the dead person must prepare for a journey to the land of the dead, and this journey is normally depicted as perilous and requires a specialist in the form of a shaman/folk magician or in some cases, a deity as psychopomp.

Separation rites surrounding death (van Gennep 1960: 164–165) include transporting the corpse in a special way, burning his possessions, killing his slaves/wives/animals, washing, purifying, and various taboos. The grave site is itself separated through various ritual means. Sometimes there are mock battles for the corpse by various family members, which seems to involve fighting against losing a beloved member, and various physical methods for separating the components of the corpse into its various parts of body/soul. Incorporation rites usually involve stories about the journey to the dead and often involve a specialist reciting a vision or story of the deceased joining with the ancestors.

In this chapter we will be exploring how rituals deal with grief and mourning. Mourning, the cultural complex of behaviors and expectations following the death of a loved one, normally facilitates the transition from the disturbed state of bereavement to a restoration of normal functioning, and this transition is accomplished in many ways worldwide. If, however, this transition is not accomplished, the more troublesome state of complicated grief (CG) can develop. In his essay *Mourning and Melancholia* (Freud 1914–1916), Freud proposed that loss of a loved one sets up a double-bind in the bereaved that, if not resolved, can lead to what we would now likely identify as CG. According to Freud, the unresolved double-bind describes a persistent ambivalent state in which the bereaved simultaneously refuses to accept the loss of the loved one while also recognizing the stark reality of loss.

The literature on CG since Freud is vast. Nevertheless, much has been written since Freud on the subject of mourning and its complications, particularly the work of John Bowlby (1982) and others (cf. Wallin 2007). Briefly, in the psychological and psychiatric literature, there are a variety of ideas currently in development with respect to normal mourning and CG, both in terms of facilitating normal mourning and identifying the risk factors for CG. We will of course look cross-culturally at ways humans have tried to deal with the challenges of death and loss.

The Double Burial

Anthropologist Robert Hertz's classic essay on mortuary ritual (Hertz 2009) complements van Gennep's analysis. Hertz reviews the variety of cultures that practice "double burial"; a practice in which the newly dead corpse is buried (or exposed) for a time in a separate and special location (an example of the transitional state), then exhumed after a prescribed amount of time and buried again somewhere else. The practices Hertz based his analysis on were observed in Indonesia predominantly, but they are by no means exclusive to that region and can be found in many areas around the globe. Here we can see evidence of van Gennep's tripartite structure, with the first burial representing a liminal state between newly dead and permanently buried. There are further subdivisions evident as well, between newly dead and quickly separated from the group, followed by a variable-length liminal state where relatives often keep vigil with the deceased, followed by burial.

One widespread belief during the time when the corpse is newly dead is that at certain times the corpse is *vulnerable to attack and must be defended* by various means such as not only standing vigil but keeping a fire or incense burning, protecting orifices to keep spirits from entering the corpse and possessing it, and so on (Hertz 2009: 199). This particular cross-cultural theme, that of *helping the deceased*, is very prominent and will play a large part in our comparative analysis later. During this dangerous transitional state, the corpse not only needs help from the bereaved, but is also potentially dangerous itself when in this state living marginally in two worlds; the condition of being dead is in many places seen as a cause of suffering that the deceased wants to share with the living. In many cultures, close relatives *share* this state and must abide by numerous taboos to symbolize the shared state of death, which are then lifted when the time of temporary burial is over. Variations on the practice of temporary burial and its symbolism are found all over the world from Central Australia to Polynesia and North and South America, with temporary treatment ranging from burial to exposure under various conditions.

As mentioned, a very important part of the transitional state is the practice of *helping and/or appeasing the deceased.* For example, many funerary practices include keeping a fire lit. This fire near the corpse is interpreted in a variety of ways from keeping demons at bay to warming the soul of the deceased. Cremation is a close analog with similar meanings, as these transformations change the character of the corpse, turn "it into a new body and [are], consequently, a necessary condition for the salvation of the soul. This is precisely the meaning of cremation: far from destroying the body of the deceased, it recreates it and makes it capable of entering a new life" (Hertz 2009: 202). This pattern can be found historically as well, as in the Viking funeral described in the tenth century by Ibn Fadlan (Lunde and Stone 2012), where a Viking king is temporarily buried, then subjected to various ritual practices, then finally cremated—thus the double-burial/transitional state has examples across the globe and across history. The primary symbolism in these various themes is that decay and destruction symbolize the change of status of the soul, and therefore represent not a sudden change but a gradual, processional change. Furthermore, this transition is not destruction but rebirth (Hertz 2009: 201–203). All these practices provide the bereaved, in physical, concrete terms, a vivid picture of what is going on with the deceased's soul, as the body and its processional change is seen as a symbol of what the soul is going through.

As in other cultures, Hertz observes that among the Indonesian peoples he observed, violent sudden death, death in childbirth, drowning, death by lightning, and suicides are often given special treatment, as their bodies "inspire the most intense horror and are got rid of precipitately . . . their bones are not laid with those of other deceased members of the group who have died a normal death" (Hertz 2009: 211). Later, we will see that, in Western psychological terms, such deaths are associated with higher rates of CG. Hertz argues that this distinction is made in many societies because of the intensity of the emotion impressed upon the survivors, for whom no rite can alleviate their suffering. This belief has parallels, contrasts, and variations in other areas, such as in the Americas (Hultkrantz 1979), where there are separate otherworlds and afterlife fates for those who die in such a manner.

Hertz next reviews the final ceremony that follows the transition period, which signifies the final transition to the land of the dead. This corresponds to van Gennep's incorporation phase, wherein the soul of the deceased is transitioned to its final place of residence in the otherworld. These rituals often involve great expense (normally beyond a single family's capacity), orgies, feasts, and merriment. "The final ceremony has three objects: to give burial to the remains of the deceased, to ensure the soul peace and access to the land of the dead, and finally to free the living from the obligations of mourning" (Hertz 2009: 204). These are three obviously very important functions and emphasize the intensely social nature of mourning rituals, where life and death are social categories as well as (but more important than) physical categories. Note again the importance of the bereaved role in *helping* the deceased through various rites and actions.

In any case, the final resting place is not a permanent condition, but frequently seen as a new birth—death/birth symbolism is seen in all kinds of rituals globally, and funerary rites are no exception. Comparing numerous mourning rituals, including Christian ones, Hertz concludes: "at whatever stage of religious evolution we place ourselves, the notion of death is linked with that of resurrection; exclusion is always followed by a new integration" (Hertz 2009: 208). This is supported by the related cross-cultural link between death of the body and death of the cosmos, where the mourning ritual centers around the idea that the body is a symbol of the cosmos, so its death comes to be symbolized by the destruction and rejuvenation of the universe (Parry 2009: 266–268), providing an important *narrative restructuring mechanism*, which is another important theme.

Traveling to the Land of the Dead

As mentioned, the journey of the deceased through various incorporation rites from the dangerous transitional period to their final resting place is cross-culturally very commonly seen as requiring strong magic involving mighty psychopomps, priest/priestess participation, songs, altered states, and so forth, as the road is often pictured as fraught with peril. Among the Dyak of Borneo, for example, rice is prepared for the souls of the dead and for evil spirits. Then one of the participants makes offerings of these and states "I place here your food; by this I crush all resistance, all that is impure, all bad dreams, and I set an end to all tears" (Hertz 2009: 205–206). Note especially this second factor that is common in mourning rituals—*the social constraining of emotional response*, in this case, tears. This charm is followed by the priestesses singing songs to lead the souls into the celestial city of the dead. One aspect of the release of the kin from mourning is depicted as a *removal of impurity*—we will see this theme again and again later on. This purification is accomplished with rites such as those above, of sacrificing/giving offerings. Other means by which this is accomplished are swimming in rivers (sometimes with the blood of sacrificed animals), after which evil is purged by way of waving torches or brooms—these acts free the living of the deathly contagion and serve to further make physical the conceptual distinction between the living and the dead. The conceptualization of evil is an important one—whether it is witches, evil spirits, or Satan, cultures which have a clearly defined concept of evil as malicious cause of death and misfortune must be protected or even challenged by such rites.

Thus death challenges the very structure of society and its understanding of suffering, and cultures respond with a restructuring of meaning. Hertz explains the very human and social nature of the cosmic themes engaged with in ritual:

> When a man dies, society loses in him much more than a unit; it is stricken in the very principle of its life, in the faith it has in itself . . . It seems that the entire community feels itself lost, or at least directly threatened by the presence of antagonistic forces: the very basis of its existence is shaken.
>
> (Hertz 2009: 208)

Those who pass to the land of the dead are then free to live there eternally or to be reborn as a human or animal at some later point, often as a descendant of the deceased. They are also often attributed divine status and thereafter worthy of offerings themselves, periodically intervening in the lives of the living and taking part in their struggles, only this time in a more distant, less potentially dangerous, role. The important theme here is the *restructuring of the relationship between deceased and bereaved.*

Note that though these themes are extremely widespread, there are always cultural variations. A few examples are illustrative. The Iban of Borneo, for example, rapidly carry off a corpse to a graveyard where it is placed in a rough hollow log coffin, then buried in a shallow grave with various grave goods, whereupon the funeral party returns to the community longhouse. The hurried nature of this practice stems from the belief that the dead struggle with the living for the body, but that once the person dies, the community has lost the struggle and should rapidly give over the body to avoid any more trouble from the ghosts of the dead. Three days after burial, a ceremony is conducted from the longhouse which formally introduces the deceased to the spirits of the dead, and offerings of food are thrown from the longhouse and imagined to be carried to the land of the dead via a bird (Metcalf and Huntington 1991: 103–105).

By contrast, the Mambia, also from Indonesia, speak of the spirit of the dead person journeying to the mountain of the dead in "the west," with a pole erected next to the corpse so it can journey through the roof. Periodically, however, there are great festivals honoring the dead where deaths are re-enacted, and the betel nut bags that belonged to the deceased are buried in a symbolic second burial, whereupon the recently dead travel from the mountain to the sea, transitioning to their final resting place (Metcalf and Huntington 1991: 106). All of this reflects Mambai cosmology, which states that Mother Earth, impregnated by Father Heaven, gives birth to the mountains, trees, and people, then dies after informing the people about mortuary rituals (connecting birth and death). Her body continues on, providing food for all life. Returning the corpse to the earth repays Mother

Earth. Such narratives provide *context and meaning* to the death, which we will see appears to be an important aspect of the prevention of CG.

The idea of a journey to the land of the dead is not present in the rites of the peoples of Madagascar. For them, the dead reside in the local tomb in which they are placed, where they continue to live with the tribe in a non-physical manner. The Bara of Madagascar practice drunken revelry at funerals in order to entertain the isolated and lonely deceased. Metcalf and Huntington (1991: 112–113) point out that the particular juxtaposition of death with sex and revelry (a theme seen in unrelated cultures across the globe), however, is not arbitrary, but is required to balance out the opposing forces at work: the absolute order of death, sterility, and the tomb, versus the absolute vitality of birth, fecundity, and the womb. Among the Bara, death is an instance of excessive order that must be counterbalanced by an overflow of life and vitality.

At death, for the Bara, a male and a female house are selected. The corpse rests in the female house where women gather and keep vigil with ritual weeping. At the male house, men receive male visitors and accept stylized condolences from others. There the men direct the burial arrangements. At night, girls leave their house and sing and dance in the courtyard, and young men join in gradually. Over time, rum and food are served, and the funeral becomes something like an orgy. On the third day the men take the corpse from the women's house and a boisterous funeral procession ensues, with youths (with sexual experience only) leading the relay to the burial site and involving racing and cattle wrestling. During this time the practitioners must observe numerous taboos and carry protective charms. After the corpse is buried, an extravagant feast is held—a conspicuous display of wealth, during which time drunken revelry ensues and occasionally fights break out, and practical jokes are played. Metcalf and Huntington comment: "It is not enough merely to bury someone . . . The survivors must bring about the renewed conception and rebirth of their deceased kin into the world of the ancestors . . . Should it fail, the consequence is nothing short of catastrophic infertility" (1991: 129). Here again we see the importance placed on *helping the deceased*, and in this case it is amplified to where the survivors' actions are *necessary in order to avoid catastrophe*. In other words, *obligation* (so important in the previous chapters on building identity) again is noted as ritually reinforced and healing.

Cross-Cultural Themes: The Dangerous Dead

Mourning rituals have long contained two major elements: the first is the ritual containment of the fresh corpse with various methods used to keep the restless soul at bay, and the secondary rites, which occur some weeks to years later (depending on the status and power of the dead individual, as well as culture of origin), where the dead are firmly incorporated into the realm of the ancestors. Archeologist Timothy Taylor recognizes that these themes are extremely old and enduring (Taylor 2002: 27). The second state—the transitional state—is recognized by the overwhelming majority of cultural data to be the most dangerous state, wherein the dead can wander and wreak havoc on the living (Taylor 2002: 118). Other parallels exist in history. Evidence of rites of passage and second burial, for example, have been found in Natufian culture (Taylor 2002: 226), and second burial has been observed in Central Asia, North and South America, Melanesia, and Greece, among other places (Metcalf and Huntington 1991: 35).

In Hindu belief, as in many others, violent and sudden death is believed to cause the deceased to be bitter and liable to torment the living either with nightmares or evil events (Parry 2009: 271). Proper rituals must be performed to prevent this, and usually involve the survivors *sharing in the deceased state symbolically* through not shaving, washing, wearing shoes or shirt, sleeping on the ground, avoiding hot food, and abstaining from sex. Such a state is usually associated with an uncanny power for mourners and for ascetics who adopt such practices permanently (Parry 2009: 277).

Cross-Cultural Themes: Ritually Sculpting the Emotionality of Mourning

In many cultures, the closest survivors of the deceased share in his/her fate and are subject to quarantine and taboos (Metcalf and Huntington 1991: 90–95). As pointed out by anthropologists Bloch and Parry (1982), the two primary objectives apparently associated with cross-cultural death rites is to facilitate the transition of the dead from the world of the living to the otherworld, however visualized, and to facilitate survivors' acceptance of the death and alteration of social life subsequent to it. The Wari, an Amazonian tribe, for example, for months after a death will go to all the places frequented by the deceased (favorite hunting, fishing, or sitting spots), then cut the vegetation in a wide circle, burn it and sweep over the circle. As they do this they report thinking about the dead person, recalling and honoring their life, then afterwards report that "there is not much sadness there" (Conklin 2009: 250).

What becomes evident is the many ways mourning rituals appear to serve grief processing. Grieving is a very natural process observed in numerous social animals (Panksepp 1998), but in humans is elaborated in a great number of different ways. These variations are numerous, but not arbitrary, and constrained by various biological and psychological universals that work in concert with surrounding cultural ideas (also so constrained) to produce the varieties of mourning rituals that exist. Though by no means limited to mourning, one commonly discussed purpose of funeral rites is to help participants express and process their grief in meaningful ways.

The example of the Tlinglit, a North American coastal tribe documented in the nineteenth century, is illustrative. Like so many unrelated cultures, the practice of taking the body out of a side door, mourners cutting their hair, fasting, painting themselves black, and singing death songs are also observed among the Tlinglit (Kan 2009). The Tlinglit also invoke the ancestors by speaking their names and recalling their deeds (Kan 2009: 289), and grief is expressed by mourners in sacred and highly treasured crying songs, by the sanctioned flow of tears during specific times, and by the male mourners striking the floor with their staffs four times, where they are instructed to pour all their grief into the act of striking the ground (Kan 2009: 291). Note the especially psychological advice and *symbolization of emotion in physical action here*, as well as the culturally sanctioned, but strictly bounded expression of emotion.

Warmth and comfort are equated as the hosts clothe the mourners in various garments during the ceremony as a way to symbolize and concretize providing comfort to them, and reinforced by the exchanging of gifts (sometimes accompanied by rubbing the gift on the forehead of the recipient). Funerals are, as in other places, associated with competitive games among families of the deceased as well as feasts, both of which emphasize the unity of them while allowing them to jockey for political position in a non-violent manner. Tlinglit oratory is described as a great art form based on the idea that words have the power to heal or harm; thus speeches were used to smooth out, strengthen, and heal the mourner's "inside" (Kan 2009: 295), an idea not too distant from the concepts of many kinds of psychotherapy.

The Tlinglit began such speeches with genealogical lists (not unlike those found in ancient European literature), which had the effect of connecting the speaker's ties with others present, and with culturally ideal typical emotions inherent in such links such as a father's love for his children. Next the speaker presented a story from his clan, of someone in great peril that is saved by some kind of mythical helper (god, animal spirit), with the host's sorrow equated with the hero's suffering, the guest's love with that of the mythical helper. Grief and non-grief are then pictured as opposites, compared with hunger/eating, light/dark, wet/dry, war/peace, and so on, and finally the story is ended with the hero being saved by the mythical helper and the opposites reconciled. Love songs are then recited, bringing in images of reconciliation, fertility, and so forth.

This is but one example among many such rituals that appear to deal directly with the symbolization, enactment, visualization, and concretization of grief and existential dread (among many other things). Anthropologists Robert Jay Lifton and Eric Olson, for example, "believe [the] influence of death on psychological life is due to the importance of symbolization in mental activity rather than to what Freud called a death instinct" (Lifton and Olson 2009: 32). Lifton and Olson draw from Freud and Jung in their conception of the meaning of mourning ritual symbolism and argue that it aims toward "symbolic immortality," expressed in many ways. This sense of symbolic immortality is necessary to normal functioning; without it, everyday living is challenged, as is the capacity to feel at home in the world (Lifton and Olson 2009: 34). These various forms of immortality are expressed through the survival of descendants and tribe members, through the production of cultural expressions such as art and music that survive one's physical body, through self-conscious theological speculation, through communion with Nature—since the processes of Nature carry on independently of humankind's activities and so represent revitalization and renewal, and experiential transcendence through altered states of consciousness: "However it occurs, experiential transcendence involves a sense of timelessness, of which Jung spoke. There does seem to be a universal psychic potential and even need for occasional suspension of ordinary awareness of time" (Lifton and Olson 2009: 37). This observation connects with concepts of social bonding and group identity—without social connection, obligation, structure, and identity, insignificance and despair result, and so part of the function here is to (at least momentarily) provide such things ritually to alleviate those feelings that the lack of them typically engender.

For Lifton and Olson (as with many other scholars of ritual) the ritual becomes *highly analogous to psychotherapy*:

> The process of therapy in psychiatry involves a symbolic reordering analogous to that which occurs in experiential transcendence. When therapy is successful, a patient feels a widening of the space in which he lives. It is as if the narrow images through which he has seen reality have been reorganized so that the past appears more coherent and the future more inviting. Death imagery is reconceived, and life imagery of connection, integrity, and movement becomes dominant.
>
> (Lifton and Olson 2009: 38)

This corresponds to the ever-recurrent linking of death to sexuality, fertility, and to vigorous assertions of continued life among the bereaved. I would add, however, that Lifton and Olson neglect the important effect of focusing the bereaved on the needs of the deceased in deflecting the sting of death as it becomes a restructuring of the relationship between the two in which such transcendence can be shared.

Cross-Cultural Theme: Cultural Beliefs and the Emotional Expression of Mourning

The way participants in mourning rituals express emotion varies widely from dramatic outbursts of vehement emotional expression to self-consciously stoic non-expression. What is universal is that emotion must be dealt with in some manner or another; it cannot be ignored, and each culture over time develops a particular technique or belief system to "sculpt" the raw emotionality of mourning and loss. Several examples will suffice to illustrate the ways in which the emotion of loss is processed, constrained, enhanced, diminished, and/or otherwise transformed via ritual expression.

The relationship between emotion and ritual is complex—it is not a simple matter of one causing the other. In studying various cultures, Metcalf and Huntington (1991) note that ritual weeping is closely and tightly structured within each culture at funeral rites. Many cultures have nearly on-cue weeping, but only at specifically outlined times, such as when the body is in a specific hut, just before the secondary burial, or when specialists recite highly poetic and/or theatrical lamentation performances. Amid all the variation, weeping occurs in carefully specified contexts, and is a symbol with meaning and not necessarily a spontaneous show of emotion that is related to indigenous beliefs (Metcalf and Huntington 1991: 47). Metcalf and Huntington summarize their assessment of the way grief and mourning rituals interact: "It was and is our opinion that the psychic process of grieving only partially intersects with the performance of death rites. As we plainly say, it may be that ritual sometimes aids the process, but it could as easily be no help at all, or even an extra burden to bear" (Metcalf and Huntington 1991: 5).

Among the Northern Cheyenne, grieving and weeping over the dead is expected to end in four days, lest mourners be given "something else to cry about," for death is seen as a release from a life of hard struggle, rewarded with reunion with the departed and a beautiful abode with the Creator god and the culture hero Sweet Medicine (Straus 2009: 75). Here we see, again, that the actions and emotional behaviors of the bereaved are connected to the deceased in a spiritual manner and the bereaved are called upon to *act in a manner which emphasizes the needs of the deceased.* Among the Andaman Islanders studied by A. R. Radcliffe-Brown, weeping has a strong ceremonial character to it that is, in relation to death, confined to certain events, including weeping over the corpse after death, over the bones of the dead man when they are recovered for purposes of second burial, and at the end of the mourning period as joined by those who have not wept yet (Radcliffe-Brown 2009 [1922]: 151). Weeping accompanies other occasions such as the reunion of separated friends, and weddings, and is "obligatory, a matter of duty" (Radcliffe-Brown 2009 [1922]: 154). Here we see that the expression of tears as having important spiritual consequences for the deceased is a powerful cross-culturally resonant idea.

The question of whether or not mourning rituals are merely primitive defenses has been fielded by a number of scholars. Anthropologist Nancy Scheper-Hughes (2009), for example, describes how while the poor of Bom Jesus, Brazil angrily cite extreme poverty, poor and inadequate food, water, medical care, and clothing as reasons for their high infant mortality rate, when a specific infant or very young child dies, there is *not* outrage. The baby is described as an *anjinho* or "little angel," "blameless" and innocent, who is returned to the Blessed Virgin from whence they came. Unlike the proscribed weeping of other rituals discussed, weeping in this instance is forbidden because a mother's tears are believed to make the angel-baby's path to the Blessed Virgin more difficult for him or her (a belief we have seen echoed in numerous cultures). Note again the recurrent theme that links the bereaved emotional expression with the spiritual fate of the deceased. Mothers are expected to be happy their child will be waiting for them in Heaven, free of suffering. But are not these responses merely "defenses" imposed by culture upon the true feelings the bereaved possess but are not "allowed" to express due to cultural imposition? Scheper-Hughes examines such common explanations given for this behavior as "a defense" against mourning and finds them wanting. Rather than unfettered sorrow, mothers express pity for the dead child, and weeping is forbidden, reinforced by a folk belief that for the few hours the infant is in the coffin (i.e. the transitional state), she is neither child nor angel but a spirit-child trying to leave this world to find the next. She must climb a dark path, and tears can make it difficult by dampening their wings or making the road slippery.

Scheper-Hughes argues that explanations of "defense" underestimate the ability of cultural expression and powerful belief systems to influence the mother's grief by identifying that there

> is a presumed binary split between public sentiments and private feelings, between what is cultural and what is "natural" . . . I have no doubt (and have gone great lengths to show) that the local culture is organized to defend women against . . . grief, I assume that the culture is quite successful in doing so . . . One need not speak of "masks" or "disguises" or engage in second-guessing on the basis of alien and imported psychological concepts of the self . . . [such beliefs] projected a very secular view of religious belief as a superficial feature of the interior life, rather than as a powerful force that penetrates and constitutes the person.
>
> (Scheper-Hughes 2009: 188–190)

Another example of how a culture sculpts the emotionality of mourning can be found in the Warramunga. The Warramunga, along with several other Australian tribes, engage in extremely violent rites when a village member dies. "People gouge their faces, slash their thighs, burn their breasts, and attack their friends. Much of this activity is so ferocious that it is not uncommon for mourning to add to the death toll. But the violence is not as random as it appears; on the contrary, it is meted out according to definite rules" (Metcalf and Huntington 1991: 49). Sorrow and anger dominate the scene, both encouraged by and contributing to the chaos, until eventually the din dies down and the bereaved begin to sing together, slowly transforming the scene into a jubilant celebration that emphasizes love conquering death.

To further contrast, Clifford Geertz (1973) describes the funeral ceremonies of the Javanese as "a calm, undemonstrative, almost languid letting go, a brief ritualized relinquishment of a relationship no longer possible" (1973: 72). Geertz observes that in one case when a young girl was caught crying after her father died suddenly, others gently reminded her not to cry because such *tears made it difficult for the deceased to find his path to the grave*. This response corresponds to the Javanese fatalism about death, and the belief that death is felt to be a good state that is devoid of desire and striving (Metcalf and Huntington 1991: 60). Thus it seems the emotionality of death, and the raw feelings it evokes, are often transformed and even partially created or destroyed by the cultural elements in the collective and personal psyche of participants.

Mourning in the West: Historical Examples

A large number of the above themes found in widespread areas can also be found in the ancient cultures of the West. Among medieval European cultures, for example, excessive weeping was believed to cause the deceased extreme discomfort in the next world and would result in the dead visiting the living in anger (LeCouteux 1996: 223)—we saw this idea among the Northern Cheyenne. The idea of the journey to the land of the dead also existed among the ancient Germanic and Celtic tribes of Northern Europe (Cunliffe 1997; Davidson 1968, 1988, 1993; Monaghan 2008; Turville-Petre 1964).

The belief that the newly dead were in an uncanny and dangerous (to the living) state, for example, was extremely widespread:

> a potentially vast number of revenants and ghosts existed: the deceased who sought vengeance or someone to avenge them or that aspired to ritual burial. They were discontented and envious—therefore evildoing dead. These beliefs can be found among all Indo-European peoples.
>
> (LeCouteux 1996: 16)

In both Germanic and Roman folk beliefs, the dead could always return to plague the living if the form of their deaths and the behavior of the living were not pleasing to them—again revisiting the resonant theme of the helpful bereaved, and the perilous state of the newly dead. Historian Claude LeCouteux observes that in European folk practice and lore, those who died in uncanny or sudden ways (women who died in labor, the stillborn, victims of drowning, murder victims, the unbaptized) *inspired the most terror* and ritual action to defend against—this is a theme we have seen before in the above study of Indonesian and Native American practices. Often rituals used to quieten the dead involve decapitation or dismemberment of the corpse, pinning or staking the corpse in place (to prevent it from walking around on its own), or cremation (LeCouteux 1996: 19–31). Additional ritual effort was often made (as in cases cross-culturally) in situations of uncanny or emotionally intense deaths (LeCouteux 1996: 29, n.23). Also prevalent are the themes of the helpful bereaved and a focus on the needs of the deceased.

Other common beliefs that we have seen reported in other cultures appear in European folklore, saga, and folk practice across many centuries (collected by LeCouteux 1996: 32–44) and include the following –

Practices that seek to help the spirit of the deceased in their confused newly dead state:

- The corpse's eyes and mouth had to be closed, in order to prevent the spirit from leaving the corpse prematurely, as this occurred at common orifices.
- The dead body needed to leave the house where death occurred through an unusual opening (like the side of the house) that was rapidly closed up. This was done to confuse the corpse's spirit to keep it from returning.
- The dead were often bound either in a pinned or stitched shroud, or their limbs corded together with various sacred or profane ties to keep the spirit from reanimating the corpse. Stakes were often used to pin the corpse in place.

Practices that seek to soothe the spirit of the deceased and aid their journey to the otherworld:

- Vigils for the recently dead are common, often including singing, games, and dancing.
- Food, tokens, favorite objects, and tools are buried with the corpse; also money, along with slaughtered animals and/or sometimes a slave or spouse ritually killed beforehand, in the case of high-ranking dead. Subsequent dead could be given any forgotten items with the idea that they would be given to those who predeceased them in the next world (LeCouteux 1996: 159).
- Means of transportation, from boats to new shoes, are provided to the corpse to ensure safe travel to the otherworld.

Beliefs that emphasize the occult powers of the deceased, which encourage proper treatment of the corpse with spiritual rewards or punishments (i.e. to restructure the relationship of the bereaved to the deceased):

- Honoring the dead is a duty that brings with it blessings of good harvest, luck in battle, and so on, and maledictions when breached or ignored.
- The dead have power over animals and local vegetation, and local weather patterns.
- The dead can take animal form—often marked by a characteristic color (often gray or red).
- The dead could cause madness in the living if displeased.

Interestingly, despite great effort on part of the clergy, throughout medieval Europe, many of these beliefs and practices surrounding the dead persisted even though they had a markedly "pagan" character to them; that is, they did not usually conform to established priestly dogma concerning the dead. For example, a nineteenth-century Icelandic text describes how to awaken a corpse in order to ask favors of it (described in LeCouteux 1996: 73, n.41), and the ritual involves carving runes on a staff, performing an incantation, as well as warnings as to the dangerousness of this activity, centuries after the Eddas were written down describing this practice as performed by the god Odin. Common syncretistic beliefs emerged that strayed little from the original beliefs, thus demonstrating high degrees of psychological resonance. In Western industrialized nations, of course, such practices and beliefs are encountered very rarely, though they often crop up in spontaneous fantasies and dream material clinically.

Example across Time: Miscarriage

The tenth-century charm "against a miscarriage" is a particularly poignant example of the emotional resonance of these rituals. The charm itself has symbolic actions of superiority over death, statements to that effect, and symbolic actions to that effect, both before and during the pregnancy. Initially, in this charm (Storms 1948: 200), a newly pregnant woman who has already suffered a miscarriage begins fasting and goes to an altar and thanks Christ for the pregnancy. Likely Christ replaced the god Ingunar-Freyr of the Inguaeones to which the Saxons belonged. Afterwards, once certain of the pregnancy, she "puts away" the sorrow of the lost child by taking earth from its grave, wrapping it in black wool and selling it to merchants to sell yet again, thus objectifying the grief and allowing it to disappear, essentially taking it out of her sight and out of mind, and carrying with it the dark spirit and getting it lost (recall the similarity of this practice to the Rwandan method of eliminating depression—giving ritually treated millet to a stranger—in Andrew Solomon's autobiographical account). Finally she must ensure enough milk for her new child by filling her mouth with the milk of a cow of one color—the rarity of such a cow, and the work involved in finding one, certainly contributes to the magical power of such a cow. Then she must go to a running stream and spit out the milk, ladling the "pure" flowing water into the same hand and drinking it which expels the evil spirits (a purification rite). She then speaks the galdor (translated by Storms from the alliterated Old English verse): "Everywhere I carry with me this great powerful strong one, strong because of this great food; such a one I want to have and go home with." Next, the woman must leave the brook "along a different road" so no new evil spirits can enter her, and she must remain silent and not look about—these two especially are psychologically significant to maintain concentration and presumably protect her baby in her imagination. Finally she enters a different house than she came from to further confuse the evil spirits. She arrives, therefore, in a psychologically "pure" state and finally is allowed to eat. All during this last "lactating" part, she is fasting, which will intensify the sensory impression of the milk and water, and finally the food which she eats at the end. The fasting would therefore be more likely to create strong memories. The ritual is clearly finished with the boundary action of eating at a neighbor's house—a reincorporation/reconnection rite. An important theme here is the *ritual enactment of emotional processes*.

Contrast this with the previous example given of grieving described by psychoanalyst Orlandini (2009). Recall that in this case, the psychoanalyst and her patient co-constructed a ritual to help alleviate the grief of a miscarriage. In that ritual, the participant symbolically buried dolls that represented the lost children, along with a letter she wrote to her children. This ritual was followed by a significant reduction in psychological distress and CG. Over a thousand years separate the psychotherapist's patient and the women who practiced the Anglo-Saxon charm "against a miscarriage"; however, we can see numerous similarities, though notably the ancient charm is far more elaborate, containing a great deal more pageantry. As Orlandini's ritual had a powerful effect on her patient's psychiatric symptoms, we can reasonably guess that the ancient charm was also effective in this manner—perhaps even more so.

Death Ways in Modern Nations

Historian Claude LeCouteux argues that many of the above kinds of beliefs and practices about the dead such as the dangerous transitional period, the ability of the dead to affect the land, and the many needs of the dead from the bereaved are eroded by industrialization and disconnection of humans from the land. Such practices typically "exist wherever a human community lives closely connected to nature or withdrawn into itself. The farmer, the mountain-dweller, and the sailor have experienced ghosts and tend to believe in them" (LeCouteux 1996: 226–227). This is no doubt part of the picture. The massive economic, cultural, and technological changes undergirding modern industrial society likely play their part as well. Furthermore we see here how *disconnection* erodes the natural human tendency for Personification, one of the 7Ps that I argue may assist in ritualizing.

It is interesting, however, that in the United States, despite the vast number of cultural backgrounds present, there is remarkable uniformity in the method of death rite, and though exceptions exist, they are rare and limited to small, tight-knit, isolated communities. As ever, we will see that this uniform death rite is ritually impoverished. In the main for Americans, a dying person is sequestered in a sterile environment such as a hospital or nursing home, in which the rest of the bereaved are removed from the dying process. Then, a doctor pronounces a person dead at an agreed-upon time, whereupon the corpse is rapidly removed to a funeral parlor, with embalming, institutionalized "viewing," and disposal by burial or unobserved cremation (Metcalf and Huntington 1991: 194). This commonality of practice exists despite widely disparate cosmology and beliefs about the afterlife, and very commonly no beliefs or extremely vague beliefs are all that are held among participants: "Just how Americans conceive of death [is] a thorny issue. Few seem able to adopt a thoroughgoing agnosticism, and yet the majority seem shaky in their faith in a Christian afterlife" (Metcalf and Huntington 1991: 196). Since afterlife beliefs appear to be such an integral part of what is helpful in the grieving process, as well as the known effect of belief on physiology, this high level of agnosticism is of concern.

Archeologist Timothy Taylor argues furthermore that the sheer level of insulation from death experienced by the typical modern is excessive, unprecedented, and probably unhealthy psychologically (Taylor 2002: 277). "This is a reversal of the common practice in tribal societies, where the care of the corpse is specifically the duty of the nearest relatives and the idea of a stranger being involved would be deeply offensive" (Taylor 2002: 279). While perhaps not going this far, Metcalf and Huntington do observe that:

> In contrast to medieval Europe, the nuclear family in America has been invested with enormous sentiment that was formerly dispersed over a wider group. Yet in a country where "togetherness" is a national fetish, no phase

> of the most severe crisis of the family's existence takes place at home. The oddest feature is that a society that provided harsh living conditions and little chance of mobility for its members stressed a positive role for them in death, whereas a country that emphasizes individual achievement allows only a passive role to the dying.
>
> (Metcalf and Huntington 1991: 208)

This approach to death is not unique to America, and can be observed in the non-identical but heavily overlapping situation observed in other highly industrialized nations, which suggests economic factors are behind it. Traditional Japanese culture, for example (Lock 2009: 103–106), included the beliefs that proper ritual separation of soul and body was necessary at death and that harsh treatment of a corpse is repulsive and disrespectful—beliefs that have survived a considerable amount of Western influence, judging by surveys done in the 1980s which showed the majority of Japanese still performed daily rituals at their homes and at the graves of their deceased parents and grandparents (Lock 2009: 104). Like those in ancient Northern Europe (Davidson 1968) and many other cultures, the Japanese believed that ancestors continued to act in the everyday world, but eventually drifted into the world of nature spirits, forming a connection between spiritual, social, and natural domains. Such a transition from ancestor spirit to nature spirit existed in folk beliefs of the pre-Christian Celts and Germanic peoples of Europe, and archeeologist Timothy Taylor notes that local nature spirits appear in numerous cultures.

There are a number of typical and universal thematic elements in the above. In modern commercialized settings, however, this situation is interpreted differently by participants than in the more rural communities from which it evolved. In older communities, reports anthropologist Hikaru Suzuki (2009), mourning rituals such as washing the corpse were done to ensure the purity of the corpse, and to protect it from the evil spirit *onryo*. In modern settings, however, the ritual is explained by the funeral industry as something far more vague and diluted, designed simply to "bring family members together in the ceremony." Like many cultures, an all-night vigil is carried out with the body, though this practice was dwindling in urban communities when Suzuki originally reported it in 2000. This may be because of the beliefs behind the practice: in rural communities, the vigil was believed essential to protect the deceased's soul from evil spirits from entering the body. In modern urban settings, this belief has dwindled, and the deceased is felt to be "taken care of by professionals." There as here, we seem to have better things to do than tend to the dead. Thus, the absence of beliefs about impurity, death pollution, and evil spirits makes such practices "optional," which typically leads to people opting out of the practice. Thus the example of Japanese mourning rituals provides further evidence, in comparison with old and new, that (again) the role of *helpful bereaved* has eroded completely, giving way to a more passive role for the bereaved, as "experts" take over the process, separating the bereaved from the deceased.

Comparing Cross-Cultural Analysis with the Clinical Study of Mourning and Complicated Grief

Normal mourning and CG are related phenomena. In general, many researchers recognize that CG results from a failure of normal mourning. In other words, CG can be viewed as abnormal mourning, rather than as an unrelated phenomenon. I suggest that inadequate ritualization of the normal mourning process may contribute to the occurrence of CG and that examination of strongly recurrent themes may help us understand what elements of mourning ritual may minimize the development of CG. The clinical manifestations of CG, as outlined by various researchers on the subject (Maercker and Lalor 2012; Simon 2013; Nakajima *et al.* 2012; Alves *et al.* 2014; Eisma *et al.* 2013; Bogensperger and Leuger-Schuster 2014), gravitate around a number of common features. These include preoccupation with the deceased, a paradoxical denial of or refusal to accept the death combined with avoidance of reminders of the death, persistent yearning for the lost loved one, detachment from others, feelings of emptiness or meaninglessness, and inadequate adaptation to the loss. All of these symptoms must persist longer than six months to one year after the death to qualify as CG. Currently the prevalence of CG is estimated to be 4.8 percent for the general United States population, with an incidence of between 8 percent and 25.4 percent among those currently experiencing grief (Simon 2013; Newson *et al.* 2011). Among clinical populations, of course, the rates are much higher.

As usual, much of the presumed potency of ritual acts is likely enhanced by the public nature of such rituals, as they force participants to perform and utter the prescribed actions before an assembly of the like-minded. Like all rituals, these communications reinforce pervasive myths and beliefs, create a sacred space and time, and connect the abstract and ineffable to the concrete and physical, all of which helps to facilitate the transition in the minds of the bereaved in a visceral and material manner, connecting inner feelings with outward objects and materials—for example, the decay of the body signals in an unambiguous way that the deceased has traveled to the otherworld, which is both an event in whatever spiritual dimension believers acknowledge, and also an event intrapsychically in the bereaved. In any case, something sensorily concrete and not generated by the individual is interpreted as a sign from the physical world that the intrapsychic event has occurred. Meanwhile, variably circumscribed expressions of emotion accompany such rituals, providing for either a controlled explosion of emotionality, or a heavily transformed expression of a conspicuous *lack* thereof (which may be entirely the point). Both kinds of practice appear to be capable of actually up- or down-modulating such emotion; the emotion is not seen as primary or secondary. It is simply seen as irreducible.

In any case, it appears throughout the foregoing that Freud's analysis presented a broadly accurate but incomplete picture of the main universal problems arising in grief that we can elaborate upon in clinical practice:

1. A refusal to let the deceased go emotionally and/or fully accept the fact of the person's death.
2. A pronounced tendency to avoid reminders of the reality of the deceased person's death. These first two opposing tendencies create a double-bind which, if left alone, will allow grief to continue indefinitely (a situation analogous if not identical to CG).
3. An inability to "make sense of" the death.
4. An inability to sufficiently modulate the intense emotionality of grief.

These problems have already been recognized as indicators of CG. Of course CG is not a new phenomenon, but probably is as old as humanity itself. Thus, it is unsurprising that cross-culturally, a number of themes in mourning rituals likely evolved over generations to perhaps deal with these problems, as cultural practices that help participants function better may be more likely to be passed on to future generations (Goodwyn 2013) due to resonance. As we have seen, the themes most commonly encountered cross-culturally in mourning rituals include some or all of the following:

1. Provide a cultural container for the raw emotionality of grief that puts it firmly into a culturally defined context.
2. Force acceptance through intense, extended close contact between the deceased and the bereaved.
3. Contain a collection of important tasks for the bereaved to accomplish to help the deceased transition into the next world.
4. Recognize the especially vulnerable state of the bereaved and the community closely following a death.
5. Recognize the even more vulnerable state following a violent/unexpected death.
6. Create a framework to destroy, and then reframe and reorganize the relationship between bereaved and deceased in the minds of the bereaved.
7. Employ methods to physically enact, but also contain and channel emotional expression in culturally specific ways.
8. Employ methods to integrate the death into a coherent narrative that is compatible with surrounding belief systems.

Here is the problem for us: the most commonly encountered death ways in the United States and other industrialized societies *do not have many of the above elements*. US death ways, for example, do not have clearly defined beliefs or traditions that circumscribe and define the "proper" emotional expression of the bereaved. One possible exception to this is the clinical definition of CG itself, which is under continual debate and is primarily limited to healthcare professionals. It should be noted that theme 5 (extraordinary death) *is* a noted and identified risk factor for CG (Simon 2013), but in this case it is not seen as "spiritually dangerous," but rather only more potentially emotionally upsetting. This lack of spiritual interpretation may reduce the overall impact on the bereaved since it goes unaddressed and/or undefined.

Furthermore, while wake traditions bring the bereaved near the deceased for a brief period of time, this amount of time is minuscule compared to other cultures and continues to shrink with industrialization and modernization, as evidenced by the changes occurring among the Japanese. With few exceptions, there are no tasks for the bereaved to accomplish that are believed to help the deceased in the United States, and there is no recognition of any sort of vulnerable state for the deceased or the bereaved that must be addressed ritually. Furthermore violent/unexpected deaths do not receive any sort of special treatment in general. There are moreover very few methods specifically aimed at physically enacting/channeling emotional expression. And as mentioned by Metcalf and Huntington (1991), coherent narrative systems are also commonly lacking or excessively vague, so integration with them is impossible.

Conclusions

What does clinical work tell us regarding these processes and CG? There is some empirical and theoretical work that suggests that the above cultural themes, nearly all of which are integrated into most traditional mourning rituals, have been independently discovered/invented by therapists in an attempt to deal with CG after the fact, rather than preventatively as traditional rituals do. In a widely recognized approach to treating CG, M. Katherine Shear advocates using imaginal and in vivo techniques that involve confronting the deceased and "revisiting" the deceased, as well as various interventions that aim toward redeveloping a psycho-spiritual connection with the deceased (Shear *et al.* 2005). These interventions are clearly variants on the above processes found in many world rituals, including themes 2, 6, and 8 (forcing acceptance, reorganizing relationship with deceased, narrative-forming). Another approach advocates not only confrontation but the establishment of rituals to commemorate the deceased (Wagner *et al.* 2006), in which one can see themes 2, 6, and 7 (forcing acceptance, reorganizing relationship with deceased, and physical enactment of emotion), but with the non-spiritual "commemorate" connotation instead of a spiritual interpretation, such as aiding the dead in their final journey. This is a step in the right direction, but I think the distinction may make a significant difference because commemoration is passive, whereas spiritually motivated ritual involves an intent to act for the deceased's benefit. However, for agnostics it may be a hard sell, so we have to work with what we have.

The concept of "sense-making" has been recognized by some investigators (Nakajima *et al.* 2012), particularly in the case of violent/unexpected death, which addresses themes 5 and 8 (extraordinary death and narrative-forming), though again in a manner that leaves spiritual interpretations undefined or unaddressed. Some investigators (Bogensperger and Leuger-Schuster 2014; Neimeyer 2000) propose that an important aspect of recovery from CG is "meaning reconstruction" and "sense-making" processes, which reflects theme 8 (narrative-forming) and appears to be important for reorganizing the bereaved's relationship with the deceased in a positive manner, which supports the importance of theme 6 (reorganizing relationship with deceased).

Support for the importance of theme 3 (bereaved helping the deceased) is probably the most profound deficit we have in American death ways. Hints at its importance can be found in study of rumination and CG (for example, Eisma *et al.* 2013). In this work, recurrent self-focused negative thinking is commonly identified as a risk factor for CG, presumably because it interrupts problem-solving, blocks instrumental behavior, and drives away social support. The excessively self-absorbed nature of such thinking furthermore can be seen as a way of avoiding painful aspects of the loss. This relentlessly self-focused dwelling on the bereaved's feelings and reasons why the loss occurred increases and perpetuates psychopathic grief responses not only because it distracts from confronting the loss, but also because not doing so makes ruminators feel disloyal to the deceased (Stroebe *et al.* 2007). I argue that theme 3 (bereaved helping the deceased) specifically addresses these concerns and may be a protective factor that can reduce the risk of ruminative thinking because such practices force the bereaved to spend a great deal of time and activity *helping the deceased.* Such ritual acts may assuage the grief because they concretize the emotions and structure the guilt, providing concrete ways in which it can be dealt with. Having provided spiritual services for the deceased, the bereaved can reassure themselves that they have done what has been agreed upon *a priori* by the culture for the deceased and helped them achieve their final destination. It also prevents ruminative avoidance of the reality of the death in the same manner that close proximity does, by occupying the bereaved in continual activity that registers on multiple (self-)communicative channels (Rappaport 1999).

Finally, support for the importance of theme 8 (narrative-forming) may be found in the study of narrative reconstruction in CG (for example, Alves *et al.* 2014). In this framework, the normal transitioning of acute grief to integrated grief is seen as a process of continual self-narrative formation that is interrupted if the bereaved is unable to reconceptualize his or her own life narrative in light of the new death. Since death often temporarily makes the bereaved's self-narrative incoherent and unstable, increased mental resources are required to create a new self-narrative, but in CG this process is interrupted and stagnates, so that the bereaved is in a continually incoherent self-narrative state that allows psychopathology to continue. Alves *et al.* (2014) found empirically that changing self-narrative co-occurred with therapeutic change, supporting the theory. These results suggest that ritual mechanisms aiming toward that end, such as the elaborate integration of the death into established cultural narratives, cosmology, and mythology, may achieve the same results.

These observations raise many concerns regarding the adequacy of American death ways to handle the stress of mourning and help prevent CG. Unfortunately, there are no rigorous cross-cultural studies to my knowledge that compare the rates of CG in cultures that have the above factors incorporated in their death ways. Such studies would be challenging to perform for a variety of logistical and conceptual reasons. Nevertheless, we can see that the most common death rituals are probably inadequate and may contribute to the rates of CG that we have.

These various findings provide preliminary support for the idea that traditional mourning rituals may prevent CG through highly concentrated non-verbal and verbal acts of symbolism, belief, and spirituality. By comparison, the best studied treatment for CG in the United States is a targeted cognitive behavior therapy modality (Wittouck *et al.* 2011) that involves "loss processing and restoration of life without the deceased" (Simon 2013: 420) and hence presumably only addressing themes 2, 8, and possibly 6 (forcing acceptance, narrative-forming, and reorganizing relationship). Such therapies may benefit from the addition of the other themes because they currently lack substantive cultural consensus on the "proper" parameters/boundaries of emotional expression (theme 1), they lack significant tasks for the bereaved to accomplish in the name of the deceased due to their vulnerable/dangerous state (themes 3–5), and they lack non-verbal, symbolic, and/or physical means to enact grief and other emotional or intangible expressions (theme 7). Furthermore the focus is typically non-spiritual and/or spiritually neutral in content, which questionably assumes that an individual's religious/philosophical beliefs can be extracted and treated as a neutral independent variable. This practice may unintentionally cut off the inherent capacity of firmly held spiritual belief to structure life experience and aid in the healing process.

Mental health professionals and pastoral counselors should consider these factors when helping patients who are struggling with mourning. Since the most commonly encountered setting is one where there are no established traditional answers to the above factors, of course, we will find additional difficulties—a legacy of our largely anti-ritual culture. In this case the therapist may benefit from working with their patients to attempt to co-create these factors when addressing CG in a non-invasive manner that honors a patient's personal autonomy. This can be accomplished by gently probing the patient's own intuitions on such issues and working closely together to ritualize the mourning process with the above factors in mind. Whether or not this frankly "reinvention of the wheel" technique will be as good as what can be provided in a more culturally/traditionally rich context remains an open question, but it may help considerably nonetheless.

Clinical Applications

All cultures have developed (with varying degrees of self-awareness) ways to handle the universal problem of mourning. While not all cultures have *all eight* of the above themes in their mourning rituals, many cultures have most of them. In the rapidly expanding world of the modern nation, it is possible that these themes have disappeared simply because the cultural and psychological forces that shaped them originally have not had enough time to "catch up" with the massive cultural changes brought about by the technological and political movements of the last 150 years. Perhaps these factors also explain the shift toward runaway sincerity in our time.

As we saw in the last chapter, there are advantages that ritualism can provide when it comes to role transitions; these advantages also apply to death rituals. In societies with low levels of ritualism, however, I think grief may have more opportunities to grow to pathological proportions. This is due to many factors. First, the creation of semi-permeable boundaries helps the bereaved formulate, express, and accept in resonant terms the new *difference* between the bereaved and the now dead loved one. The liminal period also allows them time to really process their grief and in fact *forces them* to think about it continuously for a time. It allows them to enact these differences in spatial, verbal, and bodily areas, letting them sink into their bones. At the same time, however, these boundaries are transcended but not erased, as the dead who have been incorporated into their final resting place can still communicate with their loved ones. The boundary is not absolute, but it is not non-existent either.

CG and Meaningful Coincidence

> *Death leads to the beautiful question: who died?*
>
> – Poet David Whyte (personal communication, April 2015)

Pathological grief or CG is something I have observed countless times in clinical practice, and involves both extremes of boundary-making. At the same time the bereaved is partially convinced that the loved one is not "really" dead, they are also convinced that the separation between them and the loved one is insurmountable and eternal. Both exist at the same time and create a double-bind. Patients imprisoned by pathological grief navigate this impossible situation by denying the person is dead—by either endlessly ruminating on the past before the death, or by continually insisting that the person is still with them in some mysterious way—often they have uncanny experiences or ghost encounters to corroborate this feeling. The sheer number of times this is reported to me never ceases to amaze—I encourage all therapists to ask their grieving patients if they have uncanny experiences, feel the presence of the dead loved one, and so on. I do *not* recommend worrying about whether or not such experiences are "real"—that is a blind alley. In any case patients are often reluctant to share this information because they do not want to be thought of as "crazy." It is important to normalize this by addressing its commonality (as well as its universality) because we can *use* these experiences to help our patients.

A clinical case is illustrative. Mr. B's mother died one year ago, and he reported to me that he was still experiencing severe grief and anger toward his mother, because she had been "doctor shopping" for addictive sedatives, and she subsequently overdosed and died. While alive, Mr. B had a very close relationship with his mother and they communicated often, and he had warned her against such behavior. After building the appropriate trust, Mr. B confided in me that in the year since she died he had continually experienced uncanny events, such as objects in his house being moved around, or a stack of papers moved from a curio cabinet to the desk when he *knew* he had put them in the cabinet and he lives by himself. He also often woke up in the middle of the night to feel her presence, and his nine-year-old daughter told him that *she* had seen her deceased grandmother and her grandmother had asked for forgiveness. Rather than worry about whether Mr. B and his daughter were psychotic, I explored Mr. B's beliefs concerning the dead, as he (like so many Americans) had a very vague and ill-defined spirituality. In these situations I always ask (1) if the patient believes in life after death and (2) if the deceased can somehow "hear" them. Rare indeed is the patient that says "no" to these questions (I will explain what to do in this case momentarily). Given "yes" answers, the next step is obvious: we explore the narrative that his mother is still alive and is "trying to communicate." Since I know theme 3 is particularly helpful in bereavement, I ask if he thinks his mother "needs his help" getting to heaven, or (at the very least) there is "unfinished business." The theme of needing help traveling to the final location in the otherworld is so resonant it is rare that a patient does not latch on to it. Furthermore, this conversation is much easier since we have already established that the deceased survives death and can hear the bereaved—it is a logical next step to ask, "OK, so what do they need from us?"

Tellingly, Mr. B stated he had avoided attempts at communication because of his anger with her. I then suggested that perhaps she is "sticking around" and haunting his house because she needs him to tell her how he feels. It is important here to encourage the bereaved to imagine the deceased's point of view. After all, no matter how tough loss is, she's dead—and let's face it, that sucks. Put less cheekily, the idea that the dead are traumatized and confused or sad that they have died is nearly universal and highly resonant—it will be easy for patients to latch on to that idea, and help to reconnect them with the deceased. Together, we decided that Mr. B's mother was unable to get to heaven because she felt guilty for making her son angry. Notice how powerful Personification is here—now we have Mr. B interacting with these uncanny events as if it were his mother, which allows for meaning-making. Whether it "really is" her mother is clinically not relevant. From there we co-created a makeshift ritual, to allow Mr. B to express his emotions to her *in order that* she might be allowed to pass on through the liminal phase she is in to her final destination: "heaven," whereupon she can look down upon Mr. B and his family from a place of peace and stop haunting them. In this particular case, the ritual succeeded dramatically. Of course some cases will be more difficult—in these situations, the solution is to continue narrative-making. In other words, co-create an explanation for the failure in the usual terms. If the haunting is not finished, the deceased must still be bound to this world and need more help, more interaction with the bereaved, and so forth.

For agnostics/atheists experiencing such "hauntings," we simply explain that these are very common psychological experiences, and while "scientifically" we cannot prove the existence of ghosts, our primitive emotions and intuitions clearly believe they exist. They are therefore explained as grief-induced dreamlike experiences that need to be addressed through psychological "exercises" (code word for "ritual"). Such exercises consist of treating such experiences as real, imagining the deceased as present, and interacting with them *as if* they were real in order to assuage our grieving unconscious and primitive selves. Some variation on this kind of explanation typically satisfies and allows the bereaved to carry on like a believer would.

An old Irish saying is that when someone dies our relationship with them matures, rather than ends. That the Irish are famous for their extended funerals and their "closeness" to their dead is another testament to the power of ritual in facilitating the transition from acute bereavement to integrated grief. Though the above interventions are no proof against CG, I think they add clinical tools to help in the ongoing quest to help our patients function better.

Further Benefits of Ritualizing

In CG, the bereaved often will fantasize that the deceased is "not really gone," and uncanny haunting experiences that are not handled properly using the above techniques will work only to reinforce this fantasy. But of course this fantasy does not satisfy because simultaneously another part of them is overwhelmed by the stark finality of death and its irreversible consequences, and the rage and grief churn endlessly with nowhere to go. The ritual, by contrast, enforces a separation between living and dead through various undeniable, physical means—participants are forced to acknowledge the separation through their stylized verbalizations, "viewings," and physical actions which cannot be falsified (whether one believes in the efficacy of the action, one nevertheless cannot deny that one has performed them). But at the same time, these rituals allow a continuation of relations with the deceased *as if* they were still alive, but in a different way. Conversations are carried out, caretaking is performed, protection from evil spirits is enacted. The bereaved is allowed to share in the death, and to feel it themselves—the mutual projections are activated. So too the bereaved is required to *help* the deceased journey to their final resting place; the focus is therefore directed away from the bereaved to the plight of the dead. This phenomenon is facilitated by the externalizing bias and lets the bereaved care for a part of themselves through their behavior to the deceased and encourages a reunion of the split-off parts spoken of above.

Which leads to the next benefit enabled by ritualism—its emotionally transformative possibilities. While no ritual can achieve perfection, ritual effects discussed throughout this volume clearly make containers for the raw emotional energies that roar to the forefront for the bereaved, and offer means to externalize them, narrativize them, psychologize them, and symbolize them along multiple verbal and (more importantly) non-verbal channels. Everywhere constraints and rules are placed on the expression and processing of grief and anger, ranging from placid acceptance, to forcefully channeled but intense action, all the while with an over-arching narrative explanation guiding such expression. In all cultures studied, excessive grief is prohibited—importantly *not* usually because it is seen as "morally wrong" (which would likely invite rebellion), but inevitably because it causes harm to the *deceased.* This clever shift of concern is difficult to argue with: because the grief is stimulated by love for the deceased, such practices therefore acquire an acceptable and powerful reason to curtail such feelings. If my grief is an expression of my love, but too much grief hurts my loved one, my love will have to conquer my grief. And of course, this acknowledges that love and grief are two sides of the same coin; grief cannot exist without love. As discussed, ritual can affect physiology through belief, symbol, image, and story, so it is plausible such interventions actually transform the way the primitive affective brain centers responsible for mediating grief and rage behave. Finally, the externalizing tendency of ritual allows one to see overwhelming emotion as something external that has invaded oneself—this allows me to ritually expel it and offers hope of relief.

Contrast these benefits of ritualism with that of the sincerity-dominated anti-ritual society. In this case, all there is to discuss is the sincerely felt grief and rage. Excessive grief cannot harm the deceased, so it is *encouraged* (if unconsciously) in order to show how truly sincere the love was. Since boundaries are left stark or undefined, separation and reconnection on a new level are both nearly impossible for the bereaved. No ritual mechanisms can be utilized to modify unchecked primitive emotions, and separated regions of the psyche are left disconnected from one another. As no resonant narratives are entertained (as these *as-if* constructions are seen as empty, inauthentic, or illusory), no meaning can be attached to the loss, and the bereaved cannot help the deceased—which means they cannot help the projected image of the deceased within them either. As the bereaved cannot help the deceased without the boundary defining and transcending action of ritual, they are left with no reason to constrain their primitive grief, and no opportunity to transform it. It remains endless, meaningless pain and suffering. They are permanently cut off from the deceased, and at the same time they are unable to differentiate themselves from the deceased, whom they have introjected psychologically. They become stuck in the liminal state, unable to transition from the state of being connected to a living loved one to the state of being *connected to a loved one now in another state of existence.* As we saw, many anthropologists are concerned that the modern death ways as practiced are inadequate and insufficient to foster a healthy, human, and non-pathological grieving. I can say from clinical experience: I share this concern.

Part IV

Conclusions

Thus far we have taken a long journey through rituals both ancient and modern, spanning many cultures across the globe, and found that despite the wide distances in space and time, rituals have many similar structures and characteristics, yet each has a rich uniqueness as a cultural expression. We find in this data a way to transcend the universalist vs. particularist dichotomy by realizing that the focus of each is different and contributes to a more complete and holistic understanding of what rituals do and how they do it.

In the final part of this volume, we will look at where new rituals come from and discuss the ritual expert, and how this person is treated in a variety of cultural contexts. Then we will finish by examining in greater depth the stable elements across time and culture, in order to gain a better understanding of ritual mechanisms and effects in the interrelated biological, psychological, and cultural spheres. This will better equip us with ways to help incorporate the power of ritual into clinical work.

Part IV

Conclusions

Chapter 11

The Technology of Ritual and the Ritual Expert

There are no peoples however primitive without religion and magic. Nor are there, it must be added at once, any savage races lacking either in scientific attitude or in science.
– Malinowski (in Bell 2009: 48)

Ancient and Modern Approaches to Medicine

Modern medicine has elements of ritual within it. But cultural beliefs surrounding our medical rituals often focus solely on the mechanistic aspects of treatment, often in the language of neurochemistry or biology. It is clear that in the case of medical treatment, the ritual surrounding the giving of a medical treatment complements the medication; the two work together to create a cure, and in practice it is often difficult to separate the two. And as we saw, even placebo-controlled, double-blind studies, which are the so-called "gold standard" of medical research, have their problems, and we are only now working out the numerous effects rituals have on a person's biological, psychological, and cultural self. Most ancient and/or so-called primitive cultures, however, have no such qualms, and *know* how powerful rituals are. This leaves us with the curious conclusion that though our tool-making technology has advanced considerably over the centuries, it appears that this has come at the cost of our ritual technology.

I say "technology" because rituals are tools like spears and machine guns—they help bring certain situations into being for better or worse, and have a number of effects on many different levels of human interaction and activity. Also like tools, rituals range in their effectiveness from that of the spear to that of the machine gun (and arguably far beyond), and new technologies are being constructed all the time. Ritualizing behavior is apparently a part of the human condition, as are all forms of technology.

Further, like all forms of technology, ritual can be misused, misapplied, and believed in too strongly, as Catherine Bell observes:

> When groups resort to violence to effect [an apocalyptic] new age, it was not uncommon for them to use ritual procedures to make themselves invincible.

> At this point, however, ritual reaches the limit of what it can do. The Papuans who attacked Japanese warships during World War II with nothing more than a few canoes and some wooden guns expected their holy water rituals to make them invulnerable to machine guns; they were wrong. In the same way, many Plains Indians believed that the "ghost shirts" revealed by the dead in the course of the Ghost Dance would render them invulnerable to all weapons.
>
> (Bell 2009: 134)

These are, of course, examples of taking ritual images too literally, a problem that plagues religious thinking in many ways (discussed more in Goodwyn 2012); nevertheless, it is clear that ritualization is a tool used throughout history, and always in creative, and even playful ways by humanity.

Ritual Generation and Transformation

As we look cross-culturally, we can see new rituals emerge from a variety of sources and practices. Particularly resonant dreams, for example, will inspire ritualization and new ritual construction; this has been documented among many Native American tribes, where it has been observed that vivid dreams can quickly "become property of the whole tribe and are surrounded with elaborate rituals, often inspired by the dreams of leading personalities" (Hultkranz 1979: 80). Ritual objects such as sacred poles, hats, arrows, wheels, pipes, and so on, appearing in the dreams are often sacralized by various taboos. One such taboo, echoed in countless cultures, is when an item is forbidden to touch the earth. This effectively suspends the object in air—worldwide symbolically equivalent to the spirit realm. Another taboo often observed is forbidding an object to be looked upon. This has a similar effect, in that it prevents observers from making too literal that which is purported to be divine and transcendent, while at the same time still providing the advantage of concretizing the idea. Items are routinely mythologized by embellishing them with flood or creation myths; examples of these activities come from Kiowa, Omaha, and Arapaho tribes, among others, particularly in (but not limited to) the Great Plains region of North America. New rituals can easily emerge if a few people agree on the existence of certain counterpart connections, include the infusion of magical agency and embed it as the instrumental cause in an event frame (Sørensen 2007a: 187).

Among Native American cultures, levels of specialization in and degree of access to the divine realm vary. In some cultures, all members have access to various magical activities; in others, such activities are largely the purview of specialists, known variously as "shamans" and "medicine men." A spectrum exists, however, in that the medicine man is often merely an expert in skills everyone has to one degree or another, representing differences of degree rather than kind (Hultkrantz 1979: 85). Generally a review of the American religions "illustrates how common and fundamental the shamanic complex is in America. Its absence among some of the marginal peoples in South America is no doubt due to cultural loss, [or] cultural depletion" (Hultkrantz 1979: 87).

By contrast, in agrarian societies, according to Hultkrantz (1979: 146–156), myths serve the same function they do in hunting societies—providing a self-contained symbolic system—but also serve to legitimize the faith and cult of the more collective and organized social structure. Here yearly festivals are conceptually linked to planting/harvesting/rites of passage, and man is seen as originating like a plant and dying back into the ground to the realm of death, all of which coincides with centralizing social structure such as sacral kingship and centralizing temple constructions, with shamanistic medicine men evolving into priests. These practices sometimes subsequently "rub off" on surrounding nomadic hunting cultures, who transform agrarian rain and fertility rites into healing rituals. Alternately, formerly agrarian rites transform into the hunting form when tribes are forced into the hunting lifestyle, as seen in the case of the Algonquin and Sioux Indians when they became hunting tribes for ecological reasons—in this case the previously agricultural Sun Dance became a rite for the duration of buffalo herds. Tellingly, this change in material means corresponded with an increase in individual visions as well (Hultkrantz 1979: 150). An increase in the valuation of individual ecstatic visions is also seen in cultures that are oppressed or when tradition-bound cultures experience hard times—a process analogous to what occurs within the psyche as observed by depth psychologists (Jung 1954); that is, an individual who is imprisoned by rigid attitudes and negative beliefs sometimes has violent eruptions of emotion and dream imagery that remind one of *communitas*, anti-structure, imagistic modes, and millennial rejuvenation.

Hultkrantz has pointed out that while large-scale upper-class mythologies and elaborate priestly systems often develop over a clearly identifiable folk religion, it is ironically the folk religion which, though often heavily influenced by the conquering and subsequently solidifying upper structure, more often survives in the long term when the upper echelons transform or collapse due to large-scale political or martial changes (Hultkrantz 1979: 190–193). In Peru, for example, there existed three strata of (1) conquering state gods, (2) gods of the defeated states and tribes subordinated to the Inca gods, and (3) the folk religion of the masses. Of all these, only "the lowest one has survived to our time. It is relatively unaffected by the political upheavals of the centuries, even if much of its practice today takes place in Catholic guise" (Hultkrantz 1979: 192). We have seen this elsewhere in the histories of the Anglo-Saxons and the Irish. All across the Americas, the favored gods of the common cultivators have survived the coming and going of the priestly civilization and have continued into the modern era, such as in Yucatán, where pagan rain gods mix with Catholic saints, but gods previously associated solely with priests, political hierarchy, and warriors have vanished, a fact likely more to do with socio-economic changes rather than "Christianization."

Religious scholar A. M. Hocart (1998: 149) shows how though Buddhism emerged *c.*500 BCE, and preached that enlightenment was achieved by escaping pain and sorrow by tracing them to their source psychologically and letting go of attachment to them, subsequent generations developed a new ritual tradition that was based on the life of the Master and quickly acquired a more traditional ritual character complete with various deities and rituals. New ritual construction has been observed in many cases, sometimes from dreams of important people, as in the case of "primitive" cultures especially (Lincoln 1935; see also Morgan 1936; Kluckhohn 1998: 318; Haile 1940). The Ghost Dance and Peyote Cult are also examples among many of new ritual systems emerging in historical time. Religious scholar Clyde Kluckhohn puts it this way: "man, as a symbol-using animal, appears to feel the need not only to act but almost equally to give verbal or other symbolic 'reasons' for his acts" (1998: 322).

Catherine Bell observes that constructing new rituals "is not just a modern phenomenon, although the degree to which people now feel free to eschew any claims for ritual antiquity may be relatively unprecedented" (Bell 2009: 225). Bell provides numerous examples of this phenomenon in a variety of modern settings. "There is increased pressure for the invented rite to show that it 'works'; this is what legitimates the rite since there is no tradition to do this" (Bell 2009: 241). Bell reviews a number of theorists who feel the upsurge in new ritual construction in the modern context is a reaction to prevalent Western philosophical (i.e. utilitarian and individualistic) attitudes: "The older conviction that increasing modernization, rational utilitarianism, and individualism would inevitably do away with most forms of traditional ritual life has given way to a heroic championing of ritual as the way to remain human in an increasingly dehumanized world" (Bell 2009: 258). These statements corroborate our earlier concerns about runaway sincerity in a culture. Furthermore, we can see that incorporating ritual into our therapeutic techniques is neither new nor especially unprecedented. It has been coming for a while.

This process of desolation–rejuvenation is not at all new: an excessive tedium effect can create a subjective experience for the practitioners of any given religion, making them feel the world is without meaning—it can foster a sense of alienation and emptiness, leaving one longing for more emotional engagement with life. In this situation the high-sensory pageantry/imagistic mode of religion is very attractive: "Due to the very structure of our cognitive system, the disenchantment of the world . . . is always followed by a re-enchantment, creating new ways of infusing our everyday world with magical agency" (Sørensen 2007a: 191).

Ritual Experts

The functions of the "shamanic complex," meaning ritual/magical/religious specialization and expertise, vary with lifestyle; typically in hunting cultures such functions are available to nearly everyone, whereas in more agricultural and industrialized settings these functions get taken up by specialists. Whether it be accessible to all members or only a few, this complex consists of curing the sick, acquisition of power through innate capacity or from a guardian spirit of some kind (or god), and either visionary capacity (light trance) or ecstatic proclivity (associated with deep trance, spirit journey, and possession).

On the hunting end of the spectrum, even when all members are considered to have access to the divine realms, ritual experts exist who are simply viewed as superlative members when it comes to magic/religious knowledge. In these cases, the ritual expert relies on spontaneous expressions of the psyche such as dreams or visions, or a relatively informal training by an elder ritual expert. For example, while dreams inspire the techniques proper to the medicine man, as in the case of Mohave magicians, "as a rule in both North and South America the medicine man receives his training from an older, experienced colleague or in a sort of school for medicine men . . . where the novices by asceticism and the drinking of tobacco juice evoke hallucinations of the supernatural powers" (Hultkrantz 1979: 96).

Hultkrantz observes that in the myriad cultures reviewed in North America, there is a clear and gradual transition from the spontaneous visionary expressions of the medicine man to the dogmatic and performative expressions of the priest, generally following the transition from hunter to cultivator society—this pattern holds cross-culturally in general (Hultkrantz 1979: 126). Cognitive scientist Gilbert Lewis agrees, and observes that:

> the general effect of the priest in his role as religious specialist [is] an increasing rationalization of religion, the justification of doctrine, the ironing out of contradictions, and the making of coherence . . . In matters of doctrine, claims to have authority turn on access to sacred texts, an original myth or charter, secret knowledge, or special qualification.
>
> (Lewis 2004: 168)

Ritual experts can have a powerful influence on a culture overall. Hultkrantz observes that among the American Indians a large number of spirit beings can be traced to the visions of medicine men, and these spontaneous elements are more highly valued in hunter–gatherer cultures than among cultivators (Hultkrantz 1979: 143). Hence as we travel from individualistic hunter society to collective cultivating society, the religious climate shifts from one of the primarily more imagistic and spontaneous experiences available to everyone, with some members seen as especially gifted and sometimes loosely referred to as "shamanistic," to a more dogmatic and performative experience in which only a select few are seen as having true access to the divine sphere. We have seen this pattern before in the observations of Mary Douglas (1996), who linked religious changes to changes in increasing grid and group characteristics. Here, however, it appears to also be linked to the type of subsistence strategy involved (which may, of course, indirectly or directly affect grid and group, and/or vice versa).

In any case, as the collective comes to dominate, we see the gradual emergence of the formation of clan fetishism, totemism, and secret societies, and a downplaying of individual vision/dream experience. The ecstatic "shaman" gradually transforms into a person who relies more on initiation and knowledge than on direct experience of the supernatural; gradually the miracle worker is replaced by the priest (Douglas 1996: 145). As Mary Douglas (1996) and Catherine Bell (2009) have observed, modern urban American society is associated with the low grid and group setting that is normally associated with an individualistic attitude toward ritualism and ritual expertise. Hence, to me it appears that the modern urban American society is religiously becoming more akin to the ancient hunting society—but only in some ways, for as Seligman *et al.* (2008) have noted, the sincerity mode has likely never been quite so dominant. Given the widespread anti-ritualism in the face of a breakdown of collective constructions, we appear to be in the midst of a transition to a place where hunting-society spirituality may become the norm. Moreover, this observation may help to explain the increasing popularity of various neo-pagan traditions as well as various "New Age" styles of spirituality that emphasize trance techniques, imagistic expression, and so forth. Whether these spiritualities will be replaced yet again in the setting of continual reform advocated by runaway sincerity modes is difficult to say—I will explore what I see as the possible courses in the final chapter.

For now, what many of these various "new" movements (new being a relative term) share is an increasing value placed upon spiritual beliefs and ritualized behavior. These movements, however, are not yet the norm, and only time will tell if they will coalesce over time into something more permanent, or if the endless quest for greater sincerity will continue to push eternal reform and casting away of even only slightly older structures. Ultimately, I hope that introducing the study of ritual into therapy will help us both understand the mental health practitioner as a new iteration on an old thing—the ritual expert—and help us to be more conscious of how to craft new rituals. As Bell (2009: 225) pointed out, creating new rituals is not novel; what is different about the modern construction of new rituals is the relaxation of the need to justify their performance "since time immemorial" with a made-up back story—this has been the typical way of accomplishing new ritual formation in an attempt to provide it with legitimacy.

For now, mental health practitioners are not the ritual experts of our time. Though physicians and other mental health professionals go through a lot of formal training to heal the mentally ill, the particularly ritualistic/spiritual dimension of healing is left out of medical training or is minimal in comparison. That leaves this dimension of healing to be performed by others. Given the wealth of evidence reviewed in this book, however, we can conclude that it is probably a mistake to leave this technology out of mental health training. Mental health practitioners can and should receive better training in the effects of spirituality and ritual because they work and are important.

We can and should justify this with the long tradition of empirical research from the biological, the psychological, and the cultural spheres reviewed here. When this occurs, the source of legitimacy in new ritual formation does not *require* a made-up back story and tradition that supposedly existed "since time immemorial," because the collective element of the psyche *itself* becomes the source of legitimacy. This happens when we recognize that given the phenomenon of psychological resonance, the dichotomy of "old" vs. "new" is a false one. Creating a new ritual using themes that are intensely resonant is, in effect, performing something which has been done "since time immemorial"—it's just not in as literal a sense. But it does draw upon the timeless and universally emergent structures of the human psyche.

Ritualism in Therapy

We have so far discussed how ritualism in mental health settings can provide additional tools for us to help our patients improve their lives. Through the unique characteristics of ritual, we have seen how to use objects, indexical enactment, the 7Ps, and many other factors to strengthen the ego, create permeable boundaries and structure, and many other things. We have seen how ritualism can help create meaning and a sense of the sacred, build narrative, and help with difficult life transitions, including bereavement. But there are other common challenges ritualism can help with as well.

Low Self-Esteem

In clinical populations, who doesn't have it? Its commonality is only exceeded by its common intractability. The typically encountered scenario is patients with chronically low self-esteem or worse, self-hatred, with its concomitant self-injuring behavior. Note how our sincerity-based therapies typically handle this problem. In cognitive-based therapies, for example, we are instructed to seek out negative core beliefs such as "I am a bad person/parent/child/sibling" so we can challenge their rationality. In other forms of therapy, we seek out the "source" of poor self-esteem, usually settling upon a past trauma of some kind. We offer lots of understanding, acceptance, and (hopefully Platonic) love.

These are good starts, but I think we can do more. Our sincerity-based answer to these problems is naturally more love, more acceptance, and more soul-searching for one's "true self." Alternately, in cognitive settings, the answer is more thinking, challenging of beliefs for their "truth value"—i.e. the same advice but from the rational angle that seeks the One Truth in the sincerity mode. Neither of these approaches is wrong. But by themselves, I believe they are incomplete.

Ritualizing adds what is missing through its focus on three important actions: *physical action*, *participation in something greater than oneself*, and *resolving ambiguities*. This is accomplished with ritualized communication to self and other. It means constructing non-ambiguous definitions and distinctions, and creating structure. Thus, *in addition to* challenging false beliefs, offering unquestioned acceptance and seeking out narrative traumas, we should ask our patients: "OK, so you believe you are a bad person, tell me what a *good* person does?" Note I said "does," not "is." The question "what is a good person?" invites overly analytical, intellectualizing, or abstract conversations that are not likely to yield much clinically. Instead ask "what does a good person *do*?" Very often our patients are troubled with low self-esteem because their idea of "good person" is so vague, and plagued with a sincerity-based obsession with plumbing the eternal depths of this mystery. Telling this person to continually "look within" for the answer is likely to be an endless exercise.

Instead, force the patient to spell out what good people/parents/friends/siblings actually *do*. Usually this will result in a list of activities that involve helping others—recall that identity is contributed in no small measure by our obligations to others. Do not be distracted by vague responses: "taking care of one's family members," for example. What does that entail? What specific deeds qualify? When, where, and how often? A single parent who doubts his ability to raise his little girl, for example, will benefit from the questions: what is a "good parent" supposed to do, then? Bathe her nightly? Ensure she has a meal every night? Take her to visit her grandparents once a month? If the answer to these questions is "I don't know," the natural response is "then how do you know you're not good enough?" and "how can we find out what *actions* are required? What sources do you trust?" In settings of low grid and group, these questions will be tough and require work and time, but they will be worth it. Without concretizing the feeling into physical acts, however, patients remain in ambiguity and doubt, and they may even experience role confusion. The physical enactment of "parental" things, however, will strengthen this person's role and help to create identity and resolve ambiguity of boundaries—especially when they are done *with this goal consciously in mind*. That is because when it is a self-consciously intentional act, it becomes more ritualistic through its "set apart" (i.e. sacred) nature.

The inclusion of ritualizing will moreover give both patient and therapist a list of concrete acts that one can build a sense of self-esteem from. Often, simply creating such a list can be helpful, as the patient will already be doing these things. From then on, every time they do them they will be communicating to themselves and others "this is what a good person does." It *imbues* the act with ritual significance, putting psychological ego-strengthening power into something as simple as going to bed at a reasonable hour, resisting the temptation to smoke, paying one's child support on time, or who knows what else.

It has another advantage: it makes patients ask how much is *enough*. Commonly patients feel low self-esteem because they think whatever they are doing is never enough. Obviously telling them over and over that they are loved and accepted will not help this situation. Nor will pointing out just how irrational they are being. No, *definition* and *physically enacted action* is what is needed. They need to know what is required, and they need to know how much is not enough and how much is too much. Those raised in ritualistic settings have a major advantage in this area, because all these "rules" are already internalized. They go unspoken and are never questioned. Those from settings of runaway sincerity, however, learn to "question everything" and endlessly search for the Truly Authentic. Such a search is certainly worthwhile, but it should be balanced when possible—you have to start somewhere knowing how to be and what to do, otherwise you are just lost. In most cases, when you ask a patient, "how much is enough?" you will be met with a blank stare; that is because in a setting of runaway sincerity, all many hear is "look inside yourself." But if that advice yields only more confusion and doubt, we cannot simply say "look inside yourself *harder*!" No, at some point, reference to something *outside* oneself is needed, whether it is a philosophy of living, an ethnic tradition, a religious belief system, a resonant myth outside a particular religion, a community of trusted others, or (most often) simply a trusted parent/grandparent/mentor. Even a patient's dreams can be used in this manner. Some patients use divination methods—a ritual tradition with millennia of history which I did not have space to explore in this volume. The common theme is that it is OK to go outside oneself for reassurance and/or confirmation. One should never underestimate the power of finding outside support.

In a setting of high grid and group, all these rules for correct conduct are already laid out in advance, and everyone in such settings absorbs them as they grow up, never needing to question them. This is the advantage they gain by being comparatively more rigid and "judgmental." In those cases, role confusion, chronic self-doubt, guilt, and/or paralyzing ambiguity are much less likely. It is a trade-off. In the setting of runaway sincerity, however, all such rules of conduct are considered suspect, tyrannical, and in need of constant reform and analysis. Therefore they tend not to last and are not available, making the therapist's job more challenging.

Chapter 12

Summary

According to anthropologist Clifford Geertz, rituals apply meaning to life and calm "deep disquiet," as well as allow us to attach emotions to symbols and manipulate them in space. Thus far we have seen how this is done by connecting emotion, spirituality, culture, and biology. Moreover, myths and rituals have recurrent motifs, which often can be thought of as originating from the collective element of many psyches, where culture and neurobiology combine in reliably emergent ways to create resonant expressions. In this final chapter, we will look at all the branches of our dynamic interdisciplinary model of ritual, to highlight its main points and review its most important elements. Hopefully from this the reader will have a host of new tools from which to draw in order to co-create a more balanced and fulfilling life for her/his patients.

Biological

From the biological branch we have it *that imagery, drumming, dancing, chanting, fasting, sleep deprivation, and ritual ordeals* can reduce pain, improve autonomic nervous system balance, improve immune activity, and all tend to increase right-brain holistic, associative, and participatory processing. Rituals use myths—sequences of resonant images—in order to enact and live them in a physical manner. Rituals can affect the physiology of the brain, immune system, cardiovascular system, respiratory system, gastrointestinal tract, and skin, and it appears that these effects are accomplished through vivid imagery, color, resonance, narrative, belief, touch, eye-gaze, and intrapsychic elements such as complexes.

Cognitive

Ritual is significantly influenced by universal mental tendencies and can influence the way a person constructs his/her mental world. Humans are universally equipped with biases in ritual construction and tend to create rituals along some lines over others, with "rules" about how they should work, the order things should proceed in, roles that participants should play, and where points of variability are allowed. Thus we all come with some basic intuitions about rituals already within us.

Psychologically resonant images used in ritual are the "stickiest" images because they fit easily into these universal mental proclivities. Such images and story themes are resistant to change, are transmitted easily, and are more likely to be used in ritual. Our interdisciplinary model predicts that the most resonant images will have a number of characteristics: they are predicted to be *sensually vivid, minimally counter-intuitive, emotionally evocative, tend toward extremes, be atemporal, use mid-level categories, describe simple characters with simple motives, have strongly rhythmic and prosodic elements, contain simple plots and reversals of fortune, and foster a sense of interconnectedness in their events*. Because of their resonance, I hypothesize that resonant images as described above are more likely to be able to affect physiology, be used to act out in ritual, and generate placebo effects.

Rituals are important because of their effects on *memory* and the organizing effect memory has on the mind—particularly the developing self or ego. Rituals achieve high memorability via either *high sensory pageantry* or *high repetition*. Repetition risks the tedium effect and pageantry risks sensory overload and diminishing return. Hence ritual expression can be imagistic or doctrinal. The imagistic mode will tend to use psychologically resonant expressions, use spontaneous emotionality and imagination, and be highly creative and intensely affective—all of these qualities contribute to such rituals' resilience and memorability, and hence long-lasting effect on participants. But ritual expression can also be doctrinal, achieving its long-lasting impression through rote memorization and repetition. Most ritual systems have a dynamic interplay between these modes, but sometimes imagistic expression can cause splinter groups in ritual expression, and these often later solidify into more doctrinal modes or they burn out from sensory overload and diminishing returns, both of which are constrained by universal emotional processes.

Rituals are generally constrained by universal cognitive processes such as intuitive physics, folk biology, concepts of *mentality*, essentialism, an equation of origins with essence, image schemata, force dynamics, force = effort equivalencies, origin = essence equivalencies, conceptual blending, and use iconic and *indexical symbolism* over purely semantic symbolism. Moreover, ritual language favors non-linguistic use of verbal behavior. The more resistant to explanation a ritual is, the more effective it will be deemed. Explanations in particular will favor gods, spirits, and so on, particularly when phenomena are complex, unpredictable, dramatic, causally mysterious, and appear purposeful. This explains the power of *personification* to organize and coordinate connection between the divine/idea/abstract and the visceral/biological/personal.

Psychodynamic

Images link to deeply emotional, embodied, and non-verbal aspects of the mind. Ritual connects the sublime, the divine, and the pure with the physical, the visceral, and the emotional, idealizing the base and low while materializing the ideal through images and non-verbal expression. Projection and *projective identification* are likely occur to a significant extent in ritual, in an instrumental manner which connects the intrapsychic contents with others and with material ends. Such projections can be processed and manipulated through ritual.

Narrative is tightly associated with a coherent and focused self and is not only used in ritual, but is *created by* ritual in physical space and embodied action. Greater focus and functionality (to whatever ends) is associated with more coherent internal states, and narrative is a part of this because greater functioning is associated with a greater ability to switch points of view in narrative, a more persuasive narrative, and a more organized narrative. Explanation of suffering leads to relief because it connects us with the collective understanding of something or fosters trust in the universe—suffering is explainable, hence the gods allow it. Explanations justify what has occurred and reassure us that though the world may be painful, it is nevertheless understandable. Ritual uses narrative to achieve all these ends, and enacts them out in space and action to create new narrative in real time. Ritual often fosters a heightened sense of *meaningful coincidence* which also brings narrative ideas into concrete physical reality, again connecting the ideal with the visceral. A heightened sense of meaningful coincidence subsequently can lead to better mood and vitality, an ability to notice mundane coincidences, and increased intuition and engagement with life. Ritual facilitates all these things.

Life and trauma tend to dissociate the individual mind, which is prone to it, and rituals reconnect the mind, particularly in rituals involving altered states of consciousness, and so ritual reassociates through the process of *decentering and reorganization*, fostering a greater sense of unity, better overall mood, heightened sense of sacredness, better insight, paradoxicality, ineffability, positive attitude, a greater sense of personal power, theory of mind, appreciation of music and sexuality, and greater use of symbolic activity.

Cultural

Arnold van Gennep has observed a tripartite structure in ritual, highlighting the way rituals transition participants from clearly defined roles and states using vivid imagery, symbolism, and physical action. Rituals have a (at least near-)universal *separation–liminality–reincorporation structure*.

Roy Rappaport showed how ritual negates the universal drawbacks of complex symbolic communicative ability: deception and alternative. Rituals establish convention, seal social contracts, construct and frame time and Eternity, represent (re-)creation, create a sense of the sacred (which they then refer to), evoke a sense of the numinous and awareness of the divine, make ordered meaning, and transcend semantic meaning. Rituals are communicative acts to self and others, made obviously so by their odd posture/language use. Rappaport furthermore shows how ritual resolves social, physical, and mental ambiguities into strict either/or states—thereby creating information and order from chaos. They connect participants and undeniably reinforce the mythic canon associated with them. They take abstract, ineffable subjectivities and blend them with material objects, making them concrete and sensual, and impose recurrence on non-recurrent processes, thereby structuring time and creating a sense of Eternity. Rituals connect intrapsychic parts as well as the psyches of participants.

Mary Douglas shows how ritual is connected to *grid and group*: high grid and group cultures and subcultures have a high degree of formal ritualism, a wariness of altered states of consciousness, a strong sense of personal identity, and coherent explanations for suffering. Low grid and group entities eschew formal ritualism for spontaneous expressions, encourage altered states, emphasize the individual over the group, have poorly defined senses of identity, and vague or ambivalent explanations for suffering. High group is associated largely with ritual expression of group membership, mutual obligation, and a clear in/out boundary. Low group is associated with ritual expression of lack of obligation and valorized individualism. High grid is associated with ritual expression of role and trust in hierarchy, whereas low grid is associated with ritual expression of rebelliousness, universal equality, and anti-structure. Ritual contributes to and reflects these cultural states.

The risks of high grid and group include disillusionment with ritual forms and resentment of structure, which can be stultifying, excessive paranoia over group loyalty (accusations of "witchcraft" or equivalent), over-involvement of members, and excessive obligation, whereas the risks of low grid and group include alienation, rootlessness, poor sense of identity, anomie, and lack of narrative tools to explain suffering. *Rituals are used to create, reflect, change, and express these cultural states*. Ideally, I think, the human soul needs a balance of all these elements to avoid these risks.

Victor Turner describes the mental state of *communitas* associated with liminality, both in transitional and in extended states. States of *communitas*, for Turner, emphasize the triumph of Nature over culture, of the unkempt over the kempt, of the paradisiacal future Utopia over the Eternal Order, and are typically rejuvenating but incapable of long-term stability on their own. States of *communitas* are liberating and emotionally satisfying, but unsustainable without some kind of reinforcing structure. Furthermore, Turner observes how rituals play out or instantiate various intracultural and intrapsychic forces and conflicts, as if to make them more concrete or to channel them into one type of structure over another. These psychological forces and internal pressures and conflicts manifest themselves as the collective elements acting in concert to push people into roles in the public arena, providing praxis for them as "ritual dramas." Thus ritual dramas create the narratives of nations.

Catherine Bell observes that rituals do all the above things, and moreover have a number of structural properties cross-culturally. Hence Bell's analysis gives us clues as to *how* rituals do the above. These include *formalism, traditionalism, invariance, the use of sacral symbolism, and an emphasis on the performative aspect*; the performative aspect in particular allows ritual to constellate all the intrapsychic and intracultural forces into embodied action in physical space.

Ritual Modes

Looking over the various types of rituals, their functions, modes, methods, and purposes, produces several lines of parallels and similarity that can be represented in a table which correlates the biological, cognitive, psychodynamic, and cultural commonalities.

Anti-Structure	*Structure*
The imagistic mode	The doctrinal mode
Low grid, low group	High grid, high group
Spontaneously/emotionally driven	Deliberatively/analytically driven
Communitas	Clearly defined social structure
Liminality	Well-characterized social/mental status

The strengths and functions of anti-structure and structure in ritual are as follows:

Anti-structure	*Structure*
Destroys empty forms and rigidity	Creates order from chaos
Refreshes emotionality and meaning	Reinforces pragmatic ability and organized function
Universalizing/frees from obligation	Creates identity through obligation and belonging
Connects with utopian future	Connects with divine past, dream time, Eternal
Provides utopian vision of the ideal world	Provides explanation for suffering and remedies
Frees from oppressive hierarchies	Provides roles, rules, and stable predictability
Images of fertilizing death	Images of creation and rebirth
Imagery of Nature overwhelming culture	Imagery of culture taming Nature

It can be a helpful simplification to visualize your patients along these axes, in order to see what type and kind of ritual may be useful for therapy interventions. When it comes to types of ritual and modes of ritual behavior, it seems that half of the human heart wants structure, whereas the other half wants *communitas* and anti-structure, and these two forces dance back and forth in varying ways depending on particular cultural settings, either in an endless ping-pong of splinter group separations, followed by petrification, or in more stable dynamic balance over centuries.

Participation

The common theme in all branches of ritual study reviewed here, however, is *participation*. Participation is a special state of mind fostered and perhaps partially created by ritualized behavior. It emphasizes connections, connecting the ritual practitioner with other practitioners, with tribe, with the Eternal, with the Divine, with the universe, with all humankind, with animals, with Nature, and with all the parts of oneself.

From the biological branch we see that ritual connects participants by way of shared imagery, which as we have seen can alter physiology. Biogenetic structuralism proposes that the drumming, dancing, and synchronized, stylized movements along with other techniques shift processing to the more participatory style of the right brain, and so participants come to share in the same physiology to a certain degree. Even solitary rituals can put one into a participatory frame of mind –participating in collective element contents like narratives and gods which come from many minds operating over long periods and wide areas.

From the cognitive branch, we see that such contents of the collective element are both absorbed and self-generated during development in the practitioner's mind. Such contents will fall into resonant patterns and give rise to recurrent motifs found in rituals all over the world. Since these elements are so much more collective than personal, they enhance the participatory mode of thought by de-emphasizing the personal element (another way of looking at the decentering effect). Resonant stories *feel* like they come from "somewhere else," because they are so collective, and hence amplify the participatory mode. The collective elements are dominant in participants, further emphasizing the participatory style of thinking, because everyone seems to be "on the same wavelength."

From the psychodynamic branch, the phenomenon of projection—seen not just as a defense but as a natural mode of human thought and behavior—allows ideas, emotions, and aspects of the self to be concretized as material symbols. These symbols will be either other participants or ritual objects and places. Projecting aspects of the self into these is a type of participation that reflects back at the participant during ritual and allows him/her to manipulate aspects of the mind along non-verbal, imagistic, and emotional channels through physical action in space. The participatory mode is essential for this process to work, as projection is a type of participation. Projective identification is an even more powerful type of projection that requires and/or evokes an even more profound sense of participation, as it stimulates another person's mind to identify with the projection. Projective identification is likely a major component of the events Turner has observed concerning ritual drama. The aspects of narrative, synchronicity, and dissociation also utilize participatory thinking to varying degrees. Narrative aligns participants with resonant and hence collective stories, deepening participation by evoking a sense that one is living a shared life experience with something greater than oneself. Synchronicity strengthens this process through participatory thinking, allowing one to feel one is part of a story being told by the mysterious purposeful powers that shape events. Dissociation and reassociation require participation as well; pathological participation links one with one's traumatizer, with a specific event in the past they cannot escape, or with worries about an imagined future. Functional participation is required to heal these fractures by bringing the dissociated mind back together with all one's other parts, and with one's surrounding culture, time, and environment.

Finally, all the cultural data we have reviewed point to a strong participatory mode of thought in ritual by connecting participants with not only other aspects of themselves but with other participants in a culture. Ritual reinforces grid and group structure within a culture when it exists. In low grid and group, the individual is primary, and so ritual aims to connect participants with ideas of universal love, equality, and the entire world, or with the divine realm, which is elevated far beyond the material world. Spontaneous ritual dramas, likely utilizing projective identification on a massive scale, connect cultures in turmoil and transition, but it is likely that projective identification is a part of all ritual activity.

Hence, participation is a key element of human thought processing that is heightened and perhaps maximized by ritual techniques. It is connective on levels other kinds of activity cannot be, because it allows practitioners to participate in non-verbal, physical, emotional, and symbolic channels of connection and embodied action. In this manner it connects the spiritual to the material.

A Dynamic Interdisciplinary Road Map for the Ego and the Collective Element

The foregoing is a lot to absorb. It is evident that ritual is a fundamental and powerful method of ordering human experience in a huge variety of ways. How can we put this all together into some sort of unifying framework that will help us know how and when to use ritualism in clinical work? Consider the following story. Let us say I am a member of a subculture which is going through some sort of upheaval. Old ways are seen all around me as desiccated, stifling, and oppressive. I feel they are empty and rote for whatever reason. Let us furthermore consider my mind to consist of two primary elements: my personal ego and the collective element. My personal ego will be composed mainly of my own personal narrative, my system of values, and my identity, which is the collection of obligations and relations I have to others in my community: i.e. my many roles and ranks. The collective element is something I experience directly but cannot honestly attribute to myself, as it is derived from universal emotional and cognitive elements as well as multi-generational constructs. Both of these aspects of the collective element generate resonant narratives either spontaneously or through reliable cultural transmission. Furthermore, since they are resonant, they are hard to get out of my head. Thus the collective element I experience is something I did not create, but yet provides my ego with the raw materials of which I am made. It is like the root structure of the aspen grove: from this structure come countless aspen trees. These trees (the ego) live and die, but the roots live on, sometimes for tens of thousands of years. We see here that the ego is only partially separable from the collective element. It is partially overlapping. In any case, my ego then has the choice to accept this content from the collective element, reject it, modify it, or what have you.

Because I feel empty and that the current system is not working, I plunge into the collective element. I am in a cultural situation of crumbling grid and group because of the upheaval. I am in a time of millennial, utopian visions, of *communitas*, of liminality, of the imagistic mode and anti-structure. I am drawn strongly to the sincerity mode that seeks the "real" truth and the authentic feeling I have been craving. Thus my descent into the collective element continues. From that place I am visited by an upsurge of new ritual forms, new resonant narratives (either from the past newly engaged, or from spontaneous dreams or undirected fantasy), and I see resonant characters (heroes, gods, spirits) in a new light, or a powerful and impressive vision or dream emerges.

From here there are three possible cases. In case 1, I live in an environment of runaway sincerity. In this case, I will reject these new ritual forms not long after I experience them. Thinking them mere illusion or wishful fantasy, I will continue to plunge "deeper" into the collective element to slake my thirst for new meaning and even *more* authentic feeling. And in this endless loop I will stay indefinitely, with all the many pitfalls that entails. In case 2, I will be drawn to the initially new ritual forms. I will play with them and create new rituals. I will find like-minded people who share in my vision, or maybe even follow me, and together we will carefully draw more from the collective element to expand this raw material into a new ritual system. In this case I am drawn into a dogmatic mode, seeking to systematize and create a strong, coherent structure. I seek beauty, symmetry, completeness, and non-contradiction. I seek identity, role, and hierarchy, to fill my ego with a new identity using these newly created ritual forms. Here I drift toward the Eternal, toward a union of heaven and earth, and toward a stable, long-lasting structure. Here I may stay for generations, gradually drifting away from the original upsurge of collective emotional creation (whether for economic/environmental reasons or simply religious drift) until eventually the new forms become old forms, and the original surge of vitality and imagistic ecstasy desiccates and becomes a rigid structure unable to withstand the tedium effect. This leads me back to where I started, resulting in either a collapse of the new-old form, or in the creation of an imagistic splinter group. Alternately this second case can be smashed to pieces by radical ecological/economic changes, forcing me to seek out new ritual forms to recreate myself through a return to the wellspring of the collective element. Hence I return to where I started also. The final possibility for case 2 is that I find a way in the new solidifying structure to allow—in a controlled fashion—a return to the liminal, the imagistic, the sincere, the emotional uprush and incorporate it *into* the larger structure. This is truly the most stable possibility over centuries. This periodic dip into the collective element rejuvenates the old forms, giving them new life and brightening them with revitalized meaning. Finally is case 3. Here I create just enough nominal structure to maintain a minimal degree of longevity, all the while staying close to the anti-structure, the low grid/group, and the imagistic. Because of the chaotic nature of this case, countless "denominations" will constantly emerge, and no cohering framework will ever arise, as very little effort is put into this part of the process. Thus I will end up a member of a relatively small collection of participants with numerous low grid/group ways of being that will continually differentiate, held together very loosely by (endlessly reinterpreted) sacred texts or a loosely conceptualized "tradition." I will remain one step above the situation of runaway sincerity, but I will remain close to the wellspring of life and spontaneous fertile chaos, and my craving for meaning (if not long-term stability) will be satisfied, though in a far-off, utopian way that values the spirit far above the material world. I will remain in a liminal state of *communitas* indefinitely (though this is difficult to sustain for long periods of time due to burnout). This stable-instability will continue until I feel the draw of the Eternal and the desire to enspirit the world, which will pull me toward the dogmatic structural mode, leading to case 2. If this does not happen, I may become disillusioned with the chaos and drift back to case 1.

What Rituals Do: Cultural, Psychological, Biological

Depending on what kind of ritual structure I now have in my hands, and which path among the above cases I traverse, the ritual system itself is the central creative piece of the puzzle. Though it derives from the collective element, it requires egos to use this raw energy to craft it into some kind of ritual structure. From here the ritual system that is crafted will subsequently *create* grid, group, and social structure through its forms, to whatever level it can. These things I have helped make will then feed back into my psychology, as I will absorb both grid and group into my ego to help me form an identity. In conditions of low grid and group, this effect will be minimal. In conditions of runaway sincerity, it will barely exist at all. Sacred narratives I will incorporate into my own narrative, further altering my own ego definition. Value systems will be created by ritual also, along all the channels discussed so far, and these I will incorporate into my ego also. The ritual efficacy, however, goes even deeper than that. The rituals I use will be able to alter my very bodily function. The physiological behavior of my brain, my immune system, my cardiovascular and digestive system, and even my skin can be affected by this new ritual system. Everything about me is affected, and will continue to be affected as long as I continue to choose to participate in this ritual system. As I feed back into the powerful collective element I encounter the home of the gods themselves, from which the dangerous and powerful fertile chaos of creation emerges, to be subsequently "captured" and channeled to whatever degree the ritual system is able. Both demon and saint dwell in this collective element. Both shattering emotional turmoil as well as sublime genius of the heavens emerges from here. I must treat it with care and seriousness, for even my beliefs can affect their own outcome.

Rituals can alter my role in a culture by changing the way everyone looks at me and the way I look at myself. My own ego structure (narrative, value system, and identity) can be drastically changed by this new ritual system. The disparate parts of my ego—the emotional, the spiritual, the intellectual—can be tied together through ritual. The projections I engage in, and those in which I participate, can be manipulated by ritual. Even my very physiology can be altered, down to hormonal expression and tissue physiology, by this ritual system I am in. And, through my own participation in the ritual, I create these changes in others. Rituals, therefore, are the central element in the dense interactivity of mind, culture, and body, and they are co-crafted by the egos involved and the collective elements. They have the ability to cure both mind and body; in the case of body, they can help cure physical ailments. In the case of mind, they can cure anomie, rootlessness, emptiness, and role confusion. On the other side of the spectrum, they can cure the feeling of being rigidly oppressed or trapped in outmoded ways of being. They can help us transition from immature to mature being. They can help us find meaning in suffering, and help us deal with the grief and rage of traumatic loss. They can even reframe our cognitive world, giving us new as-if worlds of meaning that we can use to understand existence. They can alter our perception of experience and connect us to the events we feel powerless over.

Of course, rituals are not limitless in their power. Their limits exist at the boundary of concrete literalism. Rituals can improve one's fighting ability but they cannot make one invincible. They can improve the chance of healing from illness, but they cannot cure everything without fail. They can help us transition into new roles and ways of being, but we must still work on them ourselves. They can force cultural consensus but they cannot erase private misgivings. They can dramatically alter perception but not without limit.

Nevertheless, I hope it is evident that rituals are a resource that we can use in clinical work. Here I have laid the groundwork for much future elaboration. I do not feel I have exhausted all the possibilities by any means. Surely some may want to take this work to the extreme—I again feel caution is in order. Ritual is a powerful technology; it should be used with only the utmost of ethical care. That said, in total I have recommended ways to construct ritual objects, ways to diagnose and treat patients with ritual solutions including the 7Ps, tripartite structures to help in identity, self-esteem, and relationship problems, and in the case of grieving, the eight themes of successful grieving practices. Many other suggestions exist in this volume and many more could be made.

Afterword

Everything I have discussed in this volume naturally applies to the charm that was used to cure my grandfather. Old Eeky, of course, was a staunch ritualist. His background was in the Mexican folk culture of his day. My great-grandparents came from a different perspective, perhaps one steeped in a greater degree of sincerity rather than ritualism, since it was one heavily influenced by the Enlightenment and Protestantism. My grandfather, however, was an impressionable child, and so his young, developing ego was rather "close" to the collective element from whence resonant things like impressive folk charms emerge and are maintained. Thus in his way Old Eeky engaged with, manipulated, and participated in the biological, psychological, and cultural effects of the deceptively humble healing charm he used to remove the dreaded *ojo*. My grandfather ends the chapter that talks about his brush with diphtheria and *ojo* with a wink: not committing himself to either side, he presents the arguments of the physician and Old Eeky—the doctor said the serum healed him, whereas Old Eeky said the charm did it. Like my grandfather, I also refuse to take sides in this false dichotomy, but not because it is a clever way to end the story (and my grandfather was extraordinarily clever), but because in truth it is highly plausible that *both* the medicine and the charm cured him. Thus both my great-grandparents and Old Eeky were wrong to assume it had to be either one or the other.

Throughout this volume we have seen how rituals can affect many densely interacting layers of the human experience. This applies to my grandfather as well. There is no doubt he desperately needed the serum to survive—but would it have been enough on its own? Alternately, might the serum have been *too much* without the charm? We'll never know for sure. In my training I have helped take care of severely immuno-compromised patients and this experience has taught me that our common conception of the power of biomedicine is often a serious overstatement. I know this because such patients, when infected, rarely respond to even the strongest antibiotic regimens. The reason for this is that antibiotics rarely kill infecting organisms. Rather, they stall them, and give the immune system time to mount a truly lethal defense. In immuno-compromised patients, however, this necessary factor is nearly absent, with often fatal results. It is Nature, not we, who heals. We are Her assistants, *not* the other way around. Therefore, in the case of my grandfather, the ritual could have "pushed" his young, impressionable immune system through various non-linear mind–brain–body paths just enough to (in concert with the serum) kill the diphtheria and/or avoid lethal serum toxicity. One does not need to be a true believer of any faith to see why this is so, as we already know the mind, beliefs, resonant narratives, and so forth can affect many aspects of physiology, including the immune system. Whether spirits or "magic" can affect the body is not the point because it has already been demonstrated that a *belief* in spirits and magic *can*. Thus, in the end, at least in part, it is very likely that I am alive because of a magic spell.

At least for now.

Bibliography

Ader, R. (ed.). 1980. *Psychoneuroimmunology.* New York: Academic Press.

Ader, R. and Cohen, N. 1982. Behaviorally conditioned immunosuppression and murine systemic lupus erythematosus. *Science* 215: 1534–1536.

Alves, D., Fernández-Navarro, P., Baptista, J., Ribeiro, E., Sousa, I., and Goncalves, M. 2014. Innovative moments in grief therapy: the meaning reconstruction approach and the processes of self-narrative transformation. *Psychotherapy Research* 24: 25–41.

Ammirati, F., Colivicchi, F., and Santini, M. 2001. Permanent cardiac pacing versus medical treatment for the prevention of recurrent vasovagal syncopy: a multicenter, randomized, controlled trial. *Circulation* 104: 52–57.

ARAS (Archive for Research in Archetypal Symbolism). 2010. *The Book of Symbols.* Cologne: Taschen.

Ashe, G. 2003. *The Discovery of King Arthur.* Stroud: Sutton.

Ashliman, D. L. 1987. *A Guide to Folktales in the English Language.* New York: Greenwood.

Atran, S. C. 2002. *In Gods We Trust: The Evolutionary Landscape of Religion.* Oxford: Oxford University Press.

Avis, J. and Harris, P. L. 1991. Belief–desire reasoning among Baka children: evidence for a universal conception of mind. *Child Development* 62: 460–467.

Bach, E. 1987. *Collected Writings of Edward Bach.* London: Ashgrove Publishing.

Badone, E. 2009. Death omens in a Breton memorate. In A. C. G. M. Robben (ed.), *Death, Mourning and Burial: A Cross-Cultural Reader.* Malden, MA: Blackwell, 65–70.

Bandura, A. 1997. *Self-Efficacy: The Exercise of Control.* Cambridge: Cambridge University Press.

Barrett, J. 2007. Gods. In H. Whitehouse and J. Laidlaw (eds.), *Religion, Anthropology, and Cognitive Science.* Durham, NC: Carolina Academic Press, 179–208.

Bauschatz, P. 1982. *The Well and the Tree: World and Time in Early Germanic Culture.* Amherst, MA: University of Massachusetts Press.

Bayly, S. 2004. Conceptualizing from within: divergent religious modes from Asian Modernist perspectives. In H. Whitehouse and J. Laidlaw (eds.), *Ritual and Memory: Toward a Comparative Anthropology of Religion.* Walnut Creek, CA: AltaMira Press, 111–134.

Beinenfeld, D. 2005. *Psychodynamic Theory for Clinicians.* Philadelphia, PA: Lippincott Williams & Wilkins.

Beitman, B. D. 2009. Brains seek patterns in coincidences. *Psychiatric Annals* 39: 255–264.

Bell, C. 2009. *Ritual: Perspectives and Dimensions.* Oxford: Oxford University Press.

Benedetti, F. 2009. *Placebo Effects: Understanding the Mechanisms in Health and Disease.* Oxford: Oxford University Press.

Benedetti, F., Mayberg, H. S., Wager, T. D., Stohler, C. S., and Zubieta, J.-K. 2005. Neurobiological mechanisms of the placebo effect. *Journal of Neuroscience* 25: 10390–10402.

Benedetti, F., Lanotte, M., Lopiano, L., and Colloca, L. 2007. When words are painful: unraveling the mechanisms of the nocebo effect. *Neuroscience* 147: 260–271.

Benson, H. and McCallie, D. P. 1979. Angina pectoris and the placebo effect. *New England Journal of Medicine* 300: 1424–1429.

Black, P. H. 2002. Stress and the inflammatory response: a review of neurogenic inflammation. *Brain, Behavior, and Immunology* 16: 622–653.

Bloch, M. 2004. Ritual and deference. In H. Whitehouse and J. Laidlaw (eds.), *Ritual and Memory: Toward a Comparative Anthropology of Religion.* Walnut Creek, CA: AltaMira Press, 65–78.

Bloch, M. and Parry, J. (eds.). 1982. *Death and the Regeneration of Life.* Cambridge: Cambridge University Press.

Blum, R. 2008. *The Book of Runes.* New York: Thomas Dunne Books.

Bogensperger, J. and Leuger-Schuster, B. 2014. Losing a child: finding meaning in bereavement. *European Journal of Psychotraumatology* 1: 1–9.

Bourguignon, E. 1972. Dreams and altered states of consciousness in anthropological research. In F. Hsu (ed.), *Psychological Anthropology*, 2nd edn. Cambridge, MA: Schenkman, 403–434.

Bowlby, J. 1982. *Loss: Sadness and Depression.* New York: Basic Books.

Boyer, P. 2001. *Religion Explained: The Evolutionary Origins of Religious Thought.* New York: Basic Books.

Brandon, S. G. F. 1998. The myth and ritual position critically examined. In R. Segal (ed.) *The Myth and Ritual Theory.* Oxford: Blackwell, 388–411.

Bretlau, P., Thomsen, J., Tos, M., and Johnsen, N. J. 1989. Placebo effect in surgery for Meniere's disease: nine-year follow-up. *American Journal of Otology* 10: 259–261.

Briere, J. 2006. Dissociative symptoms and trauma exposure: specificity, affect dysregulation, and posttraumatic stress. *Journal of Nervous and Mental Disorders* 194: 78–82.

Brody, H. 1997. Placebo response, sustained partnership, and emotional resilience in practice. *Journal of the American Board of Family Practice* 10: 72–74.

Brody, H. 1999. The doctor as therapeutic agent: a placebo effect research agenda. In A. Harrington (ed.), *The Placebo Effect: An Interdisciplinary Exploration.* Cambridge, MA: Harvard University Press, 77–92.

Brody, H. 2000. *The Placebo Response.* New York: HarperCollins.

Brody, H. and Brody, D. 2000. Placebo and health: II. Three perspectives on the placebo response: expectancy, conditioning, and meaning. *Advances in Mind-Body Medicine* 16: 216–232.

Brody, H. and Waters, B. 1980. Diagnosis is treatment. *Journal of Family Practice* 10: 445–449.

Brooke, R. 2009. The self, the psyche and the world: a phenomenological interpretation. *Journal of Analytical Psychology* 54: 601–618.

Brown, D. 1991. *Human Universals.* New York: McGraw-Hill.

Brown, D. 1999. Human nature and history. *History and Theory* 38: 138–157.

Brown, D. 2004. Human universals, human nature and human culture. *Dædalus* 133: 47–54.

Brüne, M. (ed.). 2008. *The Textbook of Evolutionary Psychiatry: The Origins of Psychopathology*. Oxford: Oxford University Press.

Bruner, J. 1998. *Acts of Meaning*. Cambridge, MA: Harvard University Press.

Buss, D. (ed.). 2005. *The Handbook of Evolutionary Psychology.* Hoboken, NJ: Wiley.

Cann, D. R. and Donderi, D. C. 1986. Jungian personality typology and the recall of everyday and archetypal dreams. *Journal of Personality and Social Psychology* 50: 1021–1030.

Cherry, J. L. 1992. Animism in thought and language. PhD dissertation, University of California, Berkeley.

Christopher, J. C., Bickhard, M. H., and Lambeth, G. S. 2001. Otto Kernberg's object relations theory. *Theory and Psychology* 11: 687–711.

Cirlot, J. E. 1971. *A Dictionary of Symbols.* New York: Dover.

Clover, C. J. 1993. Regardless of sex: men, women and power in early Northern Europe. *Speculum* 68: 363–387.

Cohen, D. B. and Cox, C. 1975. Neuroticism in the sleep laboratory: implications for presentational and adaptive properties of dreaming. *Journal of Abnormal Psychology* 84: 91–108.

Cohen, E. 2007. Witchcraft and sorcery. In H. Whitehouse and J. Laidlaw (eds.), *Religion, Anthropology, and Cognitive Science*. Durham, NC: Carolina Academic Press, 135–160.

Coleman, S. L., Beitman, B. D., and Celebi, E. 2009. Weird coincidences commonly occur. *Psychiatric Annals* 39: 265–270.

Colloca, L. and Benedetti, F. 2005. Placebos and painkillers: is mind as real as matter? *Nature Reviews Neuroscience* 6: 545–552.

Colloca, L., Lopiano, L., Lanotte, M., and Benedetti, F. 2004. Overt versus covert treatment for pain, anxiety, and Parkinson's disease. *Lancet Neurology* 3: 679–684.

Colloca, L., Siguado, M., and Benedetti, F. 2008. The role of learning in nocebo and placebo effects. *Pain* 136: 211–218.

Conklin, B. A. 2009. "Thus are our bodies, thus was our custom": mortuary cannibalism in an Amazonian society. In A. C. G. M. Robben (ed.), *Death, Mourning and Burial: A Cross-Cultural Reader*. Malden, MA: Blackwell, 238–262.

Cosmides, L. and Tooby, J. 1992. Cognitive adaptations for social exchange. In J. H. Barkow, L. Cosmides, and L. Tooby (eds.), *The Adapted Mind: Evolutionary Psychology and the Generation of Culture*. Oxford: Oxford University Press, 163–228.

Csordas, T. J., Storck, M. J., and Strauss, M. 2008. Diagnosis and distress in Navajo healing. *Journal of Nervous and Mental Disorders* 196: 585–596.

Cunliffe, B. 1997. *The Ancient Celts.* Harmondsworth: Penguin.

Danforth, L. 2009. Metaphors of mediation in Greek funeral laments. In A. C. G. M. Robben (ed.), *Death, Mourning and Burial: A Cross-Cultural Reader*. Malden, MA: Blackwell, 156–166.

d'Aquili, E. and Laughlin, C. D. 1979. *The Spectrum of Ritual.* New York: Columbia University Press.

Davidson, H. E. 1968. *The Road to Hel: A Study of the Conception of the Dead in Old Norse Literature.* Westport, CT: Praeger.

Davidson, H. E. 1978. *Patterns of Folklore*. Cambridge: D. S. Brewer.

Davidson, H. E. 1988. *Myths and Symbols in Pagan Europe.* Syracuse, NY: Syracuse University Press.

Davidson, H. E. 1993. *The Lost Beliefs of Northern Europe.* London: Routledge.

Davies, O. 2003. *Popular Magic: Cunning-Folk in English History.* London: Hambledon Continuum.

Deacon, T. 1998. *The Symbolic Species.* New York: W. W. Norton.

De Pascalis, V., Chiaradia, C., and Carotenuto, E. 2002. The contribution of suggestibility and expectation to placebo analgesia phenomenon in an experimental setting. *Pain* 96: 393–402.

Douglas, M. 1996. *Natural Symbols.* Abingdon: Routledge.

Durkheim, É. 1915. *The Elementary Forms of Religious Life.* London: Allen & Unwin.

Eadie, M. J. 2004. The antiepileptic *Materia Medica* of Pediacus Dioscorides. *Journal of Clinical Neuroscience* 11: 671–701.

Eisma, M., Stroebe, M., Schut, H., Stroebe, W., Boelen, P., and Bout, J. 2013. Avoidance processes mediate the relationship between rumination and symptoms of complicated grief and depression following loss. *Journal of Abnormal Psychology* 122: 961–970.

Eliade, M. 1954. *The Myth of the Eternal Return.* Princeton, NJ: Princeton University Press.

Eliade, M. 1958. *Patterns in Comparative Religion.* London: Sheed and Ward.

Ellenberger, H. F. 1970. *The Discovery of the Unconscious. New York:* Basic Books.

Erikson, E. 1963. *Childhood and Society.* New York: W. W. Norton.

Evans, D. 2003. *Placebo: Mind over Matter in Modern Medicine.* New York: HarperCollins.

Evans-Pritchard, E. E. 1937. *Witchcraft, Oracles and Magic among the Azande.* Oxford: Clarendon Press.

Evans-Pritchard, E. E. 1965. *Theories of Primitive Religion.* Oxford: Clarendon Press.

Evans-Pritchard, E. E. 2009. Witchcraft, oracles and magic among the Azande. In A. C. G. M. Robben (ed.), *Death, Mourning and Burial: A Cross-Cultural Reader.* Malden, MA: Blackwell, 115–121.

Faulkes, A. 1995. *Edda.* London: Everyman Press.

Flaten, M. A., Simonsen, T., and Olsen, H. 1999. Drug-related information generates placebo and nocebo responses that modify the drug response. *Psychosomatic Medicine* 61: 250–255.

Flowers, S. 2010. *Runes and Magic.* Smithville, TX: Runa-Raven Press.

Foulkes, D. 1969. Drug research and the meaning of dreams. *Experimental Medicine and Surgery* 27: 39–52.

Frazer, J. 1921. *The Golden Bough.* Oxford: Oxford University Press.

Freeman, W. J. 1999. Consciousness, intentionality, and causality. *Journal of Consciousness Studies* 6: 143–172.

Freud, S. 1914–1916. Mourning and melancholia. In S. Freud (ed.), *On the History of the Psycho-Analytic Movement: Papers on Metapsychology and Other Works.* London: Hogarth Press, 239–258.

Freud S. 2012 [1913]. *Totem and Taboo.* York: Empire Books.

Fried, R. G., Gupta, M. A., and Gupta, A. K. 2005. Depression and skin disease. *Dermatology Clinic* 23: 657–664.

Fulk, R. D., Bjork, R. E., and Niles, J. D. (eds.). 2009. *Klaeber's Beowulf,* 4th edn. Toronto: University of Toronto Press.

Gabbard, G. O. 2010. *Long-Term Psychodynamic Psychotherapy: A Basic Text.* Arlington, VA: American Psychiatric Publishing.

Ganong, W. F. 1986. The neuroendocrine system. In R. C. A. Frederickson, H. C. Hendrie, J. N. Hingtgen, and M. H. Aprison (eds.), *Neuroregulation of Autonomic, Endocrine and Immune Systems.* Boston, MA: Martinus Nijhoff, 223–242.

Garmonsway, G. N., Simpson, J., and Davidson, H. E. 1971. *Beowulf and its Analogues.* London: E. P. Dutton.

Geertz, C. 1973. *The Interpretation of Cultures.* New York: Basic Books.

Gluckman, M. 1962. *Essays on the Ritual of Social Relations.* Manchester: Manchester University Press.

Goodwyn, E. D. 2010. Approaching archetypes: reconsidering innateness. *Journal of Analytical Psychology* 55: 502–521.

Goodwyn, E. D. 2012. *The Neurobiology of the Gods.* New York: Routledge.

Goodwyn, E. D. 2013. Recurrent motifs as resonant attractor states in the narrative field: a testable model of archetype. *Journal of Analytical Psychology* 58: 387–408.

Goodwyn, E. D. 2014. *A Psychological Reading of Beowulf.* New York: Edwin Mellen Press.

Goodwyn, F. E. 1993 [1951]. *Life on the King Ranch.* College Station, TX: Texas A&M University Press.

Gracely, R. H., Dubner, R., Deeter, W. D., and Wolskee, P. J. 1985. Clinicians' expectations influence placebo analgesia. *Lancet* 1: 43.

Gras, V. W. 1981. Myth and reconciliation of opposites: Jung and Lévi-Strauss. *Journal of the History of Ideas* 42: 471–488.

Greenwood, S. F. 1990. Émile Durkheim and C. G. Jung: structuring a transpersonal sociology of religion. *Journal for the Scientific Study of Religion* 29: 482–495.

Greenwood, S. 2009. *The Anthropology of Magic.* Oxford: Berg.

Greenwood, S. and Goodwyn, E. 2016. *Magical Consciousness: An Anthropological and Neurobiological Perspective.* New York: Routledge.

Grønbech, V. 1912. *The Culture of the Teutons*, 2 vols. Oxford: Oxford University Press.

Guala, C. 1970. Jung, Durkheim, and Lévi-Strauss: from archetypes to models. *Sociologica* 4: 119–132.

Guthrie, S. E. 2007. Anthropology and anthropomorphism in religion. In H. Whitehouse and J. Laidlaw (eds.), *Religion, Anthropology, and Cognitive Science.* Durham, NC: Carolina Academic Press, 37–62.

Haig, D. 2006. Intrapersonal conflict. In M. Jones and A. C. Fabian (eds.), *Conflict.* Cambridge: Cambridge University Press, 8–22.

Haile, B. 1940. A note on the Navaho visionary. *American Anthropologist* 42: 359.

Haining, P. 1972. *The Anatomy of Witchcraft.* New York: Taplinger.

Hall, A. 2007. *Elves in Anglo-Saxon England.* Woodbridge: Boydell Press.

Harrington, A. (ed.). 1999. *The Placebo Effect: An Interdisciplinary Exploration.* Cambridge, MA: Harvard University Press.

Harris, M. 1977. *Cannibals and Kings.* London: Random House.

Harrison, J. 1998. Themis. In R. Segal (ed.), *The Myth and Ritual Theory: An Anthology.* Oxford: Blackwell, 58–82.

Haule, J. 2011. *Jung in the 21st Century*, 2 vols. New York: Routledge.

Henderson, P., Rosen, D., and Mascaro, N. 2007. Empirical study on the healing nature of mandalas. *Psychology of Aesthetics, Creativity, and the Arts* 1: 148–154.

Hertz, R. 2009. A contribution to the study of the collective representation of death. In A. C. G. M. Robben (ed.), *Death, Mourning and Burial: A Cross-Cultural Reader.* Malden, MA: Blackwell, 197–212.

Hocart, A. M. 1998. The life-giving myth. In R. A. Segal (ed.), *The Myth and Ritual School: An Anthology.* Oxford: Blackwell.

Hogenson, G. B. 2009. Archetypes as action patterns. *Journal of Analytical Psychology* 54: 325–337.

Hollander, L. M. (trans.). 2006. *The Poetic Edda.* Austin, TX: University of Texas Press.

Horwitz, R. I. and Horwitz, S. M. 1993. Adherence to treatment and health outcomes. *Archives of Internal Medicine* 153: 1863–1868.

Howe, L. 2004. Late medieval Christianity, Balinese Hinduism and the doctrinal mode of religiosity. In H. Whitehouse and J. Laidlaw (eds.), *Ritual and Memory: Toward a Comparative Anthropology of Religion.* Walnut Creek, CA: AltaMira Press, 134–154.

Hultkrantz, Å. 1979. *The Religions of the American Indians.* Berkeley, CA: University of California Press.

Humphrey, N. 2002. Great expectations: the evolutionary psychology of faith-healing and the placebo response. In N. Humphrey (ed.), *The Mind Made Flesh: Essays from the Frontiers of Evolution and Psychology.* Oxford: Oxford University Press, 255–286.

Huston, H. 1992. Direct and indirect tests of archetypal memory. Master's thesis in Psychology, Texas A&M University.

Huston, H. L., Rosen, D. H., and Smith, S. M. 1999. Evolutionary memory. In D. H. Rosen and M. C. Luebbert (eds.), *Evolution of the Psyche.* Westport, CT: Praeger, 139–149.

Huxley, J. (ed.). 1966. A discussion on ritualization of behavior in animals and man. *Philosophical Transactions of the Royal Society, Series B* 251: 247–525.

Hyland, M. E. and Whalley, B. 2008. Motivational concordance: an important mechanism in self-help therapeutic rituals involving inert (placebo) substances. *Journal of Psychosomatic Research* 65: 405–413.

Iacobini, M., Molnar-Szakacs, I., Gallese, V., Buccino, G., Mazziotta, J. C., and Rizzolotti, G. 2005. Grasping the intentions of others with one's own mirror neuron system. *PLoS Biology* 3: e79.

Irwin, M., Patterson, T., Smith, T. L., Caldwell, C., Brown, S. A., Gillen, J. C., and Grant, I. 1990. Reduction of immune function in life stress and depression. *Biological Psychiatry* 27: 22–30.

Jung, C. G. 1919. *The Structure and Dynamics of the Psyche. The Collected Works of C. G. Jung*, vol. 8, ed. H. Read, M. Fordham, G. Adler and W. McGuire, trans. R. F. C. Hull. London: Routledge & Kegan Paul.

Jung, C. G. 1952. Synchronicity: an acausal connecting principle. In *The Structure and Dynamics of the Psyche: The Collected Works of C. G. Jung*, vol. 8, ed. H. Read, M. Fordham, G. Adler, and W. McGuire. Princeton, NJ: Princeton University Press.

Jung, C. G. 1954. *The Practice of Psychotherapy. The Collected Works of C. G. Jung*, vol. 16, ed. H. Read, M. Fordham, G. Adler, and W. McGuire, trans. R. F. C. Hull. London: Routledge & Kegan Paul.

Jung, C. G. 1956. *Symbols of Transformation. The Collected Works of C. G. Jung*, vol. 5, ed. H. Read, M. Fordham, G. Adler, and W. McGuire, trans. R. F. C. Hull. London: Routledge & Kegan Paul.

Jung, C. G. 1959a. *Aion: Researches into the Phenomenology of the Self. The Collected Works of C. G. Jung*, vol. 9, part II, ed. H. Read, M. Fordham, G. Adler, and W. McGuire, trans. R. F. C. Hull. London: Routledge & Kegan Paul.

Jung, C. G. 1959b. *The Archetypes and the Collective Unconscious. The Collected Works of C. G. Jung*, vol. 9 part I, ed. H. Read, M. Fordham, G. Adler and W. McGuire, trans. R. F. C. Hull. London: Routledge & Kegan Paul.

Jung, C. G. 1970. *Civilization in Transition. The Collected Works of C. G. Jung*, vol. 10, ed. H. Read, M. Fordham, G. Adler, and W. McGuire, trans. R. F. C. Hull. London: Routledge & Kegan Paul.

Jung, C. G. 1984. *Dream Analysis: Notes of the Seminar Given in 1928–1930*, ed. W. McGuire. Princeton, NJ: Princeton University Press.

Jung, C. G. 1997. *Visions: Notes of the Seminar Given 1930–1934*, ed. C. Douglas. Princeton, NJ: Princeton University Press.

Jung, L. and Meyer-Grass, M. (eds.). 2008. *Children's Dreams*. Princeton, NJ: Princeton University Press.

Kalsched, D. 1996. *The Inner World of Trauma*. New York: Routledge.

Kålund, K. 1907. Den Islandske Lægebog: Codex Arnamagnæanus 434a 12mo. *Det Kongelige Danske Videnskabernes Selskabs Skrifter, Historisk og Filosofisk Afdeling* 7: 355–400.

Kan, S. 2009. The nineteenth-century Tlinglit Potlatch: a new perspective. In A. C. G. M. Robben (ed.), *Death, Mourning and Burial: A Cross-Cultural Reader*. Malden, MA: Blackwell, 286–302.

Kaptchuk, T. J. Stason, W. B., Davis, R. B., Legedza, A. R., Schnyer, R. N., Kerr, C. E., Stone, D. A., Nam, B. H., Kirsch, I., and Goldman, R. H. 2006. Sham device v inert pill: randomized controlled trial of two placebo treatments. *British Medical Journal* 332: 391–397.

Kelley, E. F., Kelly, E. W., Crabtree, A., Gauld, A., Grosso, M., and Greyson, B. 2010. *Irreducible Mind: Toward a Psychology for the 21st Century*. New York: Rowman & Littlefield.

Khan, A., Redding, N., and Brown, W. A. 2007. The persistence of the placebo response in antidepressant clinical trials. *Journal of Psychiatric Research* 42: 791–796.

Khin, N. A., Chen, Y. F., Yang, Y., Yang, P., and Laughren, T. P. 2011. Exploratory analyses of efficacy data from major depressive disorder trials submitted to the US Food and Drug Administration in support of new drug applications. *Journal of Clinical Psychiatry* 72: 464–472.

Kimbali, S. T. 1960. Introduction to A. Van Gennep, *The Rites of Passage*. Chicago, IL: University of Chicago Press.

King, B. 1993. *The Elements of the Runes*. Rockport, MA: Element Books.

Kirsch, I. 1985. Response expectancy as a determinant of experience and behavior. *American Psychologist* 40: 1189–1202.

Kirsch, I. 1999. Specifying nonspecifics. In A. Harrington (ed.), *The Placebo Effect: An Interdisciplinary Exploration*. Cambridge, MA: Harvard University Press, 166–186.

Kleinman, A. 1988. *Rethinking Psychiatry*. New York: Free Press.

Kleinman, A. 1989. *The Illness Narratives*. New York: Basic Books.

Kluckhohn, C. 1998. Myth and rituals: a general theory. In R. A. Segal (ed.), *The Myth and Ritual School: An Anthology*. Oxford: Blackwell.

Kluger, H. Y. 1975. Archetypal dreams and "everyday" dreams: a statistical investigation into Jung's theory of the collective unconscious. *Israel Annals of Psychiatry* 13: 6–47.

Knox, J. 2003. *Archetype, Attachment, Analysis: Jungian Psychology and the Emergent Mind*. New York: Routledge.

Koshi, E. B. and Short, C. A. 2007. Placebo theory and its implications for research and clinical practice: a review of the recent literature. *Pain Practice* 7: 4–20.

Kradin, R. 1997. The psychosomatic symptom and the self. *Journal of Analytical Psychology* 42: 405–422.

Kradin, R. 2004. The placebo response complex. *Journal of Analytical Psychology* 49: 617–634.

Kradin, R. 2008. *The Placebo Response and the Power of Unconscious Healing*. New York: Routledge.

Kradin, R. 2011. Psychosomatic disorders: the canalization of mind into matter. *Journal of Analytical Psychology* 56: 37–55.

Krell, H. V., Leuchter, A. F., Morgan, M., Cook, I. A., and Abrams, M. 2004. Subject expectations of treatment effectiveness and outcome of treatment with an experimental antidepressant. *Journal of Clinical Psychiatry* 65: 1174–1179.

Kriebel, D. W. 2002. Powwowing: a persistent American esoteric tradition. *Esotericism, Art and Imagination* 4: 16–28.

Kriebel, D. W. 2007. *Powwowing among the Pennsylvania Dutch.* University Press, PA: Pennsylvania State University Press.

Laidlaw, J. and Whitehouse, H. 2007. Introduction. In H. Whitehouse and J. Laidlaw (eds.), *Religion, Anthropology, and Cognitive Science.* Durham, NC: Carolina Academic Press, 3–34.

Lakoff, G. and Johnson, M. 1980. *Metaphors We Live By.* Chicago, IL: University of Chicago Press.

Lakoff, G. and Johnson, M. 1999. *Philosophy in the Flesh.* New York: Basic Books.

Lakoff, G. and Johnson, M. 2003. Afterword to *Metaphors We Live By*, 2nd edn. Chicago, IL: University of Chicago Press.

Lang, A. R., Goeckner, D. J., Adesso, V. J., and Marlatt, G. A. 1975. Effects of alcohol on aggression in male social drinkers. *Journal of Abnormal Psychology* 84: 508–518.

Laughlin, C. 1990. Ritual and the symbolic function: a summary of biogenetic structural theory. *Journal of Ritual Studies* 4: 15–39.

Laughlin, C. D., McManus, J., and d'Aquili, E. 1990. *Brain, Symbol and Experience.* New York: Columbia University Press.

Leach, M. and Fried, J. (eds.). 1984. *Funk and Wagnalls Standard Dictionary of Folklore, Mythology and Legend.* New York: Harper & Row.

LeCouteux, C. 1996. *The Return of the Dead.* Rochester, VT: Inner Traditions.

Lehner, E. 1956. *The Picture Book of Symbols.* New York: William Penn.

Lehrer, P., Feldman, J., Giardino, N., Song, H. S., and Schamling, K. 2002. Psychological aspects of asthma. *Journal of Consulting and Clinical Psychology* 70: 691–711.

Leuchter, A. F., Cook, I. A., Witte, E. A., Morgan, M., and Abrams, M. 2002. Changes in brain function of depressed subjects during treatment with placebo. *American Journal of Psychiatry* 159: 122–129.

Lévi-Bruhl, L. 1985. *How Natives Think.* Princeton, NJ: Princeton University Press.

Lévi-Strauss, C. 1955. The structural study of myth. *Journal of American Folklore* 68: 428–444.

Lévi-Strauss, C. 1966. *The Savage Mind.* Chicago, IL: University of Chicago Press.

Levy, R. L., Olden, K. W., Naliboff, L. A., Francisconi, C., Drossman, D. A., and Creed, F. 2006. Psychosocial aspects of the functional gastrointestinal disorders. *Gastroenterology* 130: 1447–1458.

Lewis, G. 2004. Religious doctrine or experience: a matter of seeing, learning or doing. In H. Whitehouse and J. Laidlaw (eds.), *Ritual and Memory: Toward a Comparative Anthropology of Religion.* Walnut Creek, CA: AltaMira Press, 155–172.

Lidstone, S. C. and Stoessl, A. J. 2007. Understanding the placebo effect: contributions from neuroimaging. *Molecular Imaging and Biology* 9: 176–185.

Lifton, R. J. and Olson, E. 2009. Symbolic immortality. In A. C. G. M. Robben (ed.), *Death, Mourning and Burial: A Cross-Cultural Reader.* Malden, MA: Blackwell, 32–39.

Lincoln, B. 1991. *Emerging from the Chrysalis: Rituals of Women's Initiation.* Oxford: Oxford University Press.

Lincoln, J. S. 1935. *The Dream in Primitive Cultures*. Baltimore, MD: Wilkins & Wilkins.

Lock, M. 2009. Displacing suffering: the reconstruction of death in North America and Japan. In A. C. G. M. Robben (ed.), *Death, Mourning and Burial: A Cross-Cultural Reader*. Malden, MA: Blackwell, 91–112.

Lunde, P. and Stone, C. 2012. *Ibn Fadlan and the Land of Darkness*. London: Penguin Classics.

Luparello, T. J., Lyons, H. A., Bleecker, E. R., and McFadden, E. R. 1968. Influences of suggestion on airway reactivity in asthmatic subjects. *Psychosomatic Medicine* 30: 819–825.

Luparello, T. J., Leist, N., Lourie, C. H., and Sweet, P. 1970. The interaction of psychologic stimuli and pharmacologic agents on airway reactivity in asthmatic subjects. *Psychosomatic Medicine* 32: 509–513.

Lüthi, M. 1982. *The European Folktale: Form and Nature*. Bloomington, IN: Indiana University Press.

Lüthi, M. 1984. *The Fairytale as Art Form and Portrait of Man*. Bloomington, IN: Indiana University Press.

Lyerly, S. B., Ross, S., Krugman, A. D., and Clyde, D. J. 1964. Drugs and placebos: the effects of instructions on performance and mood under amphetamine sulphate and chloral hydrate. *Journal of Abnormal Social Psychology* 68: 321–327.

McCauley, R. N. and Lawson, E. T. 2002. *Bringing Ritual to Mind: Psychological Foundations of Cultural Forms*. Cambridge: Cambridge University Press.

McDowell, M. J. 2001. Principle of organization: a dynamic-systems view of the archetype-as-such. *Journal of Analytical Psychology* 46: 637–654.

MacLeod, M. and Mees, B. 2006. *Runic Amulets and Magic Objects*. Woodbridge: Boydell Press.

McNamara, P. 2009. *The Neuroscience of Religious Experience*. Cambridge: Cambridge University Press.

McRae, C., Cherin, E., Yamazaki, T. G., Kiem, G., Vo, A. H., Russell, D., Elgring, J. H., Fahn, S., Greene, P., Dillon, S., Winfield, H., Bjugstad, K. B., and Freed, C. R. 2004. Effects of perceived treatment on quality of life and medical outcomes in a double-blind placebo surgery trial. *Archives of General Psychiatry* 61: 412–420.

Maercker, A. and Lalor, J. 2012. Diagnostic and clinical considerations in prolonged grief disorder. *Dialogues in Clinical Neuroscience* 2: 167–176.

Magnar, E. L. 1998. *Runor*. Falun: Historiska Media.

Malinowski, B. 1925. *Magic, Science and Religion and Other Essays*. New York: Free Press.

Malinowski, B. 1935. *Coral Gardens and their Magic*. London: Allen & Unwin.

Malley, B. 2004. The doctrinal mode and evangelical Christianity in the United States. In H. Whitehouse and J. Laidlaw (eds.), *Ritual and Memory: Toward a Comparative Anthropology of Religion*. Walnut Creek, CA: AltaMira Press, 79–87.

Maloney, A. 1999. Preference ratings of images representing archetypal themes. *Journal of Analytical Psychology* 44: 101–116.

Manousakis, E. 2006. Founding quantum theory on the basis of consciousness. *Foundations of Physics* 36: 1–41.

Marlatt, G. A. and Roshenow, D. J. 1980. Cognitive processes in alcohol use: expectancy and the balanced placebo design. In N. K. Mello (ed.), *Advances in Substance Abuse: Behavioral and Biological Research.* Greenwich, CT: JAI Press, 159–199.

Mawdsley, J. E. and Rampton, D. S. 2005. Psychological stress in IBD: new insights into pathogenic and therapeutic implications. *Gut* 10: 1481–1491.

Mayberg, H. S., Silva, J. A., Brannan, S. K., Tekell, J. L., Mahurin, R. K., McGinnis, S., and Jerabek, P. A. 2002. The functional neuroanatomy of the placebo effect. *American Journal of Psychiatry* 159: 728–737.

Mead, M. 1928. *Coming of Age in Samoa*. New York: Morrow.

Mead, M. 1935. *Sex and Temperament in Three Primitive Societies*. New York: Morrow.

Mech, L. D. and Boitani, L. 2007. *Wolves: Behavior, Ecology, and Conservation*. Chicago, IL: University of Chicago Press.

Meir, C. 1968. *Ancient Incubation and Modern Psychotherapy*. Evanston, IL: Northwestern University Press.

Mello, N. K. (ed.). 1980. *Advances in Substance Abuse: Behavioral and Biological Research*. Greenwich, CT: JAI Press.

Mestrovic, S. G. 1985. Durkheim's renovated rationalism and the idea that collective life is only made of representations. *Current Perspectives in Social Theory* 6: 199–218.

Mestrovic, S. G. 1988. *Émile Durkheim and the Reformation of Sociology*. Lanham, MD: Rowman & Littlefield.

Metcalf, P. and Huntington, R. 1991. *Celebrations of Death*, 2nd edn. Cambridge: Cambridge University Press.

Mitchell, R. and Thompson, N. 1986. *Deception*. Albany, NY: State University of New York Press.

Moerman, D. 2002. *Meaning, Medicine and the 'Placebo Effect'*. Cambridge: Cambridge University Press.

Monaghan, P. 2006. *The Encyclopedia of Celtic Mythology and Folklore*. New York: Checkmark Books.

Morgan, W. 1936. Human wolves among the Navaho. *Yale University Publications in Anthropology* 11.

Morris, D. B. 1999. Placebo, pain, and belief. In A. Harrington (ed.), *The Placebo Effect: An Interdisciplinary Exploration*. Cambridge, MA: Harvard University Press, 187–207.

Moseley, J. B., O'Malley, K., Petersen, N. J., Menke, T. J., Brody, B. A., Kuykendall, D. H., Hollingsworth, J. C., Ashton, C. M., and Wray, N. P. 2002. A controlled trial of arthroscopic surgery for osteoarthritis of the knee. *New England Journal of Medicine* 347: 81–88.

Nakajima, S., Masaya, I., and Takako, K. 2012. Complicated grief in those bereaved by violent death: the effects of post-traumatic stress disorder on complicated grief. *Dialogues in Clinical Neuroscience* 2: 210–214.

Neimeyer, R. 2000. Searching for the meaning of meaning: grief therapy and the process of reconstruction. *Death Studies* 24: 541–558.

Newberg, A. 2006. *Why We Believe What We Believe*. New York: Free Press.

Newson, R., Boelen, P., Hek, K., Hofman, A., and Tiemeier, H. 2011. The prevalence and characteristics of complicated grief in older adults. *Journal of Affective Disorders* 132: 231–238.

Nisbet, R. A. 1969. *Social Change and History*. Oxford: Oxford University Press.

Oftedal, G., Straue, A., Johnson, A., and Stovner, J. L. 2007. Mobile phone headache: a double-blind, sham-controlled provocation study. *Cephalalgia* 27: 447–455.

Oken, B. S. 2008. Placebo effects: clinical aspects and neurobiology. *Brain* 131: 2812–2823.

Orlandini, A. 2009. The transforming power of ritual. *Journal of the American Academy of Psychoanalysis and Dynamic Psychiatry* 37: 439–456.

Page, R. I. 1987. *Reading the Past: Runes*. London: British Museum Press.

Pahnke, W. 1967. LSD and religious experience. Paper presented to a public symposium at Wesleyan University, March.

Panksepp, J. 1998. *Affective Neuroscience: The Foundations of Human and Animal Emotions.* Oxford: Oxford University Press.

Panksepp, J. (ed.). 2004. *Textbook of Biological Psychiatry.* Hoboken, NJ: Wiley-Liss.

Panksepp, J. 2005. Affective consciousness: core emotional feelings in animals and humans. *Cognition and Consciousness* 14: 30–80.

Parry, J. 2009. Sacrificial death and the necrophagous ascetic. In A. C. G. M. Robben (ed.), *Death, Mourning and Burial: A Cross-Cultural Reader.* Malden, MA: Blackwell, 265–284.

Peel, J. D. Y. 2004. Divergent modes of religiosity in West Africa. In H. Whitehouse and J. Laidlaw (eds.), *Ritual and Memory: Toward a Comparative Anthropology of Religion.* Walnut Creek, CA: AltaMira Press, 11–30.

Pennebaker, J. W. 1990. *Opening Up: The Healing Power of Confiding in Others.* New York: William Morrow.

Piaget, J. 1951. *Play, Dreams and Imitation in Childhood.* New York: F. M. Hodgson.

Pierce, C. S. 1931. *Collected Papers,* 4 vols., ed. C. Hartstone and P. Weiss. Cambridge, MA: Belknap Press.

Pinker, S. 2007. *The Stuff of Thought.* New York: Penguin.

Pollington, S. 2008. *Leechcraft: Early English Charms, Plantlore and Healing.* Ely: Anglo-Saxon Books.

Pollo, A., Amanzio, M., Arslanian, A., Casadio, C., Maggi, G., and Benedetti, F. 2001. Response expectancies in placebo analgesia and their clinical relevance. *Pain* 93: 77–84.

Pouillon, J. 1982. Remarks on the verb "to believe." In M. Izard and P. Smith (eds.), *Between Belief and Transgression.* Chicago, IL: University of Chicago Press, 1–8.

Price, D. D. and Fields, H. L. 1999. The contribution of desire and expectation to placebo analgesia: implications for new research strategies. In A. Harrington (ed.), *The Placebo Effect: An Interdisciplinary Exploration.* Cambridge, MA: Harvard University Press, 117–137.

Price, D. D., Milling, L. S., Kirsch, I., Duff, A., Montgomery, G. H., and Nicholls, S. S. 1999. An analysis of factors that contribute to the magnitude of placebo analgesia in an experimental paradigm. *Pain* 83: 147–156.

Price, D. D., Finiss, D. G., and Benedetti, F. 2008. A comprehensive review of the placebo effect: recent advances and current thought. *Annual Review of Psychology* 59: 2.1–2.26.

Propp, V. 1968. *Morphology of the Folktale.* Austin, TX University of Texas Press.

Puhvel, J. 1987. *Comparative Mythology. Baltimore, MD:* Johns Hopkins University Press.

Pyysiäinen, I. 2009. *Supernatural Agents: Why We Believe in Souls, Gods, and Buddhas.* Oxford: Oxford University Press.

Radcliffe-Brown, A. R. 2009 [1922]. *The Andaman Islanders.* In A. C. G. M. Robben (ed.), *Death, Mourning and Burial: A Cross-Cultural Reader.* Malden, MA: Blackwell, 151–155.

Radin, D. 1997. *The Conscious Universe.* New York: HarperCollins.

Radin, P. 1957 [1927]. *Primitive Man as Philosopher.* New York: Dover.

Rappaport, R. A. 1999. *Ritual and Religion in the Making of Humanity.* Cambridge: Cambridge University Press.

Robben, A. C. G. M. (ed.). 2009. *Death, Mourning and Burial: A Cross-Cultural Reader.* Malden, MA: Blackwell.

Rosaldo, R. 2009. Grief and a headhunter's rage. In A. C. G. M. Robben (ed.), *Death, Mourning and Burial: A Cross-Cultural Reader.* Malden, MA: Blackwell, 167–178.

Rosen, D. H. and Luebbert, M. C. (eds.). 1999. *Evolution of the Psyche.* Westport, CT: Praeger.

Rosenblatt, P. C., Walsh, R. P., and Jackson, D. A. 1976. *Grief and Mourning in Cross-Cultural Perspective*. New Haven, CT: HRAF Press.

Ross, A. 1999. *The Druids*. Stroud: History Press.

Rossi, E. and Cheek, D. 1992. *Mind-Body Therapy: Methods of Ideodynamic Healing in Hypnotherapy*. New York: W. W. Norton.

Ryle, G. 2009 [1949]. *The Concept of Mind*. London: Routledge.

Sapirstein. G. and Kirsch, I. 1998. Listening to prozac but hearing placebo? A meta-analysis of the placebo effect of antidepressant medication. *Prevention and Treatment 1:* 3–11.

Saunders, P. and Skar, P. 2001. Archetypes, complexes and self-organization. *Journal of Analytical Psychology* 46: 305–323.

Scaer, R. C. 2001. *The Body Bears the Burden: Trauma, Dissociation, and Disease*. Belfast: Haworth Medical Press.

Scheper-Hughes, N. 2009. Death without weeping. In A. C. G. M. Robben (ed.), *Death, Mourning and Burial: A Cross-Cultural Reader*. Malden, MA: Blackwell, 182–193.

Segal, H. 1964. *Introduction to the Work of Melanie Klein*. London: Karnac Books.

Segal, R. A. (ed.). 1998. *The Myth and Ritual Theory: An Anthology*. Oxford: Blackwell.

Segal, R. A. 2007. Jung and Lévy-Bruhl. *Journal of Analytical Psychology* 52: 635–658.

Segerstrom, S. C. and Miller, G. E. 2004. Psychological stress and the human immune system: a meta-analytic study of 30 years inquiry. *Psychological Bulletin* 130: 601–630.

Seligman, A. B., Weller, R. P., Puett, M. J., and Simon, B. 2008. *Ritual and its Consequences: An Essay on the Limits of Sincerity*. Oxford: Oxford University Press.

Shankland, D. 2004. Modes of religiosity and the legacy of Ernst Gellner. In H. Whitehouse and J. Laidlaw (eds.), *Ritual and Memory: Toward a Comparative Anthropology of Religion*. Walnut Creek, CA: AltaMira Press, 31–49.

Shapiro, A. K. and Shapiro, E. 1997. *The Powerful Placebo: From Ancient Priest to Modern Physician*. Baltimore, MD: Johns Hopkins University Press.

Shapiro, A. K. and Shapiro, E. 1999. The placebo: is it much ado about nothing? In A. Harrington (ed.), *The Placebo Effect: An Interdisciplinary Exploration*. Cambridge, MA: Harvard University Press, 12–36.

Shear, K., Frank, E., Houck, P., and Reynolds, C. 2005. Treatment of complicated grief: a randomized controlled trial. *Journal of the American Medical Association* 293: 2601–2608.

Shore, B. 1998. *Culture in Mind: Cognition, Culture, and the Problem of Meaning*. Oxford: Oxford University Press.

Simon, N. 2013. Treating complicated grief. *Journal of the American Medical Association* 310: 416–423.

Smith, R. 1998. Lectures on the religion of the Semites. In R. Segal (ed.), *The Myth and Ritual Theory: An Anthology*. Oxford: Blackwell.

Solms, M. and Turnbull, O. 2002. *The Brain and the Inner World: An Introduction to the Neuroscience of Subjective Experience*. New York: Other Press.

Solomon, A. 2008. From *The Moth* podcast, "Notes on an Exorcism", recorded October 29, 2008. http://themoth.org/posts/stories/notes-on-an-exorcism.

Solomon, A. 2015. *The Noonday Demon: An Atlas of Depression*. New York: Scribner.

Sørensen, J. 2007a. *A Cognitive Theory of Magic*. Walnut Creek, CA: AltaMira Press.

Sørensen J. 2007b. Malinowski and magic ritual. In H. Whitehouse and J. Laidlaw (eds.), *Religion, Anthropology, and Cognitive Science*. Durham, NC: Carolina Academic Press, 81–104.

Sperber, D. 1996. *Explaining Culture: A Naturalistic Approach*. Oxford: Blackwell.

Spillius, E. (ed.). 1988. *Melanie Klein Today*. London: Routledge.

Spiro, M. 1982. *Oedipus in the Trobriands*. Chicago, IL: University of Chicago Press.

Sproul, B. 1979. *Primal Myths*. New York: HarperOne.

Staude, J. R. 1976. From depth psychology to depth sociology: Freud, Jung, and Lévi-Strauss. *Theory and Society* 3: 303–338.

Stein, D. J. S. (ed.). 1997. *Cognitive Science and the Unconscious*. Arlington, VA: American Psychiatric Publishing.

Stein, M. (ed.). 2010. *Jungian Psychoanalysis*. LaSalle, IL: Open Court.

Stevens, A. 1998. *Ariadne's Clue: A Guide to the Symbols of Humankind*. Princeton, NJ: Princeton University Press.

Stevens, A. 2003. *Archetype Revisited: An Updated Natural History of the Self*. New York: Routledge.

Stockwell, R. P. and Minkova, D. 1997. Prosody. In R. Bjork and J. Niles (eds.), *A Beowulf Handbook*. Lincoln, NE: University of Nebraska Press, 55–85.

Storms, G. 1948. *Anglo-Saxon Magic*. Dordrecht: Springer.

Straus, A. S. 2009. The meaning of death in Northern Cheyenne culture. In A. C. G. M. Robben (ed.), *Death, Mourning and Burial: A Cross-Cultural Reader*. Malden, MA: Blackwell, 71–76.

Stroebe, M., Boelen, P., Hout, M., Stroebe, W., Salemink, E., and Bout, J. V. 2007. Ruminative coping as avoidance: a reinterpretation of its functional adjstment to bereavement. *European Archives of Psychiatry and Clinical Neuroscience* 257: 462–471.

Suzuki, H. 2009. The phase of negated death. In A. C. G. M. Robben (ed.), *Death, Mourning and Burial: A Cross-Cultural Reader*. Malden, MA: Blackwell, 224–237.

Talmy, L. 2000. *Toward a Cognitive Semantics*. Cambridge, MA: MIT Press.

Tambiah, S. 1968. The magical power of words. *Man* 3: 175–208.

Tambiah, S. 1985. Form and meaning of magical acts. In S. Tambiah, *Culture, Thought and Social Action*. Cambridge, MA: Harvard University Press.

Tambiah, S. 1991. *Magic, Science, Religion, and the Scope of Rationality*. Cambridge: Cambridge University Press.

Tasman, A., Kay, J., and Lieberman, J. A. 2003. *Psychiatry*. Chichester: John Wiley.

Taves, A. 2009. *Religious Experience Reconsidered. Princeton, NJ:* Princeton University Press.

Taylor, T. 2002. *The Buried Soul: How Humans Invented Death*. London: Fourth Estate.

Tetlock, P. E. 2003. Thinking the unthinkable: sacred values and taboo cognitions. *Trends in Cognitive Science* 7: 141–156.

Thomas, K. B. 1987. Medical consultations: is there any point in being positive? *British Medical Journal* 133: 455–463.

Thomas, K. B. 1994. The placebo in general practice. *Lancet* 244: 1066–1077.

Thompson, J. J., Ritenbaugh, C., and Nichter, M. 2009. Reconsidering the placebo response from a broad anthropological perspective. *Cultural Medical Psychiatry* 33: 112–152.

Thompson, S. 1960. *Motif-Index of Folk Literature*. Bloomington, IN: Indiana University Press.

Thomsen, J., Bretlau, P., Tos, M., and Johnsen, N. J. 1981. Placebo effect in surgery for Meniere's disease: a double-blind, placebo-controlled study on endolyphatic sac shunt surgery. *Archives of Otolaryngology* 107: 271–277.

Timonen, M., Jokelainen, J., Hakko, H., Silvennoinen-Kassinen, S., Meyer-Rochow, V. B., Herva, A., and Räsänen, P. 2003. Atopy and depression: results from the Northern Finland 1966 Birth Cohort Study. *Molecular Psychiatry* 8: 738–744.

Tresidder, J. (ed.). 2005. *The Complete Dictionary of Symbols*. San Francisco, CA: Chronicle.

Turner, V. 1974. *Dramas, Fields, and Metaphors*. Ithaca, NY: Cornell University Press.

Turville-Petre, E. O. G. 1964. *Myth and Religion of the North*. New York: Holt, Rinehart & Winston.

Tylor, E. 1878. *Primitive Culture*. London: Forgotten Books.

Üther, H. J. 2004. *The Types of International Folktales*. Helsinki: Finnish Academy of Science.

Vallance, A. K. 2007. A systematic review comparing the functional neuroanatomy of patients with depression who respond to placebo to those who recover spontaneously: is there a biological basis for the placebo effect in depression? *Journal of Affective Disorders* 98: 177–185.

Van der Hart, O., Nijenhuis, E. R. S., and Steele, K. 2006. *The Haunted Self: Structural Dissociation and the Treatment of Chronic Traumatization*. New York: W. W. Norton.

Van der Kolk, B. A., Pelcovitz, D., Roth, S., Mandel, F. S., McFarlane, A., and Herman, J. L. 1996. Dissociation, somatization, and affect dysregulation: the complexity of adaptation of trauma. *American Journal of Psychiatry* 153: 83–93.

Van Gennep, A. 1960. *The Rites of Passage*. Chicago, IL: University of Chicago Press.

Van Lommel, P. 2011. *Consciousness Beyond Life*. New York: HarperOne.

Vase, L., Robinson, M. E., Verne, G. N., and Price, D. D. 2005. Increased placebo analgesia over time in irritable bowel syndrome (IBS) patients is associated with desire and expectation but not endogenous opioid mechanisms. *Pain* 115: 338–347.

Verdery, K. 2009. Dead bodies animate the study of politics. In A. C. G. M. Robben (ed.), *Death, Mourning and Burial: A Cross-Cultural Reader*. Malden, MA: Blackwell, 303–310.

Versnel, H. S. 1998. Prospects. In R. Segal (ed.), *The Myth and Ritual Theory: An Anthology*. Oxford: Blackwell.

Viamontes, G. I. and Nemeroff, C. B. 2010. The physiological effect of mental processes on major body systems. *Psychiatric Annals* 40: 367–379.

von Franz, M. L. 1996. *The Interpretation of Fairy Tales*. Boston, MA: Shambhala.

von Franz, M. L. 1999. *Archetypal Dimensions of the Psyche*. Boston, MA: Shambhala.

Waber, R. L., Shiv, B., Carmon, Z., and Ariely, D. 2008. Commercial features of placebo and therapeutic efficacy. *Journal of the American Medical Association* 299: 1016–1017.

Waggoner, B. 2011. *Norse Magical and Herbal Healing*. New Haven, CT: Troth Publications.

Wagner, B., Knaevelsrud, C., and Maercker, A. 2006. Internet-based cognitive-behavioral therapy for complicated grief: a randomized controlled trial. *Death Studies* 30: 429–453.

Wall, P. D. 1993. Pain and the placebo response. *Ciba Foundation Symposium* 174: 187–216.

Wallin, D. 2007. *Attachment in Psychotherapy*. New York: Guilford Press.

Walsh, B. E., Seidman, S. N., Sysko, R., and Gould, M. 2002. Placebo response in studies of major depression: variable, substantial, and growing. *Journal of the American Medical Association* 287: 1840–47.

Welling, D. B. and Nagaraja, N. H. 2000. Endolymphatic mastoid shunt: a re-evaluation of efficacy. *Otolaryngology, Head and Neck Surgery* 122: 340–345.

White, L., Tursky, B., and Schwartz, G. E. (eds.). 1985. *Placebo: Theory, Research and Mechanisms*. New York: Guilford Press.

Whitehouse, H. 2002. Modes of religiosity. *Method and Theory in the Study of Religion* 14: 293–315.

Whitehouse, H. 2004. Toward comparative anthropology of religion. In H. Whitehouse and J. Laidlaw (eds.), *Ritual and Memory: Toward a Comparative Anthropology of Religion.* Walnut Creek, CA: AltaMira Press, 187–205.

Whitehouse, H. 2007. Towards an integration of ethnography, history, and the cognitive science of religion. In H. Whitehouse and J. Laidlaw (eds.), *Religion, Anthropology, and Cognitive Science.* Durham, NC: Carolina Academic Press, 247–280.

Whitehouse, H. and Laidlaw, J. (eds.). 2004. *Ritual and Memory: Toward a Comparative Anthropology of Religion.* Walnut Creek, CA: AltaMira Press.

Whitehouse, H. and Laidlaw, J. (eds.). 2007. *Religion, Anthropology, and Cognitive Science.* Durham, NC: Carolina Academic Press.

Wickramasekera, I. 1985. A condition response model of the placebo effect: predictions from the model. In L. White, B. Tursky, and G. E. Schwartz (eds.), *Placebo: Theory, Research and Mechanisms.* New York: Guilford Press, 255–287.

Wilson, E. O. 2013. *The Social Conquest of Earth.* New York: Liveright Publishing.

Wilson, G. 1939. *Nyakyusa Conventions of Burial.* Johannesburg: University of Witwatersrand Press.

Wilson, G. T. and Lawson, D. M. 1976. Expectancies, alcohol, and sexual arousal in male social drinkers. *Journal of Abnormal Psychology* 85: 587–594.

Wittouck, C., van Autremve, S., de Jaegere, E., Portzky, G., and van Heeringen, K. 2011. The prevention and treatment of complicated grief: a meta-analysis. *Clinical Psychology Review* 31: 69–78.

Wolf, E. 2002. *Treating the Self: Elements of Clinical Self Psychology.* New York: Guilford Press.

Wright, R. J., Cohen, R. T., and Cohen, S. 2005. The impact of stress on the development and expression of atopy. *Current Opinion in Allergy and Clinical Immunology* 5: 23–29.

Yoder, D. 1990. *Discovering American Folklife.* Ann Arbor, MI: UMI Research Press.

Young-Eisendrath, P. and Dawson, T. (eds.). 1997. *The Cambridge Companion to Jung.* Cambridge: Cambridge University Press.

Zipes, J. 2003. *Introduction to the Complete Fairy Tales of the Brothers Grimm*, 3rd edn. New York: Bantam.

Zipes, J. 2006. *Why Fairy Tales Stick: The Evolution and Relevance of a Genre.* New York: Routledge.

Index